Praise for

UNDER THE SAME SKY

"Vital to our understanding of life in North Korea." — *Washington Post*

"[A] page-turner — fast-paced, suspenseful and novelistic . . . Searing." — *Wall Street Journal*

"This book is a remarkable tale of a homeless youth's survival in North Korea, his daring escape to China, and his eventual transition to life in the United States. *Under the Same Sky* vividly describes what Joseph Kim and millions of other North Koreans endured during famines that began in the 1990s . . . Offers fascinating details about daily life in North Korea." — *Christian Science Monitor*

"Kim's harrowing memoir is the best of a trio of books published this summer by North Korean defectors . . . The real value of these memoirs is the way they describe life during one of the greatest disasters the world has ever known — and one of the most secret." — *Time*

"Few can imagine what it is like to be homeless and starving as a child. Few can imagine life in the hermit kingdom of North Korea. However, refugee Joseph Kim knows both very well and he gives us a window into those worlds." — *NPR*

"Beautifully written . . . As *Under the Same Sky* makes very clear, life for the average North Korean is hard, and good fortune in short supply." — *Mental Floss*

"[*Under the Same Sky*] paints a vivid picture of life inside North Korea that, despite the accounts of suffering, by turns surprises and enlightens." — *Acton Institute PowerBlog*

"Harrowing . . . Poignant . . . It's the life of a survivor, filled with determination and deep regret." — *BookPage*

"This short, brutish book — with chapter-ending cliffhangers presaging the next hard twist — will enlighten readers as to the devastating hardships facing those living in North Korea during the 'great famine.'" — *Booklist*

"Told with poise and dignity, Kim's story . . . provides vivid documentation of a remarkable life. It also offers an important account of atrocities committed within North Korea that have been hidden from the West — and indeed, most of the rest of the world. A courageous and inspiring memoir." — *Kirkus Reviews*

"Powerful . . . Doesn't hold anything back . . . Riveting . . . Kim's tale is a vital insight into a little-understood country and a modern-day tragedy." — *Publishers Weekly*, starred review

UNDER THE SAME SKY

*From Starvation in North Korea
to Salvation in America*

JOSEPH KIM

with

Stephan Talty

Mariner Books
Houghton Mifflin Harcourt
BOSTON   NEW YORK

First Mariner Books edition 2016

Copyright © 2015 by Joseph Kim

Library of Congress Cataloging-in-Publication Data
Kim, Joseph, date.
Under the same sky : from starvation in North Korea to salvation in America / Joseph Kim ;
contributions by Stephan Talty.
pages cm
ISBN 978-0-544-37317-4 (hardback) — ISBN 978-0-544-37318-1 (ebook)
ISBN 978-0-544-70527-2 (pbk.)
1. Refugees — Korea (North) — Biography. 2. Immigrants — United States — Biography.
3. Victims of famine — Korea (North) 4. Human rights — Korea (North)
5. Rescue work — China. 6. Christian ethics — China. I. Title.
HV640.5.K67K567 2015
362.87092 — dc23
[B]
2014039686

Book design by Chrissy Kurpeski
Typeset in Minion

Printed in the United States of America
DOC 10 9 8 7 6 5 4 3
4500674040

Author's note: Some of the individuals I knew in China and North
Korea are still at risk today. Their names have been changed.

To my sister, Bong Sook,
and to my brothers and sisters in North Korea
May you never lose your hope,
for it is what makes us live

PROLOGUE: THE GUARD

MY SECOND DAY at the Saro-cheong Detention Center, I was sent to work weeding the rice fields. The task was exhausting, slogging for hours through the flooded rows of dirt, pulling at the weeds and digging down with my fingers for the grub-white roots, but at least it got my fellow inmates and me away from the prison. Even though I'd been homeless for more than two years by then, and had dealt with gangsters and starvation, the place terrified me. The day before, I'd seen a teenager beaten so severely I was sure he was brain-damaged, and darkness had brought the shrieks of girls being raped in the next room. The detention center had once been a school, in fact the best art school in Hoeryong, but now, like many things in the city, it was broken and wild, a place of seething chaos.

Around noon, we marched under a hot sun back to the detention center for lunch. Not knowing the routine, I simply followed everyone else, trying not to stick out. After we ate our meager portions of corn noodle soup, the guard, a lean teenager with an angry face, yelled to us: "It is your break time." I watched as the other boys lay down and fell asleep, all in a matter of twenty seconds. I could tell how precious this time was by how fast they dropped to the floor. I, too, was exhausted and found a spot to lay my head.

I fell asleep soon after and dozed among the others. After I don't know how many minutes, I heard a voice calling in my dreams: "Up, up." I opened my eyes. The guard was screaming at us, kicking the sleeping boys, threatening the slow ones with the long stick — actually the handle of a garden hoe — he held menacingly in his right hand. Everyone began scrambling to find his shoes that sat in a pile at the center of the room. My hands shook. I found one shoe but not the other. I was stooped over, hunting among the remaining pairs, when something struck me between the shoulder blades with great force.

"Bastard! Why are you so slow?"

I turned, crouched in pain. It was the night guard. He'd struck me on the spine with the long stick. It hurt terribly, but I managed not to fall over. I knew that showing weakness here could mean death. I bowed to the guard, his face twisted in a bright grin, as the flesh above my spine throbbed.

"Please, sir," I said, "I'm looking for my shoes."

He raised the stick again and screamed "Bastard!" He slammed it down on my left shoulder, trying to break the collarbone. I wanted to kill him, but I thought he must have allies among the other guards and they would come for me when the sky grew dark.

From this day on, the guard chose me as his number-one victim. I learned later that his parents were middle class and could have afforded to get him out of the prison, but chose not to. The guard had been abandoned and then sent to detention, where he got a job watching over the other inmates. To show his dominance, he attacked people for no reason at all. And he made a special case out of me.

I learned to put my shoes in a place where I could find them, but the guard didn't care. Bastard was my name, and beatings were my regular fate. Sometimes he hit me with the big stick; other times he slapped my face with his open hand. I only bowed in response. But rage was building up inside me. I could feel the blood pump hot to my face when he slapped it.

Out on the streets, I was considered a good fighter for my age. I was even feared by some. But people were treated like animals at the detention center, often brutally beaten by a dozen men at a time. No one could stand up to that.

One day, after weeks of this treatment, I heard the guard approach me from behind.

"Hey, bastard," he said, almost jovially. I could feel the eagerness in his voice, the anticipation of a good slap, a release of his hatred and frustration from his skin into mine. It was almost like he craved the letting go of the dark electricity that had built up in him all morning. I could feel how he savored these moments. I had always been sensitive to others' emotions, even my enemies'.

But today, I couldn't take the thought of him touching me. I spun around.

"Why are you always picking on me?" I cried, my voice breaking. "Leave me alone, please. Leave me alone or else!" Even as I said it, I knew that I'd opened myself up to danger. But it was too late to take the words back.

The guard's face went still with surprise. Then it blushed dark and his eyes slitted.

"How dare you talk back to me!" he said in a low voice.

We began shouting at each other, the other boys gathering, wide-eyed, to watch. The team leader heard what was going on and came running over.

"What's happening?" he said, pushing boys aside. "What are you two yelling about?"

Before the guard could open his mouth, I quickly spoke up. I described what had been happening under the team leader's nose. He listened and nodded, gesturing for the furious guard to be silent. When I finished, the team leader nodded.

"I don't need to hear any more. I will do what's fair! And that means only one thing: you two will fight it out!"

The team leader looked very pleased with himself. He was clearly bored with his daily routine, and here was an opportunity for a little excitement.

I knew that losing the fight would be dangerous. The guard would have total control over me, and because I had humiliated him by defying him in public, he would show no mercy. I decided I would do whatever it took to win.

The team leader gathered all the boys together in the center of our room. I studied my opponent. He was bigger and heavier, but I knew he'd led a more privileged life while I'd been on the street. *You are mentally stronger,* I said to myself. *Whatever you do, don't give up.*

"OK, begin!"

The guard and I grabbed each other by the shoulders and arms and pushed back and forth, grunting with the effort. He quickly slipped his hand away and landed a punch on my jaw, mashing the flesh against my teeth. I tasted blood and this frightened me. I shoved him back, trying to topple him over. But he was stronger than I thought. After a few minutes of furious wrestling, my left knee gave way and I rolled to the ground. The guard's hands went to my throat as he fell on me. We rolled back and forth, punching each other and snorting for air. The minutes stretched on and on. I saw in my peripheral vision that the other team leaders had joined us. I could hear bottles of moonshine clink as they were set down on the concrete.

After twenty minutes of wrestling and blows, my arms were slick with sweat. I was exhausted. It felt as if my arms were hanging from their sockets by thin strings. But I had more to lose, and I'd always been a stubborn fighter. I threw the guard to the ground and climbed on top of him, sitting on his heaving chest. I pinned both his hands with my left hand and started punching him in the face as he turned it this way and that, trying to evade my blows. I felt no rage anymore, no emotion at all. I was like a miner gouging out a seam of coal. There was no hatred left in me, only determination.

Bang, I gashed his lower lip on his teeth. Again. I took a deep breath, leaned forward, and gritted my teeth. Bang. Harder. *Bang.* A spurt of blood drifted up, then fell to his cheek.

"I give up!" he shouted finally. A cheer went up from some of the spectators while others blew out their breath in disgust.

I rolled off the guard and lay on the floor, gasping.

I'd survived yet again.

I'd only wanted to serve my time as quietly as possible, but by winning I'd brought myself to the attention of "the gangster brothers." That afternoon, I learned my reward. I was named the new guard. This meant more and better food and freedom not to work all day in the intense heat.

The guard I'd beaten became a regular inmate, and would go out to the fields to weed. The stick was handed to me, with the understanding that I would use it indiscriminately, and with great harshness.

I didn't want the long stick, I didn't want to be a guard, but I had no choice. I vowed to be a better person than the teenager who victimized me. I hoped I wouldn't become a brutal creature, like the gangster brothers who ran the detention center. I wanted to keep a part of the old me alive. But within weeks, there were boys in that place who would probably have killed me with pleasure. Months after I left the center, I was still being chased on the streets of Hoeryong by the same boys, with the same rage in their eyes that I'd felt when the stick rapped me on the spine. We were angry, I think, because of what had happened to us, but also because of what we'd become.

The famine in North Korea killed hundreds of thousands of people. Some of their graves are still visible on the low hills outside Hoeryong. But the famine also did secret things. It dissolved families as if they'd been dipped in acid (mine, unfortunately, was a good example); it broke up deep, committed friendships over something as small as a cornmeal cake. Even if your body survived, you would find someday that your soul had been marked in ways you couldn't know until much later.

This was true of many people I met in those times. And it was true of me.

UNDER THE SAME SKY

CHAPTER ONE

As a very young boy, I was quiet and introverted. It was hard for me to talk easily with people, and this made it difficult to make friends. But I found that I'd been given something that went some way toward balancing out my shyness: an ability to gauge other people's emotions without the use of words. I think of this gift as a kind of chemical mood sensor inside me. It was as if people's feelings left their bodies as invisible particles and sailed through the air between us, passing through the pores of my skin before being absorbed into the mood sensor, which identified them for me.

At that time, my family — my handsome, confident father, my sickly mother, my beloved older sister, Bong Sook, and I — were living in a small "pigeon coop" apartment in Hoeryong, a city known for its white apricots, its beautiful women, and for having the best pottery clay in North Korea. I still remember the emotions that flowed into me then from my parents and sister. Few words we spoke come back to me now, only shades of light and blackness, sadness and joy.

My mother emitted dark energy. In the middle of the day, I would find her motionless on her sleeping mat. She would stay there for hours, completely still. Why she was like this when my friends' mothers were always bustling around, making tofu and sweet snacks, gossiping loudly in the stairwells or shooing us away from their doors, I didn't know. She did tell me once that she'd come down with pellagra — a disease caused by a lack of vitamin B_3 — while pregnant with me. She'd also eaten a fish the week before my birth and gotten really ill. "The neighbors didn't think I was going to live," my mother said. I couldn't understand what the pellagra or the fish had to do with her lying on the floor all these years later.

I absorbed her sadness into myself. When she was like this, I felt listless too. I would often lie down beside her and sink into a miserable slumber. In those rare moments when she laughed, I wanted to laugh with her.

The truth was, my mother was depressed about her life and her marriage, and this resulted in a sad and spiritless woman whose moods permeated our tiny pigeon coop. Her sickness, or her distress about her own life, also caused her to become a clean freak. "Kwang Jin," she would call to me as soon as I walked in the apartment. (My name, Kwang Jin, means "moving forward with brightness.") "Hurry up and wash your hands!"

Bong Sook, on the other hand, had the complete opposite effect on me. Seven years older than me, sweet and uncomplaining, she never failed to light up my mood sensor like sunshine. In those years, before I fell out of favor with my father, I was the prince of the family. The nice things Bong Sook did for me (and what *didn't* she do for me?) I came to expect. Whenever I was hungry for more rice, she would take some of hers and put it on my plate, saying, "Look, Daddy, you gave me too much." When she came home from school, she would be sure to bring me a little snack, ice cream or candy, from a shop along the road. When my socks needed washing, she would wash them. When I was bored, she'd sit me down and read from one of her textbooks.

Bong Sook didn't get the same love I did as the baby boy. When my father swept through the house and picked one of us up to swing around and around, it was always me. When he chose one of us to drape across his feet while he lay on his back, allowing us to feel like we were flying, I was always the one. When the family bought a new bike, it was handed to me.

But Bong Sook never got jealous or spiteful. When my father went out of town on business, he would always return with gifts (a toy gun for me, a doll for my sister) and North Korean candy — boiled sucker balls, white with light brown stripes, sticky and delicious. If he pulled ten pieces out of his pocket, I would get five and Bong Sook the same. But she wouldn't eat them. She would take one herself and hand me three, which I would gobble up in no time. The last piece she would hide away for a day when I was feeling sad. Then she would dangle it in front of my eyes and laugh before letting me tear off the wrapper and pop it in my mouth.

Bong Sook did this without the slightest resentment — or so I have long believed. But did she? Or did her heart flutter with secret jealousies? Did she long for my father to pick her up just once and swing her around the apartment, chortling with glee? I wish I could ask her now.

One of my first memories is of my sister's school uniform: a white blouse, a scarlet-red scarf tied around her neck, and a royal-blue skirt. I was out playing with my friends near the stairs of the apartment building, and I recall the whirl of activity: cars passing and honking, pedestrians pushing along the sidewalk, my friends laughing and dodging among the people. And then, through this tan-gray blur, something, just an outline of a body, appeared at a distance. Somehow I knew it was my sister. I must have been three or four years old. Out of all the cold and unfamiliar things in the world that weren't Bong Sook, Bong Sook had magically appeared. This filled me with happiness.

And my father? He provided light, kilowatts of pure energy. My father had risen far from his poor peasant boyhood, having been named the second-highest official in a district in Undok before becoming a successful accountant for a military school in Hoeryong. This had given him a shining confidence in all of life's possibilities. At least for the first few years of my boyhood, he could send a surge of hope through me just by walking in the door.

Men like my father were, I think, especially vulnerable to the storms that awaited us. It's impossible to confirm that such men died at higher rates than cynical or skeptical types — where in North Korea would one find such statistics? — but I believe they shared a dark fate. Their simple belief in life must have cost them dearly.

3

CHAPTER TWO

BY THE EARLY spring of 1994, when I was almost four years old, my parents wanted to leave the pigeon coop. We didn't pay rent; we knew an old woman who had an extra room she let us stay in. But my parents felt threatened by the woman, who was always knocking on our door and asking my mother pointed questions. Mother wasn't used to being harassed, and this upset her terribly. The old woman—she wanted, I think, to show my family who was boss—would even ask my father to bring her wood and coal and to do odd jobs around the house, hinting that if he didn't obey her, there would be consequences. My parents began to think about leaving. They wanted to go someplace where we could afford our own home.

I didn't want to go. I loved the little building where we lived. Every morning, I would tear off and go running around the apartment complex with the few friends I had, making all the noise we wanted to. We were left to our own devices for most of the day and would explore the nearby streets for hours on end. Three blocks felt like a dozen miles to us, with each more distant street full of mystery and danger and exotic smells. We would meet in the stairwell and play rock-paper-scissors, or run outside and find a tree and play hide and seek. Each tiny corner of the building's stairwell held memories embedded in the dirty, chipped cement. Here was the stair where I sprained my ankle and couldn't play for three weeks; there was the step where I ate pillow bread, a North

Korean specialty, and ice cream that Bong Sook had brought me, a rare double snack. It was the only world I knew.

There were shops along my street, everything you could want: a barber, a grocery, an ice cream parlor. There were no rich people in our neighborhood to support fancy stores and no poor people to pity. At 5 p.m., when the day's TV programming began with news and cartoons, we'd all rush over to the apartment of the one friend whose parents had managed to buy a set. There we'd sit in a row and eat homemade popcorn and candy. The residents of the apartment building were very close. All the kids would play together and anyone who had extra food would gladly share it with their neighbors.

We were all alike, one big North Korean family, or so it seemed to me. I wanted to stay.

One cold afternoon that fall, my father came home from work on his bicycle, pedaling fast. We didn't own a car—hardly anyone in North Korea could afford one—so my father's bicycle was a treasured possession. I spotted him a block away on our cluttered street, leaning over the handlebars, his lean and handsome face—so different from my round one—shining with sweat. Right away, my mood sensor understood something: my father was very excited.

"Come, Kwang Jin," he called to me from half a block away. "We're going to see the new house." He lifted me and set me down behind him on the bicycle seat. Off we flew through the loud and congested streets, headed toward the country.

My father was determined to leave the inner city. He had a good job and a spotless reputation. As far as we knew, North Korea was doing well economically, through its citizens' hard work and the generous help of food and fuel subsidies from Russia. My father was thirty-seven years old, smart, incorruptible, and loyal to the regime. He'd joined the Workers' Party of Korea at the young age of twenty-four, a major accomplishment. Everyone wanted to join, but few were accepted, and my father had no family connections to help him.

All in all, it was high time to build a house.

Now my father powered steadily through the traffic, his strong back flexing with each pump of the pedals. A couple of blocks away was a broad highway, lined by branching elms, yellow flowers, and the tall concrete statues the government put up with slogans carved into them. I knew these slogans well: CHUN LEE MAH flashed by as we sped onward. It meant, "We must work a thousand times harder than other countries!" It was one of Kim Il Sung's favorite sayings.

I held on to my father's shirt so as not to fall off. I watched the trees and buildings flow by. The small apartment buildings fell away and cars became harder to find, replaced by peasants with carts and oxen. I had never been so far away from home except for our trips to see Grandma and Grandpa for New Year's.

Our destination was an hour away: the July 8th neighborhood, named after the date Kim Il Sung came to visit. This is how many places in North Korea are named: by some event far in the past related to the Great Leader and his ministers. The farther we went, the quieter the roads became. The homes I saw now were rough-looking farmhouses with mud splashed on the walls. My father tirelessly pumped the pedals of the old black bike.

By the time we pulled up to our new plot of land, he was sweating beneath the thin material of his shirt. He turned and plucked me off the seat and set me down. Happiness and anticipation were written all over my father's face. How much this house meant to him! We walked over and inspected the site.

It wasn't much to look at, really. The foundation had been dug deep in order to keep jars of kimchi cool in the winter—in North Korea, even the houses are designed around that most sacred of foods. The walls were slowly going up. It was a two-room building with a basement. No bathroom. We would use an outhouse for that, as do most North Koreans.

There were three or four workers mixing cement to bind the cinderblocks together. And this is what my father delighted in most: the walls were surrounded by nothing but air. We were going to escape the apartment building and live in something modern and new. My father's house stood on its own, touching nothing, touched by nothing.

Father began walking the dimensions of the small plot, squatting down and pointing at something in the foundation, shouting questions at the workers. I fooled around with some loose bricks and placed one on top of two others. Then something caught my eye. Behind the rising walls of the house, I saw a hill. And on the hill were little mounds, like gophers or beavers might build, only bigger. I stared at the mounds, my nerves tingling and then suddenly still.

I knew what those shapes were. Graves.

In North Korea, a grave is just a small, round mound of earth with a stone or wooden tablet stuck into the dirt saying who is buried there. As I looked out beyond the house, I saw the rising foothills of a mountain range that reached perhaps 2,500 feet in the air, with veins of snow snaking down toward the valley. At the foot of the mountains was a huge cemetery. And next to the cemetery was our future home.

Father has decided to build a place near a cemetery, I said to myself. *Why would he do that? Does he even know about the graves?* I was afraid of the dark, and often felt panic on my nighttime trips to the outhouse. *How much worse will it be to face these graves on the way to pee every night?*

Much worse, I thought.

But I said nothing. My father was my hero; I wanted him to be happy. For him, I would live with the dead.

While my father inspected the property, I played with broken bricks and watched the men slap cement onto the walls with trowels. There was space for a big yard and garden, but all I could think of was the boys in the apartment building I was going to leave. Them and the cemetery. My father issued a few orders and then we turned around and pedaled home.

My father had many reasons for wanting the house. Somewhere in his mind, having grown up in a poor backwater like Undok, he equated unattached houses with the rich and the well-connected. Now, after becoming a rising star in our little community, he had a chance to build such a house. He was like ambitious men everywhere: he wanted his success to be visible.

But the house was also for my mother.

Years later, I visited my maternal grandparents. Several aunts and uncles were there, gathered around, talking about my mother when she was young, and how she pursued my father to the point of recklessness during the time they both worked for the same farming organization. "How you used to chase him around that office!" her brother cried out at one point, trying to coax a smile from her. What had happened to that headstrong girl, they were saying, what became of that mad love? I glanced at her face; she looked down, her lips tight. I turned to my father. His eyes were downcast too; he looked pained, uncomfortable. He didn't want to be reminded of how things had turned out. My mother didn't chase him around anymore. That feeling had died before I was born.

My father thought the reason my mom was often ill and depressed was that she had no home of her own. Or rather, he must have *hoped* the solution was so simple. In any case, with the great risk of building a house, he was taking care of her. The new place wasn't only a statement of how far he had risen from his humble beginnings. It was also, I'm sure, a message of silent concern. Of love.

Yet the July 8th house would witness great suffering soon enough.

CHAPTER THREE

WHEN WE MOVED the following spring, the house wasn't fully finished. There were more than a few things that needed fixing: pieces of flooring missing, a window with a missing pane. My father would come home in the evenings and work on the house, singing sentimental North Korean songs. When he was done, he moved on to making furniture: beautiful cabinets went up, and fine dressers made of Korean pine for our clothes. When I went to my neighbors' houses I realized that the furniture they'd bought from the store wasn't nearly as nice-looking or strong as what my father had made with a few simple tools.

Everything went well in the beginning. Bong Sook was as kind and quiet as ever. My mother's illness seemed to lift, and my father was as delighted with his new house as if it was a second son. I managed to come to terms with the people in the graveyard. When the wind from the mountain blew toward our house, I could hear the sounds of mourners. Sometimes I heard three crisp gunshots above the houses, the sign that a soldier was being buried. Instead of being horrified, I would think, *Someone actually got to fire a gun!* I was becoming obsessed with firearms and the military around that time. *Three shots*, I thought. *Lucky guy.*

All in all, when it came to the cemetery I surprised myself. Instead of always asking my father to hold my hand and take me to the outhouse, I would run there alone just before bed. When the moon was out, you could see the sloping face of the mountain and the small bumps of graves. North Koreans are very superstitious: they believe in haunted places and ghosts and omens. I wasn't afraid of the dead people beneath the mounds, but sometimes on those short walks, when the moonlight lay on the graves in a certain way, my mind would stumble across the thought, *What if you were no longer in the world, Kwang Jin? What if you stopped being?* Then I would get scared. If it got to be too much, I would call my father and he would take my hand and lead me back. He never refused.

I made friends. My best pal in July 8th was named Bae Hyo Sung. He lived a few doors down from me and we played every day. Our main game was called *Ddakji chigi,* where you compete to own beautiful strips of paper that look like origami. We were completely mad for this game. Later, many of us would rip up our school notebooks — even our textbooks — to get paper to make the intricately folded squares that we would then try to flip over with a hard slam. Kids put tiny bits of steel in the pieces of paper to make them harder to flip. I even tore up my father's copy of Kim Il Sung's memoir, which not only infuriated him but was also a crime against the state.

Hyo Sung and I were about the same height, but he was more confident than I could dream of being. Some of this probably came from his father, a city official, who was a giant: six feet at least, which made him taller than almost anyone I knew. His mom, who was kind and chatty, looked like a dwarf next to her husband.

My friend's cocksure talk electrified me. I was beginning to change from the obedient boy my mother bragged about to her friends in the street.

I started kindergarten that year and met my first school friends — and my first mean kids, too. In North Korea, when you go to school, you aren't ranked academically, but by your ability to fight. Literally. I can tell you who was the number-one boy in my first-grade class, and the number seven — and the numbers refer to only one thing: how good a battler you are, as judged by your classmates. The schools encouraged this kind of thinking: for example, when a child fails to show up for class, the teacher doesn't call the parents and ask about the absence (to begin with, there are no phones). Instead, she sends a group of the toughest students to yell at the kid. Sometimes they even beat the boy until he agrees to come back. I don't know where this mania for toughness comes from. Perhaps it's my country's history, which is full of pain and oppression.

In kindergarten no violence was allowed, but I knew that in one year the bigger kids would be sizing me up. It was in kindergarten that I acquired my first nickname outside the house: Gang Duk Gee, the name of a character in the espionage movies we all watched. Gang Duk Gee was a South Korean spy, which made it a horrible thing to call someone. Later, in grade school, I got a second nickname that was only slightly better: Yeok Do San, which referred to a big-boned Korean-Japanese wrestling champion and meant "fatty." But I wasn't fat. It was my round face, like my mother's, that earned me that name.

In any case, I knew I'd have to fight people because of my nicknames. It was inevitable.

When I went to kindergarten, I learned more about Kim Il Sung. I knew a lot about the Great Leader before I ever went to school, of course. He was our grandfather; he had magical powers; he was the smartest man in the world; and he often flew around the countryside keeping watch on all his children. Like all North Korean families, mine kept a shrine on our wall to the Great Leader and his wife. The first thing my father did in the morning, even before he washed up or ate his breakfast, was to take a cloth and carefully dust both of their portraits. Kim Il Sung looked very handsome, his face glowing with a dazzling and benevolent light, his eyes kind but also determined.

You could be sent to a prison camp for allowing dirt to gather on Kim Il Sung's portrait, or for putting it behind cracked glass. But my father cleaned the pictures out of reverence, not fear.

Kindergarten changed my view of the Great Leader. In the first few days of class, our teachers, their faces solemn and still, brought out a set of drawings and showed them to us. We crowded around to see:

a group of American soldiers with big eyes, even bigger noses, and flashing white teeth were stabbing Koreans with razor-sharp bayonets. The picture was so terrifying I thought I would faint. But I already fancied myself a soldier and would not turn away. I held my breath as the teacher explained that Americans had come to our country to massacre Koreans for no other reason than they liked to. The Americans *enjoyed* killing Korean people.

I felt a thrill of dread travel the length of my body. It came as a physical shock that there were such people in the world. We'd known that the Americans were bad. In the spy movies, it was always them or the Japanese who were trying to steal North Korea's secrets, but here was evidence of just how awful they truly were. My teacher showed us a new picture from the back of the pile. I blinked in disbelief. American soldiers were shoving pregnant Korean women into a room filled with fire. I stared at the drawing as my teacher explained that the Americans loved to roast Koreans alive or put them into gas chambers. The gas-chambers killed them faster.

Tears welled up in my eyes.

The only people who stopped the Americans from coming to my country, our teacher said, were Kim Il Sung and the soldiers of North Korea. I nodded. The Great Leader was so much more than I had ever known.

That summer, Hyo Sung and I became secret agents. We tossed our bows and arrows onto the trash pile and begged our fathers for guns. My dad had always bought me toys when I asked, but now he looked at me strangely. "Things in the market cost more these days," he said quietly. "But I'll carve you some guns out of scrap wood. How would that be?"

I felt my skin flush with annoyance. Why couldn't my father earn more money to buy me toy pistols? I began to complain, but one look at my father stopped me. I detected a sadness in him that was new. *He's worried about something,* I thought. *I wonder what.*

My father was as good as his word. He supplied me with an unending number of hand-carved pistols, revolvers, and rifles. My popularity soared. When my father carved me a gun that shot small pebbles with an elastic band, my new friends nearly died of envy.

I was a clumsy boy, always tripping and falling over exposed roots or little holes in the ground. Or I would stuff a gun in my pocket like a bandit and jam it against a doorframe when running into my room, smashing my toy to pieces. It gave me a mournful feeling to lose a gun.

When this happened, I would run to my father and say, "Could you . . . ?" The first few times, he only laughed and began fashioning a new one. But eventually he got mad at my astonishing ability to break everything in sight, and handed me a toy with no details on it, just a wood block carved into the shape of a gun. I looked at it. This was my punishment for being such a thoughtless boy. I brooded for a while, but even my father's worst pistol was better than what my friends had.

I loved those guns so much. I slept with them, and when I woke up in the morning, the first thing I would do was feel around my bed for my latest sidearm. When I touched the smooth wood, a feeling of peace would come over me. When I grew up, I was sure I would become a spy or soldier who saved his homeland from the big-nosed people.

I was very patriotic. I believed Kim Il Sung would take care of my family and me. Everyone believed this. Which is what made what was to come so hard for us to accept.

CHAPTER FOUR

HYO SUNG AND I spent our free time chasing dragonflies. As a transplanted city boy, I became obsessed with the sight of their dark glinting wings. We hunted them day after day. The bugs' favorite place to land was on the green corn stalks in the fields next to our houses. They liked the top parts of the stalks; they sat there buzzing in the heat. We snuck up behind them and clapped them in our hand-prisons. We even created our own equipment, a sort of tennis racket made out of corn stalks with spider webs draped across the middle. If you swung this in the buzzing air, the dragonfly would get caught and become your prisoner.

Just before you got to the graveyard near our house, there was an irrigation canal that supplied all the fields with water. We ran along this ditch chasing particularly beautiful dragonflies, venturing out beyond the houses, with the mountains on our right, sunlight spilling over their rounded shoulders. So long as there was sunlight, we ran and leaped and stalked our prey.

One summer day, Hyo Sung and our other friends switched to chasing frogs, which we found in the irrigation canal. The water wasn't very deep, maybe a foot, but it stretched to eternity. Despite the miles I walked that summer trying to spot the green frogs, I never got to the end of that canal.

When it crossed under a road, the water sped up and flowed down into steel pipes that angled beneath the road. My friend Chul Min and two of my other pals were hunting frogs one sweltering June day when

Chul Min jumped in the ditch—he'd spotted a toad perched on a rock. The water was running fast and Chul Min lost his footing and soon he was shooting along in the fast little rapids, screaming for help. I ran after him, my heart knocking in my chest. I knew Chul Min couldn't swim, and if he went down into the pipes he would get trapped below the road. When he got to the mouth of one of the pipes, he gripped the rim and screamed, "Help me! Help me!" The water rushed over his face, distorting his features. I didn't know what to do.

I rushed to the nearby cornfield. There I grabbed a stalk, ripping it from the ground with frenzied strength. I ran back to Chul Min. We could see the rushing current pulling him under with a giant sucking sound. On the grassy bank I lowered the stalk down to him and yelled, "Grab it!" Chul Min reached up one hand and tried to snatch at the stalk. On the third try he caught hold and we pulled until our backs ached. With a *whoosh* the water let him go and the top half of his small body collapsed onto the grass, his feet still trailing in the ditch. He was alive.

It was the first time I had felt death come close to me. And my friends and I had outwitted it. It felt wonderful.

Everyone in the neighborhood called us heroes that day. When they heard what we'd done, they actually came outside their doors and applauded us, as if we were soldiers returning from war. I became famous in July 8th as the boy who rescued Chul Min with a corn stalk.

Dinnertime was 5 p.m. in the summer. Bong Sook would be sent out to call me home. Sometimes I'd run from her, too caught up in a war game to think of food. "But it's my turn to play spy catcher!" I'd cry. I'd beg her for just a few more minutes. Other times, I would tramp home after her, hoping for *kko Jang Dduck,* a kind of corn pancake that was my favorite thing to eat. For me, those hot pancakes meant security; they meant love.

To make *kko Jang Dduck,* my mother took corn powder and mixed in saccharin (sugar was very expensive), some soda powder, and water, making a thick dough. Meanwhile, she cooked white rice in a separate pot. After thirty minutes, the rice would be almost ready, the water having boiled away. My mother then divided the dough and shaped small pieces into circles and placed them in the rice pot, slapping each pancake to the side wall. After ten minutes, the pancakes were ready. It was a simple recipe, but easy to ruin: if you put the pancakes in the pot before all the water had boiled away, they would come out soggy.

One day that July I was out playing with my friends when Bong Sook called for me, her *"Poppppp-eeeeeeee"* coming to me over the fields. I looked at the sun; it seemed too high in the sky for dinnertime. I said goodbye to my friends and headed home.

As I passed the houses on my street, I noticed that each of the rare television sets was turned on. This was nothing less than shocking. Normally, the national programs wouldn't start until five o'clock in the evening, and there would be nothing but static until then. But now I could hear the same voice coming from all the houses with TVs. And the streets, which should have been filled with people hurrying home for their lunch, were empty. It was strange; I had a queasy feeling in the bottom of my stomach. What was going on?

When I walked into my house, I found my mother sobbing, her hands clasped over her mouth. This wasn't that big a deal, actually. My mother cried at the TV all the time. She would hardly wait for the opening titles to roll on the screen before letting her tears stream down.

It was embarrassing to look at her. I used to watch my mother out of the corner of my eye and think, *Please don't cry tonight.* Why couldn't she wait until the sad scenes started, when at least one or two other people would cry, covering up her strangeness? It never occurred to me that she was sad or depressed to begin with, and that the movies simply triggered emotions she felt deep inside.

But now her eyes were red and her hands were shaking. And then I saw Bong Sook — the eternally cheerful Bong Sook — and knew something had gone terribly wrong. My sister's face was crumpled and from her lips came a wail.

It was July 8, 1994. Kim Il Sung had died.

I turned to the TV and watched soldiers marching and mobs of people in Pyongyang sobbing. I had never seen people cry so hard, shaking and beating their chests with their hands. I was afraid.

That night, the sky seemed darker than usual. Clouds covered the moon and the foothills disappeared into blackness. It began to rain, a hard, pounding rain that turned the streets into mud pools. Everywhere were the sounds of crying people, crying on the TV and crying in my own house, and outside there was the slap of rain. We believed that the earth was in mourning for our Great Leader.

Life stopped. I couldn't meet my friends for dragonfly hunting or even venture outdoors. Our only trip outside was the next day, when we went to a statue of Kim Il Sung's first wife, Kim Jong-suk, which stood in a beautiful plaza in the middle of Hoeryong. So many people thronged around the statue, scores of them in traditional Korean clothing, that you couldn't get within fifty feet of it. People laid flowers at her feet and sobbed some more. A feeling of death seemed to snake through the crowd, transmitted from person to person. My mood sensor was overwhelmed. I burst into tears, clutching my mother's hand.

Maybe some of the people in the crowd were faking, but a child doesn't realize this. I didn't even know why I was crying, really; the sorrow of the crowd was so strong, it pushed its way into my heart. We inched our way closer and I kneeled on the steps below the statue with my mom and sister, tears streaming down my face. The statue now stood in a field of flowers, seemingly floating on their bright petals.

With the Great Leader gone, the world was a scarier place. I felt his absence the way a navigator would miss a guiding star. Who would watch over us now?

CHAPTER FIVE

―――――

THE FAMINE ARRIVED. It wasn't like we opened the rice pot one day and there was nothing in it. Instead, everything disappeared slowly, as if by evaporation. There wasn't any Internet or television news or ringing telephones to warn that bad things were headed our way. Later, some people would call the famine *Gonan-eui haenggun* (the March of Suffering), which was a government slogan meant to convey that life was difficult now, but better times were coming. The government also wanted us to believe that the crops had disappeared through no fault of the state, and that everyone was suffering equally. This, I later learned, was a lie.

North Koreans never called the famine the March of Suffering. We never gave it a name. It was like a heavy, poisonous fog that enters your mouth before you can shout a warning.

What we didn't know then was that Russia had stopped sending North Korea food and fertilizer, the tons of it that had helped sustain the country for many years. The Soviet Union had collapsed in 1991. The Russia that emerged in its wake was cash poor and no longer inclined to prop up the few remaining Communist regimes, such as Cuba and North Korea. Despite the government's propaganda that emphasized a policy of *juche,* or self-sufficiency, the nation had relied on that food to survive.

To make matters worse, monsoon-like rains struck North Korea in

1995, washing away topsoil and destroying many thousands of acres of crops. The disastrous policies of the government, which had introduced farming on only a small portion of the country's arable land, caused great suffering. The government, now led by Kim Jong Il, responded with a series of patriotic campaigns. City dwellers were forced into the countryside to toil in the fields from before dawn until nightfall. The "Let's Eat Two Meals a Day" drive commenced. But corruption and a broken economic system doomed all their efforts. There were no private markets where one could buy rice and tofu; the government was the only source of food. And each month it distributed less and less.

My father, as it turned out, had chosen a terrible time to build his dream house. North Korea's economy was rapidly falling apart.

The first sign of disaster I witnessed came in late 1995, not with crop failure or anything so obvious, but with a cartoon show. It was called *Boy General*, and it was set in 50 B.C. In it, an ordinary boy wakes up one day to find he's been turned into a superhero. He flies through the air, shoots a bow and arrow, and rides a horse like he was born to it. My friends and I were obsessed with the cartoon. We would climb on fences made of plank wood that separated our yards and jump from the tops, yelling that we were the Boy General, and jump — *aiiiyyeeeeee!* The hills resounded with our blood-curdling yells.

It goes without saying that I never missed my favorite show. Then one ordinary Wednesday, when I sat down in front of our TV, nearly levitating with excitement, to watch the latest episode, the picture was wavy and there was no sound. I couldn't even hear the theme song.

Somewhere in the countryside, a TV relay station wasn't getting enough power. I was shocked. I began to make up the dialogue of the cartoon in my head, watching the characters' lips move and imagining what he or she was talking about. It was terrible. My dialogue made no sense! I grew so frustrated that I wanted to smash the set to the ground.

"Papa," I cried, "what's wrong with the TV?" My father came and adjusted the rabbit ears, but nothing happened. He stood silently for a moment, then sighed. My mood sensor picked up something unfamiliar in his expression, but I ignored that. A whole episode of *Boy General* was slipping away! I stared at the screen in mute horror. I was so annoyed. How could the adults let this happen to our national hero?

I began to notice other things. The electrical outages we had always suffered grew worse. The lights in our little part of July 8th would snap out and all you could see were things lit up by moonlight: the rooflines of houses, the hummocks of the graves on the mountainside.

Next, my mother's corn pancakes disappeared. She made them for the last time one evening and they never graced our table again. My mother said nothing. I didn't ask her when we were going to have them again. Something inside of me sensed it was not a good time to explore the subject.

Even humble corn noodles—the basis of our diet—grew scarce. Bong Sook would always "get full" first and shovel some of her noodles over to my plate, noodles I ate hungrily, but no one was getting enough. The homemade bread my mother loved to make no longer sent out its wonderful yeasty smell. White rice departed that autumn. Any kind of meat was soon a distant memory, and the entire concept of a snack, something you ate just because you liked it, became a sad joke.

With the shortage of vegetables and the stress of not being able to feed her children, my mom's illness returned. I'd find her lying on the floor when I came back from school, her eyes slits of black. The lack of food began to affect her brain. She kept telling my father she heard things moving in the walls.

My father shrugged off her fears. But my mother insisted that when I was out playing and Bong Sook was still at school, the noises would start—scrapings, rustlings, mysterious squeaks. Was it mice? Or was the new house settling?

Finally, when the noises didn't stop, my father told her a secret he had been keeping. During construction of the house, he and the workers had found something under the foundation that didn't belong there. Bones, in fact.

While my father and the laborers were digging the basement for the kimchi, they'd uncovered pieces of human skeletons at a depth of five feet. Perhaps the government had reclaimed the land from the cemetery and never bothered to remove the graves. Perhaps the bones had been washed down from the mountains many years before and covered in layers of dirt. But my father, afraid to lose his dream house, had said nothing.

This revelation affected my mother deeply. "It's because of the bones that I'm sick!" she cried to my father. "The dead have no rest. They want to find their home."

My parents were completely lost. First a famine, and now ghosts in the house. Both of these things were beyond their slight experience of the world. The government wouldn't help; the neighbors could do nothing. So my parents went to a *Mishin*.

A *Mishin* is a shaman, a figure that has been part of Korean culture for thousands of years. Despite the government's crackdown on all forms of spiritual belief, every decent-sized village still had one person, usually a woman, who was ready to intercede in the spirit world on your behalf, for a small fee. So my parents went off one evening to meet the spirit worker. They must have asked her to perform a *bhang toh*, the guiding away of a disturbed ghost.

When my mother and father got back home that night, their mood had changed. They were cheerful. As soon as they walked through the door, they got to work making a delicious meal: white rice and eggs and fried pork, and plenty of it, too. We were already suffering from hunger pangs, a scraping misery that tears at the pit of your stomach and nestles like a malevolent thing in the twists of your intestines. So I was overjoyed when I saw them cooking the food. White rice! Succulent meat! Where had they gotten it? The aroma of the pork was like a powerful potion, and I drank it in happily. But as midnight approached, my parents scooped up the delicacies and slid them into a ceramic jar, which they covered with my mother's best scarf and set in a corner of the house.

After a moment of stunned silence, I commenced wailing. Loudly. I wanted to eat the eggs and the white rice. My parents hushed me and explained that the food was prepared so the ghost in our walls would leave. I thought that was ridiculous. It was a long while before I fell asleep.

My parents followed the same ritual three times over several months, following the *Mishin*'s instructions to the letter. The second and third times, they also placed paper money with the warm food inside the jar. I thought this ghost must be very important for them to be feeding him *and* giving him cash. After we placed the jar in the corner, we would all go to sleep.

The next morning, the jar was gone, every time. My parents were highly satisfied. You could even say the ritual worked. After the third jar disappeared, my mother stopped hearing noises in the house. My parents believed that the ghost had come out of the walls and taken the food, and the *Mishin* had guided the poor spirit back to the land of the dead. We were now poorer, but no longer haunted.

What happened, really? Perhaps it was a neighbor who wanted rice or money for free. Perhaps the shaman herself came in the middle of the night to take the jar, so as to keep her customers happy and to enjoy a rare good meal.

I've always wondered about the bones and the *Mishin*. Did my mother really hear noises in the walls of our house? Or was her mind warning her about something else? Sometimes I think she saw the great hunger coming, and the voices she heard were her own mind telling her that disaster was on the way.

The ghost was gone, but the *Mishin* could do nothing about the famine, which was with us always, making us irritable and sleepy. I wanted to ask my parents what was going on — *why has all the food disappeared?* — but the dread in their eyes made me silent.

We added more and more water to our grain soup. When the grain was gone, we stirred in dandelions and green weeds to give the soup some flavor and bulk. Then one day spiky things appeared in our bowls. At first I didn't understand what they were, but after studying their shape, I realized they were soybean plants. Not *soybeans*, which tasted nice, something like peanuts, but the stalks of the plant itself. My mother had gone into the nearby hills and come back with these dry things, boiled them in water, and served them to us. My brain, as hunger-crazed as it was, said, *This is completely disgusting.*

I picked up a stalk and put it in my mouth. It dripped with water, and just by looking at it I knew it was going to taste bad. I nibbled on the end. "It's terrible!"

"Eat it," my father said quietly. He didn't look at me. He was a much more subdued person nowadays. The palpable confidence of just a year ago was gone.

I didn't want to eat it. The plant had tiny spikes along the side and it tasted like what I imagined cement would taste like. I felt the stalk crawling down my throat, the spikes jabbing the soft flesh there. I thought I would throw up, but finally managed to get a single stalk down.

Your body knows when it is eating something that's not food. It's as if some alien thing has entered your stomach. Your belly is temporarily full, but you can tell that no nutrients are flowing to your limbs, that there's no fat to make your taste buds happy. There is only a sodden arrow made of lead sitting in your belly.

This is worse than starving, I thought. But I was wrong, of course.

CHAPTER SIX

WE WEREN'T THE only ones suffering. One night I overheard my parents talking. (Our house was too small to keep secrets.) Our next-door neighbor's grandfather had died of hunger the day before.

I didn't know this grandfather; his name brought no face to my mind. But the news frightened me. I didn't know that you could run out of food and actually die. This new fact, that hunger's path led to death, was shocking to me.

In the first months of the famine, people began to panic. They didn't know what to do. It was as if they were children who'd woken up one morning to find their parents had vanished with all the rice, leaving no message behind. People in Hoeryong were bewildered, but they still feared their leaders. To cry out that your father or brother had died of hunger in a totalitarian state was to accuse the government of a serious crime: *Why did you allow this to happen?* The *Inminban*, the local committee of women who reported troublemakers to the government, kept watch over all of us. If one of these women heard you complain about the lack of food, you could get into serious trouble. So people remained silent.

Nor did we have the comfort of blaming God, as there was no God in North Korea. We had to swallow our fear and go on. The hopelessness I had once seen in my mother's face affected all of us now. It seeped into our home like a heavy gas. Our faces grew pinched and dumb.

I would catch my parents looking at Bong Sook and me with terror in their eyes. At first I thought it was strange, but gradually I realized they were observing us for signs of starvation. The thought that they might die wasn't what worried them. Their greatest fear was to not be able to feed us.

As the famine swept through Hoeryong, my parents bickered more and more. They had never been very loving toward each other. It's not the North Korean way to hug your spouse or your children and say "I love you." The marriage that was fragile to begin with grew brittle when this disaster, which would test the strongest marriage to its limit, blew down on them. Their love shivered beneath it.

My parents argued about food. It was hard to hide their worry and fear in a two-room house. "But we don't have anything left!" I would hear my mother shout at my father. "Why don't you take money from your company like other fathers?" One of the things that had made my mother fall in love with my father was his idealism. My father was the straightest of straight arrows. He refused to take bribes or steal food or use his company's money, as other families did. During that time, North Korea was a place where corruption was so common it wasn't even called corruption, it was just life. But my father wanted to walk with a straight back.

In that small house, when my father returned home from work, exhausted and gray-faced, my mom would be furious. She was the one who was forced to hear us whimper from hunger. She had to go into the hills and rip disgusting weeds out of the ground and pretend they were good for her family. So when my father walked in the door empty-handed, my mother screamed at him. "You're sacrificing your own children!"

My mood sensor absorbed my mother's resentment. Why didn't my father bring sacks of rice home? He was an important person. I couldn't yet see that my dad was a misfit in the feral world of North Korea, that his faith in the leaders in Pyongyang was a horrible curse for him. In his mind, North Korea had given him a chance to succeed, and he couldn't steal so much as a single coin from its coffers.

My mother and I didn't care about that. (Bong Sook never expressed anger at my father.) Rage built up inside us. We were dying.

The day after each fight, something else would disappear from the house. Clothes went first. My mother even sold the dress she was married in; my father's wedding suit was also sacrificed. I knew she was selling these things in the market to sustain us.

We grew thinner. Our eyeballs pushed from their sockets, or so it seemed. Really, our faces were just growing leaner. We had little energy for playing or reading books or anything else.

Bong Sook didn't need to come looking for me now at dinnertime. An hour or two before my mother would put the old battered pots over the flame, I hunched by the cold hearth waiting for food. I would sway lethargically, watching her prepare a meal out of whatever plants she could find.

One evening, my parents came back from a walk into town looking excited. "Children! Next month it's going to be better," they said. "We're going to make a lot of money!"

Bong Sook clapped her hands. "How wonderful!"

"How do you know this?" I said, ever the skeptic.

"The *Mishin* told us!" my father responded.

My parents could barely contain their excitement. They devoted the whole night to talking about what they were going to buy when the cash started pouring in. It was as if the money had already been made. The hard part would be figuring out how to spend it.

When things got worse economically, my parents sought out the shaman. Inevitably, they received good news: "In two months, the best days of your life will arrive!" "In three months, you will never worry about money again!" This optimism led my father to make bad decisions. Usually so level-headed, he got swept up in my mother's dreams. He was desperate to provide for us; he succumbed to false hope. When my mother asked him to borrow money from his company to fund a business scheme, he didn't yell at her. He got the money. Wasn't this the business opportunity the shaman had predicted?

Two months later, my father asked my mother for the loan back. My mother didn't have the money. Something had gone wrong with whichever business she was running at that time. This caused my father to fly into a rage.

This happened whenever things got desperate in my home. There would be a new scheme, a visit to the *Mishin*, ecstasy, two months of waiting, public humiliation, then horrible screaming fights. Each time, my father's debts grew and his marriage to my mother suffered another blow. We had less money to buy food, and our ribs nudged farther out from our shrunken skin.

When the confrontation came, it was made worse by the feeling my parents had of being made fools of. How could they fall for the same nonsense again? And yet there was nowhere else for them to turn. The next month, my mother would go to a new *Mishin*, and my father, unwilling at first to listen to her promises of riches, would tag along. Then came the shouts of "Where is the money?" echoing through our house.

Really, they were like lost children.

Even at that age, I knew I was different from my parents. They believed in things. My father believed in the value of hard work and the North Korean government. My mother believed in business. Both of them were crazy about "luck." If North Korea had casinos, my parents would have been their best customers.

But me? I didn't believe in luck, or miracles. My parents cured me of that. I always felt that if you wanted something, you were going to have to go out and get it yourself.

Dinner now consisted of a bite or two of corn, some watery dandelion soup, or once or twice those spiky soybean leaves that scratched my throat as I forced them down. I cried in frustration, wondering what was happening in the world to make us suffer like this.

To keep my spirits up, I would replay in my mind favorite meals from the past, the moment my lips had last touched a slice of *kko Jang Dduck*. I replayed every creamy bite in exquisite slow motion.

Those days will come again, I thought. And for the very fortunate, they did. But my family was never lucky in these things.

CHAPTER SEVEN

IN THE SPRING of 1996, we clung to the edge of life. The famine had thinned out the village, as many of our friends lost grandmothers, aunts, sons, and cousins. The graves climbed up the mountainside as if it were infected with a virus. I went to my second year of kindergarten (in North Korea, kindergarten lasts two years), but learned little. I had no energy to concentrate. It seemed that most of our strength was devoted to fighting hunger.

We ate two meals a day, then one—mostly weeds that we choked down. Finally my parents admitted that we weren't gathering enough to feed ourselves. My mother decided to visit her family in Kang Suh, a city more than five hundred miles away, to look for help. Better for my father to have three mouths to feed, she told us, instead of four. She left without ceremony and walked to the train. I missed her terribly.

Despite having just three mouths to feed, my family grew weaker. Some days we consumed nothing but a few sips of water before passing into a fitful sleep. My father began worrying that we would succumb to starvation in the house without anyone knowing. "We're going to my brother's house," he said to Bong Sook and me one day. How hard a decision that must have been for him! Only now can I appreciate it. To go begging for food from his relatives meant that he'd failed to save his own family.

Still, I was excited. A train trip! My love of travel and rail stations and the broad-backed electric trains overpowered any thought of the hunger that gnawed at me constantly. Bong Sook and I rolled up our clothes in the nylon bags we'd take on the journey, and my father bought tickets for one of the trains that were transporting whole provinces south in search of food.

We were heading for a city near Pyongyang, where my paternal uncle, a major in the Korean People's Army, lived in a big house. My uncle was a legendary figure in our family; he'd prospered in his career through the power of his winning personality. When he was a platoon leader, years before, he'd so impressed his young soldiers — most of them members of the elite — that they'd taken care of him when they rose through the ranks. Now he was living the good life.

There was no way to warn my uncle that we were coming. We had to depend on his wholesome and sweet nature. Surely such a good man would never turn us away. If he did refuse us, Kang Suh — where my mother was staying with her relatives — was close by.

In the south, I believed, lay our salvation. I began to incorporate Haeju and my uncle's great house into my daydreams. There would be food there. Mountains of food.

On the day of departure, we walked to the station in the stifling heat. There were no more scheduled departure times; with the power outages, trains simply appeared. Hundreds of people were waiting at the station, lying on the grass or sitting on benches, fanning themselves, silent and wary. I barely noticed; I couldn't wait to leave. We expected to be away by nightfall.

We sat on the concrete platform guarding our few bags. After a couple of hours, the crowd stirred. A train appeared around the bend of the southbound track. But there was something odd about it. The train itself looked misshapen — instead of the sleek tubular carriages I was used to, a thick, swollen thing chugged toward us. I realized that the swelling was actually bodies crouched on the train cars' roofs and people hanging from the cars' broken windows. I felt my stomach lurch.

Something about the train looked scary, chaotic-looking. Why were those people allowed to hang all over the locomotive? Where were the ticket takers and the conductor?

Everyone in the West talks about the oppressive, invasive government of North Korea, but what I experienced then was more frightening to a child: a complete absence of authority of any kind. A child wants someone to be in charge of the world. But it was clear from the train that the people in charge had abandoned it to the masses. No one was enforcing the rules any longer.

The locomotive heaved to a stop and the people around me surged forward, letting out a collective shriek. The sight of the only way out of the famine lands triggered a kind of hysteria in the people. "I've been waiting for days!" a woman next to me screamed, and people began to shove around me and to smack each other with their fists. My body was caught up in the swell. I was lifted toward the train, wriggling helplessly. I screamed to my father, but he was fighting his way toward the door. I struggled to keep hold of Bong Sook's hand. The people were clawing at each other from behind now, swearing and red-faced. My father fought, too, but with two children, he was overpowered by soldiers and single men. Eventually the train pulled out of the station without us, and a keening wail went up from the women left behind. I saw a look of despair cross my father's face. Perhaps we'd waited too long after all.

More trains came, one or two a day, sometimes only an hour or two apart, but it was always the same story. It seemed as if the entire north of the country was fleeing at once. We slept near the train station, foraging along the tracks for things to eat. On the second day, my father sold his favorite pen for a piece of cornbread. Vicious hair-pulling fights broke out over pots of stewed weeds.

One day, I saw a man carrying a corpse on his back, a corpse that had apparently come off a passing train. It wasn't like the other bodies I'd seen before. The top half, including the head, was burned to a blackened crisp. It looked like it was wearing some kind of costume, with the completely normal legs dressed in tan slacks and scuffed black shoes, and then the black char of the upper body that cut a line right where his belt should have been.

"Father, what happened?" I asked, my stomach growing queasy.

My father glanced at the body.

"He must have been riding on top because of the crowding. He touched the live wire."

I stared until the man with the body disappeared into the parting crowd.

On day three, when we saw a train approach around the bend, my father, knowing that to be left behind was to die, battled his way toward the closest open door, pulling my sister and me along with him. It felt as if my arm would be jerked out of its socket, but somehow I managed to keep my hand clasped in Bong Sook's as she tugged me through the crowd at waist height.

We grappled our way to the door, elbows flying and people grunting to our left and right. My father grabbed the metal handhold attached to the outside of the train and pulled us on board. We'd made it.

The train moved off, the cry of anguish from those left behind fading as the sound of steel on rails swelled in our ears.

Aboard, there was no relief from the crowds. We pushed our way toward the seats, but of course they had long been filled, so we stood or crouched, supported by the bodies of the other passengers. If you could put your feet down on the ground without stepping on someone lying there, sick or passed out, you were lucky. Those who had been squeezed out of the carriages climbed to the roofs, near the overhead cables that powered the train.

The journey to my uncle's town usually took three days. But now the train seemed to wander aimlessly across the countryside like a heat-dazed snake. The electricity went out frequently and the train would make a sad, droning noise as its systems died. Eventually it slid to a stop on the tracks. We often waited for a day or longer for the power to come back up.

There was no room for Bong Sook or me to play, and we had no books with us to help pass the time. It felt claustrophobic being stuffed into the car with so many other unwashed bodies. "The train is so slow," my father said, shaking his head. "I hope we have enough food to last."

The passengers were people like us, neither rich nor dirt poor, fleeing their homes on a rumor or a hope. "There is food in the south," one woman told us. "My cousin will welcome us." But she had no way of knowing this, not really. She was in the same situation we were: down to our last chance.

Instead of reading or playing, I watched the other passengers. They were my movies, and I studied them for hours. The first thing I realized was that the famine had produced many, many thieves. I saw people who probably had never stolen a thing before take food from the pockets of fellow passengers. Children waited for old men to fall asleep and then rifled through their pockets. People pushed their way down the aisle, noses bleeding, their faces raked with cuts, the losers in some battle over food scraps.

The mood of the crowd was sullen. It wasn't like the carefree trips I remembered. Travel, to me, had always been fun: there were cousins and aunts and presents and food waiting for us on the other end. But now we were going to my uncle's to beg. Everything was so different. People would go to sleep leaning on someone's shoulder and wake up in the morning to find that that person had died during the night and had to be pulled out of the clench of bodies. It was what I would imagine traveling during the American Depression was like. Even though Bong Sook and I were still kids, we could see the darkness in people's faces.

As the train swung southward through half-abandoned villages, we swayed along with it, staring mutely out the windows. There was very little to say. People lay in the aisles of the cars, too weak to lift their heads for morsels of food; others were taken out to the fields on either side of the railbed and left to die. As we passed stations, I saw corpses piled up outside them, people who'd been waiting and had expired in the heat. When the train passed those stations, you could smell the bodies, a stench of putrefying flesh that had one virtue: it cured your hunger pangs for as long as you breathed it in.

And yet the train pressed on. Three days, four, one week. It felt as if the city had disappeared, or the engineer could no longer find it.

After ten days we still hadn't arrived. The crush inside the train got dangerous. At every stop, more and more people clambered on to escape the stricken countryside.

CHAPTER EIGHT

THE TRAIN CHUGGED forward, on the last leg of the journey. We went through the rice and corn farms of the south, the faces of the locals registering shock at the malnourished faces in the broken windows. After three weeks, my father recognized the outskirts of my uncle's city—there were no announcements anymore—and with a feeling of exhaustion and joy, we pushed our way off at the station.

It was just after midnight, and pouring rain. We still had five miles to go, and there was no other way to get there other than walking. That five-mile walk, dazed with heat and pain . . . it was as if it would never end. It must have been worse for my father, because it never occurred to me that we might be turned away when we reached my uncle's house. But he knew that food was scarce everywhere and that our welcome wasn't guaranteed.

When we found the house, we rushed up to the door and knocked. It felt like I would collapse unless the door opened that very instant. Finally, when it did, my uncle stood in the doorway, staring at us in shock and surprise. He was dressed in sporty clothes that looked foreign and new. His expression changed to one of happiness and he swung the door wide.

"Brother, come in," he said.

We ate like kings that night. Seafood, noodles, white rice. We stuffed our bellies and laughed. It was heaven. Before going to sleep, I fervently wished that we would never leave this place.

I was reunited with my two cousins. I explored their neighborhood hand in hand with them. I ate my first blackberry. My older cousin—he was the prince of our family, smart and handsome and destined for the army—took me on a tour of their house and, in the kitchen, proudly showed me an enormous metal box called a refrigerator. I had never seen one before. Truly, my uncle was blessed.

I saw the ocean for the first time. Everything in the south seemed bigger, richer, and happier.

After spending one week at my paternal uncle's, we went to Kang Suh, where my father dropped us off with my mother's relatives before he headed home to Hoeryong. In Kang Suh, a surprise awaited us.

We hadn't seen my mother for several months, and something had happened to her during that period. I've puzzled over this many times in the intervening years: What things did my aunts and uncles say to my mom that would end up causing such pain and disruption in our lives? Did they tell her she wasn't like her old self? Did they encourage her to stand up to my father? Did they disparage him for not taking care of his family?

Whatever it was that caused the change, my mother was a different person. She had put on a few pounds and dressed better than before. She wore shoes with heels now, and stylish, well-fitting pants, and brightly colored blouses that looked like they were from China. Obviously her family had treated her well. But it was her personality that had undergone the most startling transformation.

Somehow, my sickly mother had been replaced with a dynamo. She talked more in those first few weeks than she had in years. My mom had always been smart—she read constantly, mostly books about health and nutrition and philosophy—but now she offered us bits of wisdom she'd been storing inside all those years. "Stop eating when you feel like you want to have one more spoon of rice," my mom told me once, which I later interpreted to mean, If you fall in love with power, you'll never be satisfied and ruin your life. It's funny that I remember that particular saying above all others. She herself would soon ignore it, with dreadful consequences.

My mother had always left most of the big family decisions to my father, as was traditional in North Korea. But now she was outspoken, ambitious, fired up with the possibilities of life. I was so happy to see my mother was happier and more at peace with herself.

When my mother had arrived at my uncle's doorstep, she was a thin, depressed thirty-nine-year-old woman who was fleeing starvation and an unhappy marriage. To give her something to do, my uncle, who owned a factory that made household goods, bestowed on her his excess inventory. There were pencils, as I recall, and sunglasses and other small consumer items. In the bad economy, the stuff was just collecting dust in a building nearby.

My mother didn't see the pencils and sunglasses as throwaways. She saw them as her salvation. The famine, and the almost complete governmental breakdown that accompanied it, had given my mom the big chance she'd been waiting for all her life. Before the disaster, it was illegal to start a small business. But as the country threatened to come apart, Kim Jong Il and his ministers decided to allow a little private enterprise, so as to save at least some of its citizens. My mother leapt into the breach.

I wonder if she ever saw the irony in this: that the disaster that threatened to wipe out everyone she loved also freed her. I don't think so. There was no room for such thoughts in my mother's whirring brain. She was fighting to save us.

My mom took the items from the Kang Suh warehouse and went to rural districts where people didn't have the chance to buy such things. She sold them door to door or at small markets, making a decent profit. She was traveling, meeting new people, reinventing herself as an entrepreneur. She was as independent as she'd ever been in her whole life. From what I found out later, I'm sure my mom dreamed of becoming fabulously rich, of parlaying her meager profits from the sunglasses and pencils into larger and larger hauls.

My mother was a dreamer. She was also, it turned out, a terrible businesswoman.

After another trip to the countryside, where my mom had managed to sell my uncle's dusty old inventory, she thought, *Why should I leave this place with empty hands when I can go back to Kang Suh with unique products from the country? I'll sell them in the city and double my profits.* My mother spent the *won* she'd earned on local handicrafts and brought them back to Kang Suh.

This is where her plan backfired. The goods didn't sell. My mom had to go back to my uncle and ask for more inventory to start over again. This caused friction: my uncle wanted to know where the profits went from the first batch of goods. She defended her scheme to double down. My uncle, in so many words, told her she was acting like an idiot. The sophisticated people of Kang Suh didn't want the crude homemade things she'd brought back. But my mother had seen her fortune, and she wouldn't give up.

"She always wanted more!" my uncle cried to us.

We shuttled between Mother's relatives and my paternal uncle's house, so as not to overburden either family. On one of these trips, while we sat in the grass next to the railroad station in Kang Suh, waiting for the next train, my mother pulled out three cucumbers she'd purchased and passed one each to Bong Sook and me. We munched on the thick green vegetable, savoring the juice that flowed down our throats. That cool, tart liquid was so refreshing. We ate the cucumbers down to the bitter ends, which were inedible, and looked for somewhere to throw them.

Amid the throng of other travelers I noticed a plain young woman in her early thirties watching us. She had a baby strung to her chest, maybe one year old, very small, making no noise. The woman turned to my mother and asked for the cucumber ends.

"These?" my mother said. "But they aren't good to eat."

"They're for my father," the woman said. "We'll take anything." My mom nodded and we gathered up the six nibs. The woman bowed slightly as I tilted them into her cupped hands. I watched as she walked several yards to where someone was lying in the grass. I followed her.

After taking a few steps I saw an old man, wearing a red ribbon with thin gray stripes and a medal hanging off it, a five-pointed star in light gold on a pale blue background, surrounded by a circle and then gold bars that suggested intense beams of light. I knew this medal from the countless war movies I'd watched: it was called the Hero of the Republic, and for many years it was the highest award a North Korean could earn. Only those who'd performed some extraordinarily heroic action in the Korean War had received it.

I stared at the medal in awe. I'd never seen one in real life. Then I looked at the old man as his daughter tilted his head up and tried to feed him the bitter nibs. He spat the cucumber back up. Perhaps there was something wrong with his digestion. Or perhaps he was tired of the long journey.

The Hero of the Republic medal usually ensured respect and a comfortable life. Even at five years old I knew that. The old man and I stared at each other. He was breathing so shallowly, like a fish that has mistakenly jumped onto the shore. *If a Hero of the Republic can die,* I thought, *what chance is there for Bong Sook and Mommy and me?*

CHAPTER NINE

THE ATMOSPHERE AT my paternal uncle's had changed since I'd first visited with my father. At dinner our first night back, after our father had dropped us off and headed back home, my chemical sensor went off. I began to pick up a feeling of unease in my uncle's family.

I didn't have the words to express what I was feeling, but suddenly I knew. *Auntie wants us to leave.*

The next day, my uncle found us playing in the yard and asked if we wanted to go blueberry picking.

"Yes!" I cried. I hadn't had blueberries since I'd last been here. He smiled and went to the kitchen. "Wife, do you have cups for us to go looking for blueberries?" She whipped around.

"Why do they need blueberries? Are you going to pick everything and leave nothing for us?"

I was the baby boy, I had always been cherished, my needs seen to first. Now I felt the sting of being unwanted. Hated, even.

I didn't understand it. I wanted to leave, but to leave was to starve. We stayed there for a month or so before moving on.

I knew then the panic that I'd seen on the train had spread everywhere in North Korea. Not only had the state abdicated its role in our lives. So had family. Blood meant little or nothing. There was no force on earth that could stop the famine.

I felt older than I was. The chaos around me was so strong that its waves seemed to overwhelm my mood sensor. You couldn't help but feel them.

. . .

In August, we returned home to Hoeryong. My father greeted us at the railway station. His face lit up with joy, and he embraced us. He'd never been away from his children before, and his voice was filled with happiness as he spoke our names.

The mood in our little detached house lifted despite the gnawing hunger in our bellies. My mother now had a thousand and one schemes to save us from the famine. She would buy candy from the market and sell it in the rural villages. She would purchase corn, turn it into noodles, and make a killing in the city market. Sometimes the plans were so complex I couldn't follow them.

My mom began to go on trips to the north of the country to make her deals. She was gone for weeks at a time. Sometimes she'd say she would be back on the sixteenth of the month and not return until the twenty-eighth. At first, my father welcomed her newfound vitality, but soon I could feel the tension rise. No words were spoken, at least ones that Bong Sook and I could hear, but it was like climbing higher and higher in an airplane. The pressure in your ears begins to grow. My mood sensor was on high alert.

By the fall of 1996, my parents' dreams were collapsing, and they took their anger out on each other. My father had borrowed money for my mother's schemes, sacrificing his ideals, and she'd betrayed him. Her new name in the house became "thief." She fought back, asking why my father couldn't feed us. Her depression returned.

Their fights sometimes went on all night. It made it hard to play or to read books with Bong Sook. My sister and I were always on edge, expecting another blowup.

One night, my father lost his mind completely and began beating my mom during an argument over money. He slapped her with a thunderous crack across the nose and she collapsed to the floor. He began clubbing her with a closed fist, grunting, no longer speaking human words.

My sister and I watched, holding each other. We cried out for my father to stop, but his handsome face was like stone, dark stone.

CHAPTER TEN

WE WERE HUNGRY all the time now. Our soup, with a few bits of grain or corn in it, kept us alive, but we were desperate for something more substantial. We tried eating wild plants and raspberry leaves, which were incredibly bitter and which you had to force down your throat with water. My father, whose wages had remained constant, couldn't buy anything in the market because inflation had pushed prices beyond working people's means. We were beginning to waste away, and the dull knife of starvation probed at our guts.

One night I heard my parents whispering on the other side of the main room. I could hear the desperation in their voices, and I realized they were discussing selling the house and moving into the abandoned office where my father once worked. The company could no longer afford to pay him or any of his fellow employees, so people were taking what they could: stealing equipment or inventory to sell at a pittance.

I couldn't believe what I was hearing. The detached house was the great joy of my father's life. He'd taken such pride in crafting every piece of furniture inside, every lintel and every cabinet. I could feel his sadness in my chest.

My parents began to spread the word that they would consider offers for the house. There were no real estate brokers in North Korea, no For Sale sections in the newspaper. You had to spread the news by word of mouth. So my parents told their friends and neighbors, and my father his former colleagues, that they were selling. I don't think they put a price on the house; it was assumed they would take almost any offer.

The idea of making money from the sale of our home gave my parents hope. Unfortunately, everyone else had the same idea. People were willing, even eager, to become homeless if it meant surviving for another month. They were hawking their places for whatever they could get and moving into shuttered offices or factories or just camping out in fields. There was suddenly a glut of houses on the market.

Nobody could afford to buy our whole house, even for the price of a sack of cornmeal. After only ten days, my father divided the house in two and sold half to a young couple. The house had two rooms, and now it had two one-room apartments. The new couple were under thirty and just beginning their lives together. The price they paid was enough to buy us cornmeal for seven or eight days. Though it must have been devastating for my father, he never showed any bitterness toward the couple. In fact, they became good friends of ours. We visited them in their half of the house and shared meals with them. It felt weird, but with families camping in the wild grass, weird was better than the alternative.

Still, the famine pursued us. There were days when all we had to eat was a handful of wild mushrooms in water. So we decided to travel to my maternal grandmother's, where we hoped to find food.

Usually, my mother would have planned a trip like that for months, since it took all that time to notify the person you were going to see of your arrival, to get train tickets, and to tell the school your kids wouldn't be attending. But we didn't have normal lives anymore; your schedule was decided by what you needed to do to get food that day. It was frightening how these major decisions were made the night before, in a moment of panic.

My father told us he would be staying behind. My parents made it seem as though he had to work, but I knew they were separating again. Another mouth to feed wouldn't be welcome at my grandmother's, and my father's pride would be hurt by showing up at his mother-in-law's house, destitute.

The morning of our departure, my mother gathered our bags by the front door, one big one for each of us. My father watched us, his hands behind his back, his face lined with sadness. I'd been calm until the last moment, but as we said our goodbyes, I felt a wave of fear wash through me. "But . . . but what if we never come back here?" I said to my mother. "What if we die on the way there?" I don't know what made me say such an awful thing; perhaps it was the tofu or boiled egg that every family is supposed to eat before leaving on a journey. (Eggs roll fast, which means the trip will go quickly, and tofu is perfectly square, which means everything will go according to plan.) Since we didn't have any tofu or eggs to eat, I got nervous and blurted out the words about dying.

My mom erupted. "Are you crazy? Why would you say such things?" I looked at her, stunned by the vehemence in her voice. But nothing about the journey was right. Usually you wear your best clothes and set off with a warm meal in your belly. We were doing none of that. We'd sold our good clothes and were wearing the only outfits we had left; I was dressed in a dark coat, dark slacks, and a soiled, much-washed white shirt. Honestly, we looked like vagrants.

At the railroad station, huge crowds were waiting for the next train. My mother managed to get us on the second one that came through — when she wanted to be, she could be fierce. There was nowhere to sit down, so we stood pressed up against the people we'd boarded with.

The dumb thing I'd said at home immediately cursed the journey. As the train got under way, moving down the track at a snail's pace, the car swayed and someone dropped a huge suitcase on my foot.

"Yow!" I cried. It felt as if the bones had been smashed. My mother scolded the man with the bag, but she could barely reach me through the bodies stacked inside the car. I couldn't even reach down to massage my foot, but howled and wept as the other passengers looked at me with blank faces.

The trip should have taken an hour or two at the most. We arrived six hours later, pulling ourselves through the mass of bodies at the Hok-seung station.

The wind swept across the train platform and instantly I was cold. On past visits, we would wait for the local train that branched off and took us very close to Grandmother's house. But we saw no one waiting on that platform. "That train doesn't run anymore," an old man told us.

My mother looked at him anxiously. "What? But we have to get to Undok."

"Then you better start walking."

Our grandmother's house was a couple of hours away on foot. My mother's face grew grim and she picked up our suitcases and marched out of the station. Bong Sook and I followed, me limping on my smashed foot.

"Mother, I'm hungry," I said. Outside the station there was a street with private houses that doubled as restaurants. One house would sell soup and radish kimchi, the next corn and bread. We stopped at one and bought a bowl of soup with some kimchi, along with a couple of potato side dishes. We stood there on the road and dug in: the food was delicious, little globs of fat floating on the soup's surface.

In two minutes, the food was gone. We felt refreshed and began the long walk. We arrived at our grandmother's house around midnight and could hear the TV as we walked up the path. There were two houses in my grandmother's compound: a big one where my aunt and uncle lived, and a second, much smaller house for Grandmother. We hoped they had enough to feed us.

We knocked on the door of the big house and my aunt and uncle let us in. Exhausted, we dropped onto our sleeping mats. The next morning, Grandmother greeted us, her expression a mix of love and worry. She was in her early eighties, tiny, stooped, and skinnier than I remembered.

Mother was telling Grandma about the journey: the packed cars, the slow train, the local that didn't run anymore, the restaurant food that gave us the strength to walk.

Grandma's face froze. "Which restaurant did you stop at?" she asked.

"The second one from the station," my mother said. "Why?"

Grandmother's expression was one of fear and disgust. Bong Sook and I looked at each other. Was it wrong for us to have eaten something?

My mother and grandma disappeared into the other room, where I could hear them murmuring.

"Bong Sook, what's wrong?" I asked.

"I don't know," she said. "Go play with your cousins."

I was happy to, but Grandma's reaction still bothered me. I ran off to find my cousins.

It was a couple of days before one of them spilled the beans.

There had been rumors going around for months about a restaurant by the railroad station. They said that the owners of the place had been kidnapping homeless people and travelers and killing them. They would then chop them up, strip the meat from their bones, and add it to their soup.

"Which restaurant?" I asked quickly.

"Some say the fourth from the corner," my cousin said, watching my reaction closely. "Some say . . . the second."

I felt my stomach do a flip.

"Cousin," she said, "what shape were the fat bubbles?"

My tongue felt covered in greasy fur. Had I eaten a human being? If I did, I was now a cannibal. And what was worse, the soup, I remembered, had been delicious.

"What shape?" she repeated.

"Why does it matter?"

She looked at me hopelessly.

"When you boil meat, the fat rises to the surface."

"Yes, yes," I said. "I know *that*."

"OK," my cousin said. "But were they circles or triangles?"

"What kind of a question is that?"

She frowned impatiently. "Fat from pork, beef, or chicken forms a circle," she said, as if she was repeating some famous science equation, like the law of gravity. "Fat from a human . . ."

"Triangles?"

"Yes," she said. "Triangles."

I racked my brain to remember what the fat blobs looked like. I could see the heavy wooden bowl and the few corn noodles floating half submerged in the cloudy soup. I could see small chunks of vegetables and the tiny bits of yellowish fat on the surface. But no matter how hard I closed my eyes, I couldn't for the life of me remember the shape.

When I saw Bong Sook, we talked softly about the soup that day.

"Are you sure there were no triangles?" I asked.

"No," she said. "There weren't."

But the truth is, we couldn't remember. Some days, I would say to myself, *Who knows if the circles and triangles are even true?* But folk stories, rumors, and superstition were all North Koreans had. There was no authority to consult to see if you'd consumed a human being or not.

CHAPTER ELEVEN

I SPENT MANY SAD hours with my grandmother. Like my father, she liked to tell stories, but her tales were very different from my dad's, which were heartwarming and always triumphant. Grandma's stories were filled with melancholy. Most of them centered on how, during Japan's occupation of our country in the early twentieth century, her father had sold her off to a rich family when she was only thirteen.

It turned out that my great-grandfather was an alcoholic who sold his own children to buy bottles of corn moonshine. Grandma went off as a maid to the big house, but the family there worked her hard while feeding her only small meals twice a day, barely enough to live on. When they sent her to the river with a basket of dirty clothes perched atop her head, she would run to the foothills of the nearby mountains and desperately search for blackberries to eat. When she found enough to stop the dizziness that always afflicted her, she would go back to the house, saving the small portion of rice the rich people gave her. And what did she do with this rice? She gave it to her father.

I always wondered why Grandma did this. Was it out of love or fear? Did her father force her to give up her small pittance of rice? I'd like to believe she did it out of a noble character, saving the man who had sold her like chattel. Ironically, she would tell me these stories over meals of rice and soup, her long face creased with wrinkles. The meals were so small she would have only three bites of food before it was gone.

Though she had so little, barely enough to survive, Grandma always fed me a spoon of rice or two sips of her soup while telling me her stories. As I swallowed the soup, I thought about Grandma's life, so full of bitterness and scarcity. She'd been hungry her whole time on earth, and she was hungry now. "Kwang Jin," she said, "even though the Japanese occupation was horrible, we had more to eat then than we do now. How can this be?"

We heard more and more stories of orphans being stolen and eaten by ravenous people in the countryside. The orphan children called *Kkotjebi* ("wandering swallows"), figures dressed in dark rags who haunted the roadside markets, a consequence of the famine, were told not to sleep in the open, lest they be kidnapped and consumed. Townsfolk warned us about buying meat (as if we could afford meat!) if we didn't know where it had come from. There were cases of people eating their own newborn infants. A kind of mass insanity spread from town to town.

Soon after we arrived at Grandma's, the news came that authorities had arrested the owners of one of the restaurants near the train station for serving human meat. But there were no newspapers or official bulletins, so we didn't know which house it was. Some people said it was the first house, others said the fifth, still others the second.

It was an inauspicious omen for our stay with Grandma.

The first week or so, we ate well: cornmeal, rice, and soup, along with side dishes like radish kimchi. I would wait all day for the main meal. One day my uncle came home from work and saw me lying on the floor. "Instead of sitting around," he said, "why don't you clean up the house or chop wood for the fire? If you do this, you'll become more likable, and this will help you survive." His tone was warm and kind; he was trying to help me. That day I chopped a load of firewood, which my aunt thanked me for, smiling broadly. Everything was going well.

But as the second week began, my mood sensor felt the welcome leave the air like a fading scent. By then, we were having soup at almost every meal; the rice had disappeared. My aunt worked on a farm and my uncle worked for a coal company, and they received food as their wages, but the government didn't increase your portion because you had three relatives staying with you.

It always began at the dinner table. My aunt would snap at her older daughter, "Why are you eating so much?" Bong Sook and I bowed our heads when she said this. We knew she was really talking to us: *Why are you here? Can't you see I can barely feed my own children?* It was hard to get the food down after hearing those words.

My mom grew more tense with every passing day. So much was piled on her shoulders. Why were we here? Why couldn't she provide for her own children? Her face grew strained and pale. It seemed that my old mother—the one I knew before she went to Kang Suh—had returned.

I was getting hungrier. The pain scraped the lining of my stomach. It felt like there was no fat left for my body to consume, and the hunger was attacking muscle, which made the pain worse.

One morning, when my aunt and uncle went to work and my cousins were at school, I was alone in the big house with Bong Sook. After an hour, I couldn't take it anymore.

I looked at the clay pot that held the soup we would have for dinner with the family.

"I'm just going to have a few spoonfuls," I said to Bong Sook.

"No, Kwang Jin. You know you can't do that."

"One, then. Only one."

Bong Sook shook her head sadly at me. "You can't. Auntie will find out."

"But Bong Sook!" I whined. She was adamant. So I waited for her to close her eyes—we drifted in and out of sleep like old people—and then went to the kitchen. There was a plate over the soup pot. I lifted it and dipped the ladle in and quickly sucked in a spoonful of soup. Then two more.

My body seemed to bloom. A feeling of contentment, of sweetness in my bones, came over me. I wanted desperately to keep eating, but I knew that would court disaster. I put the ladle down and replaced the top plate.

At lunchtime, my aunt came home from work and went straight to the kitchen to begin preparing dinner. A few seconds later, I saw her standing in the doorway to the main room, staring at me. Her face was flushed, her eyes big and wet. She shot me a poisonous look, a look that said, "No better than a thief!" I dropped my eyes. And yet I was still hungry.

My aunt couldn't say anything. It was as if we were all choking on these unsaid words. The next day, my uncle came to me and said, "What is your mother's plan?"

"Uncle, I don't know."

"What is she going to do? Is your father getting money together while you're away? Kwang Jin, what is their plan?"

Why was he speaking to me? My parents had barely told me we were getting on the train to Grandmother's the day before we left! Did he think we were all in cahoots?

"I really don't understand," he said, his eyes bulging. "I feel I am suffocating."

Finally Mother couldn't take it anymore. She went out and found a job. It wasn't a real job; it was another of her crazy schemes to feed us. She would go out and buy corn powder at the factory and then sell it on the street — not even making it into noodles — hoping to make one *won* for every sale. When she'd made enough money, she would buy corn noodles and bring them home to us.

But there were very few people in the market who could afford corn powder, and many days she would come home with nothing. When this happened, her face was like a clay mask, frozen in the expression of a hopeful person. She was trying hard to convey confidence in our future. But she needn't have bothered; I felt the strain growing within her. She talked to Bong Sook about her troubles, and then both of them would wear the clay face. I felt sad that they couldn't tell me what was happening, but part of me didn't want to know.

There was one day when we felt the sting of our poverty especially deeply. My mom had four sisters and three brothers. Her second-oldest sister, whom we called Great-Aunt, was doing well even in the famine.

Her son had joined the police department, and the police always found a way to survive—either through bribery or corruption. One day my mom and my small aunt (my mother's younger sister) were invited to a birthday party for Great-Aunt's son, the policeman. They were excited to go; they hadn't seen my great-aunt in many months, and it would be a day they didn't need to worry about feeding their children. The party givers would provide plenty of food.

When you go to someone's house, even a relative's, you can't go with empty hands. So my mom worked hard to make my favorite meal: a single corn pancake. She went to the market with her last few *won* and bargained until she got the most corn powder for the money, then brought it home and pounded it into a pancake shape and steamed it. A single pancake was all she could afford. She wrapped it up in waxy paper and we headed to the birthday party, an hour away.

When we got there, I was dazzled by the large crowd. So many people, so nicely dressed! Police officials wore suits of rich wool with sharp creases down the legs. The wives of government managers wore lipstick and beautiful light clothing. We walked into the house, me in my stained white shirt and dark pants, and my mother and Small Aunt in their scuffed shoes and country clothes.

When my mother handed the corn cake to my great-aunt, our hostess wouldn't so much as look at it. Usually the host smiles and thanks you for whatever you bring, but Great-Aunt didn't even open the waxy paper to see what we'd brought. Her face never changed—she gave us a look of frozen indifference—as she handed the pancake to one of her children. I saw in her face that she was embarrassed by us, embarrassed to have such poorly dressed relatives in their drab work clothes among this glittering array of local government officials. We watched as they put our pancake in the kitchen, apart from the other gifts and dishes brought by the other guests. I saw the back of my mother's neck flush red. She turned quickly away, her eyes on the floor.

One part of the party lived up to expectations: there was plenty to eat. We found a corner of the room to sit in and tried not to make a spectacle of ourselves as we tasted things we hadn't eaten in months, if not years. Tasty, well-marinated kimchi with spices and fish! Fried pork! Beef ribs! We cleaned our plates and waited for a few minutes before going back for more, so as to look like we were perfectly capable of stopping at any time.

My small aunt sat with us, watching the guests. She was on the verge of tears. "How could you treat us like this?" she whispered, addressing her older sister across the room, more in sorrow than in anger. No one came to our corner to ask us how we were and if we were enjoying the food. Great-Aunt and her family carefully avoided us, though we saw them circulating and chatting with the more glamorous people. I was mostly unfazed—the food and its enticing aromas had given me a jolt of happiness, and I didn't care what people thought of us—but my mother and my small aunt were inconsolable. Awkwardly, I chewed on spare-rib bones and waited for the next dish to be served. To make my mother's misery complete, as we left the party, Great-Aunt handed us back the single corn pancake we'd brought, along with some leftovers.

My mother accepted it, bowed, and turned wordlessly toward the door. On the way home, Small Aunt's sorrow had turned to rage. "How dare they!" she cried. By now, Bong Sook and I were embarrassed, too.

The night was cold and I didn't have a warm enough jacket. My mother put me on her back and Bong Sook walked beside us. I could feel my mother crying, her throat working to stifle the sobs, my head resting on the back of her neck.

Years later, Small Aunt's family grew quite rich. Her husband had relatives in China, and after many attempts, he got a visa to see them. This allowed him to bring back Chinese goods, which he sold at a large markup. Their income shot up. Soon Great-Aunt went to their house looking for handouts, saying nothing of the time she'd humiliated us.

Great-Aunt was a shameless person. She wouldn't be the last one I'd meet.

CHAPTER TWELVE

As MY SEVENTH birthday approached, I saw my mother grow more depressed. I was still a boy and hoped for nice things on my special day: a small gift, perhaps, or something good to eat. I dreamed of boiled eggs, fluffy rice, sizzling pork dishes. Surely my mother would find something.

But when the day came, it was just like any other. There was the usual watery gruel for breakfast and no hint that something better was on the way. My mother didn't cry out "Save some room!" Nothing to let me know a treat had been stashed away for me. I tried to hide it, but I was disappointed that there wasn't the tiniest gift to celebrate my day. I laid my head on the sleeping mat and tried to sink into sleep.

Bong Sook was upset, I could see; her face was troubled and she spent long periods staring at the tile floor. Finally, without saying a word, she got up and ran out the door. I thought she'd gone for a walk, though there wasn't much to see around Grandma's, just fields echoing with the sound of peasants chopping wood. But an hour and a half later, the door opened and Bong Sook rushed in, holding something behind her back.

I sat up cross-legged on my sleeping mat as she approached, bringing her hands forward. In each hand Bong Sook had a rice cake. My mouth began to water.

Bong Sook thrust the cakes into my hand. "Happy birthday, Kwang Jin!"

I delayed devouring the cakes long enough to ask her one question. "But how?"

Bong Sook shook her head happily, her black hair swinging. "Don't worry about that."

Did I offer Bong Sook a bite of the cakes? I'm not sure; my memory is filled only with the joyful, drug-like recall of the sweetened rice hitting my taste buds. I was so happy. The taste, for me, literally equaled love. It meant that my birthday was still special to someone besides me. I gobbled up those cakes and pressed my fingers on the crumbs that had fallen into my lap and ate them too.

I had two or three moments of happiness before the storm broke over Bong Sook's head. When you produce unexpected food during a famine, everyone immediately becomes suspicious. Where have you been hiding it? Or what did you sell to get it, when we have nothing?

Bong Sook, it turned out, had done something rash. She'd run out to the yard and dug up some of Grandma's potatoes, the ones that were to sustain the family through the winter. Then she marched off to the market, exchanged the potatoes for some saccharin, and with part of the saccharin bought the two rice cakes.

In other words, my gift had been stolen. Worse still, my birthday would cost us precious calories in the future.

Grandma berated Bong Sook. It was the first time I'd ever seen my sister disobey her elders. But she was unrepentant. As Grandma yelled at her, and my mother watched with a wretched expression on her face, my sister stared at me. Her eyes said, *I'm happy I did it. I am.*

My mother, already depressed, had grown paranoid about the possibility of someone kidnapping Bong Sook and me. The cannibal story had burrowed itself deep in her brain. "Kwang Jin, if someone offers you candy, don't go with them. Hear me? People will offer you food if you go with them to their houses, but I forbid you!" She repeated this every couple of days, and she wouldn't allow us to go into town alone.

I just looked at her and nodded. "OK, Mom," I said. She needn't have bothered. We were hearing scary stories from our relatives, who seemed to relish telling us the grisly tales. One was about the women in the market who sold their own children. They would arrive with four kids and sell one, usually the oldest. The money they earned they immediately spent on corn, which they stuffed into the mouths of their remaining children while screaming out "I'm sorry!" as the buyer led away the unfortunate boy or girl.

I didn't believe those stories then, though many people swore they were true (and I now believe such things did happen). I didn't doubt people would sell their own children. My question was, who on earth would buy them?

This was not the only story that turned out to be true. "Did you hear about the ax man?" my older cousin asked me. "Homeless children had been disappearing from the market — to where, nobody knew. Then one boy escaped and told people a local man was offering Kkotjebi food if they returned home with him. The children who went into his house never came out. So many of them! The local people broke into his house to investigate. Do you know what they saw?"

I shook my head.

"Heads. And feet. The heads had rags stuffed in their mouths. And in the corner they found an ax with blood and brains on it."

I tried to look nonchalant, like this was old news to me, but my body began to tremble. I was very scared. Bong Sook and I weren't homeless yet, but we were just one step away. All it would take would be to lose my mother and we'd be out on the street. I already knew that my relatives were too stressed to be able to take us in.

"Why only homeless kids?" I asked.

My cousin made a face.

"Because they have no parents to go look for them!"

Some days, Bong Sook and I would lie on our mats and stare at the ceiling, daydreaming of meals we'd had: creamy corn pancakes, this or that kimchi, sizzling marinated pork. I enjoyed this immensely. I believed I could taste the corn pancakes more deeply and fully than when I'd actually eaten them, because I slowed each bite down so that it took two or three minutes to finish. But when the daydream was over, I felt hungrier than before.

My aunt came home and made those very same corn pancakes, just like my mom's. Unfortunately, there weren't enough to go around. With a heavy heart, she gave the pancakes to her children in secret, not telling Bong Sook and me about them. But we could smell the corn as she pounded it into powder, and then as the pancakes were being steamed to perfection. What torture! And our cousins, being children, would come in after eating it all up, their eyes alight, and say, "Oh, how delicious the pancakes were today! Don't you love them?"

"I'll say. I think today they were better than ever."

All the while their eyes watched Bong Sook and me.

I said nothing. I thought, *If I was in your position, I would save a bite or two for you.* But my cousins had no such compunctions. They gloated over their pancakes and the store-bought snacks their mother got for them. I hated them. I thought of ripping the pancakes from my young cousin's hands and eating them in front of his face, slowly. I was used to this kind of warfare: didn't my friend Hyo Sung and I once taunt each other in the game we played with origami paper? But it seemed crueler to me when the stakes weren't toys, but life itself.

When we felt strong enough, Bong Sook and I would go to the mountains to look for anything edible. The plant varieties here in Undok were different from the ones back home: strange-looking floppy-headed mushrooms, for example. This was the only contribution we could make to the household, and we bent over the fields searching for particularly succulent things.

"What should we look for?" I asked my sister.

"Anything a rabbit nibbles on," Bong Sook said.

"But the rabbits are all gone, Bong Sook. People have eaten them."

"Well, look for what they ate when they were still around."

I stood there.

"I never watched them when they were around. I was too busy playing. Please tell me."

So Bong Sook showed me what to look for, and I found some dandelions and a few harmless weeds. We brought them home and my mother made them into a stew. My cousins, their bellies full of more delicious things, shook their heads no when my mother asked if they wanted to taste her cooking.

This sense of not being wanted was the air Bong Sook and I breathed. For the first time in my life I wished I could turn my mood sensor off. I wanted to feel nothing.

CHAPTER THIRTEEN

THE STRANGE VISIT to my grandmother's lasted through the first half of 1997. That summer, my father came to get us. It was time to try our hand at farming.

A year or two before, after the famine began, Kim Jong Il had introduced a new approach to saving his people: "private" farms. Government officials realized they couldn't let the famine run rampant or they would lose all their citizens. I believe this was their motivation for what little they did: *If everyone dies, who will we rule over?*

One of the biggest problems for Kim Jong Il and his ministers was that hunger was killing the nation's farmers. When Bong Sook and I went foraging in the mountains, we passed through farm country. We saw fields where crops had never been planted, or where weeds had sprung up on good farmland and choked the rows where cabbage and peppers should have grown. The farmers had become too weak to work, or they were dead and buried and their families had fled to the cities. We passed row after row of attached "accordion" houses, where not a single face could be seen at the windows. Under such dire circumstances, fewer acres of farmland were being worked and less food reached the markets.

The government came up with a plan. It would grant portions of land to companies, and they would allow their employees to farm them. Each employee would get a small plot to grow his own corn, string beans, radishes, peppers, and cucumbers.

The plan did save a lot of families. It saved mine, at least for a little while.

That summer, my father, Bong Sook, and I (my mother was away with her relatives again) left for our designated plot, about two and a half hours' walk from our house. When we reached the farm, we cleared the ground by hand. It was hard, thirsty work: pulling out tall weeds by hand, removing rocks, and hoeing the dirt into rows. At the end of the day, we walked home exhausted, but finally with a bit of hope in our hearts. We did this for many days, returning to plant the seeds and give the rows a good dousing of water.

Later that summer, we returned to the farm and stayed there. There was no food at home, so we camped out beside the rustling fields, surviving on eggplants, string beans, and peppers while waiting for the main corn harvest, which would begin in mid-August. My father made a makeshift tent out of discarded plastic and wood planks, and we slept next to our farm.

We had only enough eggplants and peppers to sustain us for a few days. The only option left to us was to start looking for frogs, a great delicacy in the rural districts. When we first arrived, we could hear them croaking from the streams and the thickets of ash and poplar. But soon after amateur farmers like us began our great frog hunt, the woods went silent. One evening that first year of farming, a friend of my father's who had a plot of land near ours came by and, seeing me, assumed a worried look.

"Kwang Jin," he said, "I'm missing my number-five frog. Have you seen him?"

I was mortified. *Frogs have numbers?* I was convinced I'd eaten this man's property. He was joking, of course, and burst out laughing at my confused expression. He knew we'd eaten every frog we could find. We roasted them over the fire outside our tent. The protein made us strong enough for a day's work.

Next came grasshoppers, which we caught with our hands as they leaped through the hot afternoon air. I stuck them on small sticks and roasted them over a roaring fire. When the grasshoppers began to brown, I pulled them out of the flames and blew on them. When they had cooled down, I bit into them, their bodies crackling under my teeth. Delicious. I even ate the heads. I would have offered some to Bong Sook, but she wasn't a meat eater and the whole thing repulsed her.

Then came my first taste of what would eventually save my life: thievery. It was during our farming adventure that I first started to steal. I considered myself canny, or at least I had always wanted to be, like my friend Hyo Sung. I realized that if the three of us began eating the early corn, in a month or two most of our crop would be gone. We would have very little to bring back home for the fall and winter.

I decided we weren't going to touch our corn. I would supply all our nutritional needs by stealing from other fields. When I announced this to my father, he looked sad. I expected him to say something like, "Son, stealing isn't the right thing to do," but he was silent. As he watched me sneak away from our tent that first night, I tried to read his eyes. Was he ashamed that his son had become a thief? Today, I understand that to ask that question is to mistake North Korea for a normal country. Morals simply didn't exist there in the late 1990s. My father was a highly ethical man, but what morality is there in watching your children go hungry?

As the sun sank behind the hills, I ran off along the dusty road that bordered our little camp, putting distance between me and our farm. My father had asked me to steal from government plots and not from those owned by individual families—his last line of moral defense. He warned me especially not to take anything from the fields next to our own. Those belonged to his coworkers; he knew their families and could picture the faces of their children. I wasn't to take any corn from their mouths. But farther on were anonymous fields owned by government agencies or assigned to other companies. My father's mercy didn't extend to them.

My heart was beating like crazy. After I'd jogged for fifteen minutes or so, I turned sharply and ran into the rows of corn by the roadside. I was only a few feet into the dark rows when I began twisting the ears from their stalks. I wasn't a very sly burglar; I didn't have the technique that I would develop later on, when I'd become as close to a professional thief as you could get in North Korea.

Before the famine, we thought raw corn was inedible. No one would touch it. But I was so hungry now that I ate two ears right there on the spot, tearing off the husk and pushing the kernels against my teeth and taking that first delicious chomp. I went down the ear of corn, clearing a row. We called this way of eating "playing harmonica," because that's what it looked like.

I unbuttoned my shirt, leaving only two buttons secured at the bottom. Then I tore ears off more stalks and pushed them inside. The husks were rough and scratched my skin, but I was too worried about getting caught to care. When I'd gotten about ten ears, I rebuttoned my shirt, dashed out to the road, and hurried back to the camp.

I returned to the tent with my shirt stuffed like some monster with a giant torso. I carefully undid my buttons and the unshucked corn came tumbling out, hitting the ground with a hard thump. My father said nothing, but he and my sister each plucked a fat ear from the pile, cooked them, and began playing harmonica. I felt happy watching them. I wasn't the spoiled younger son anymore. I was helping my family to survive. To steal, I thought, was a victory.

I did make mistakes. One moonless night, I crept away from our tent and searched for a field to go into. I tried never to hit the same field twice, and so I always varied the amount of time I spent jogging down the road. This night, I turned quickly at the end of a long row and made two more turns before finding a promising field that I had never seen before. I ran in, played harmonica, and ran out with a full shirt. Every time the corn rustled, I was sure it was a farmer coming to beat me with a club. The lack of moonlight made things worse; in a cornfield, you can't see more than three or four feet ahead, and the rustling of the corn seems to cover up a dozen oncoming men. I could never relax in the rows.

Finally, I dashed out to the road, my bare feet pounding away, afraid to look back. I arrived at the tent and unloaded the corn. My father and

Bong Sook ate. My father asked me to describe the route I had taken to the farm. As he munched on the last of the ears, I told him.

He looked at me. "Son," he said, "that's our farm."

I had zigged and zagged and ended up stealing from our own crop. I felt awful.

In my second or third week as a corn thief, I found a field about half a mile from our camp and began my usual routine. I was munching on my second ear of corn when I saw movement out of the corner of my right eye. I turned my head. Something was rustling the corn, the plants shivering each in turn.

Something's coming, I thought. For a split second, I thought, *Wild animal.* North Korea has foxes and leopards and wild boar, but of course most of them had been hunted to near extinction by then.

So what is it?

I stopped eating, holding the corn next to my mouth as if I could hide behind it.

The stalks a few feet away from me parted and a woman stood in front of me, breathing hard. She looked like a giant, taller than the corn stalks, dressed in long pants and work boots. (Fear probably caused her to grow in my eyes—looking back, I'm sure she was just an average-sized woman.) My mouth was open, but I was too terrified to speak. I thought the woman was going to beat me or slash at me with a knife or do I don't know what. But instead she stared at me, and I slowly realized that her eyes weren't furious or scolding. They were sad.

"How old are you?" she said in a quiet voice.

"S-seven," I stammered out.

I had the strange feeling that she wasn't seeing me, that her gaze was regarding a different figure. She dropped her eyes.

"Go home," she said. "And don't come back here."

I dropped the half-eaten corn and ran.

I've thought about that day a lot since then. It happened to me more than once—to have an adult stare at me without saying anything, to escape punishment for inexplicable reasons. Perhaps it had to do with the fact that I rarely had the chance to bathe and my face was covered with grime, with only my eyes staring out. The dirt made every North Korean child of the same age look more or less identical.

I always had the feeling that this woman had seen in me someone she knew who had died. A son? A nephew? Somewhere, there'd been a young boy who was no longer here on earth. And she felt pity when she saw this—a child so hungry he would eat raw corn.

The famine would soon force me to become a wanderer all over the North Korean countryside. During that time, I never saw one of the haunted spirits that I'd heard so much about. My fate was different: to become a ghost for other people.

CHAPTER FOURTEEN

Back home, things fell apart again. The corn we'd saved up went faster than we could have imagined. We were forced to sell the other half of the house and leave for the neighborhood of Manyang, closer to the center of Hoeryong, where my father's former workplace was. It had been abandoned when the economy collapsed. We would now squat in his old offices.

I had to leave Hyo Sung and the dragonflies behind. I said goodbye to him in front of his house. I wasn't that sad to be leaving him, honestly. I'd never figured out how he won all those games and took all that origami from me, and that rankled me. I didn't know that I would see Hyo Sung again once our lives had changed unimaginably.

When my family first arrived at our new place, I wanted to turn around and go back. It didn't look like a house. It was a long accordion building, dark and abandoned-looking, with no glass in the windows. When we walked in the door, we discovered a wreck: there was dirt everywhere, and abandoned bits of bicycles littering the floor, along with crooked nails and old tools. This had been a combined bike and shoe repair shop before the economy had collapsed. There wasn't even a floor to sleep on. And no kitchen. Worse still, this wreck of a building was packed with human beings. Every doorway had three or four faces staring out at us, and there were more faces at the windows. I had a strangled feeling in my chest, composed of claustrophobia, humiliation, and fear. I looked at my father forlornly. How was it possible to live in such a place? He didn't meet my eyes.

My dad set to work immediately. He scrounged up scraps of wood and hammered them together to make crude bunk beds for the four of us. He found a small barbecue grill somewhere and started a fire. My mother promptly crouched over it, heating a pot of creek water over the blazing sticks of wood. Our portion of the building had four rooms, which was a change for the better, and I enjoyed roaming through this enormous space. But it was a place for desperate people. The real houses faced away from the busy unpaved road that lay fifteen feet beyond, giving their residents some privacy. Our home faced the road, like the other commercial spaces. When cars went past, billows of dust would come whirling in our doorway. And people passing by could stare in our windows as if we were for sale.

My first concern, of course, was finding a new best friend. There I got lucky. Kim Il lived maybe two minutes away; I had to wait until school started in the fall to meet him, but it was worth it. Kim Il was eight years old, like me, and we quickly became inseparable. I liked him through and through. His family was unusual. His mother was so tall and white-skinned that we called her "the Russian," and his father owned a motorcycle, which was a very exotic thing to have. His family was probably one of the richest in Manyang.

Kim Il was tall and strong. He was the number-two fighter in my school. At the beginning, I was the lowest, number forty out of forty kids. My accent, my clothes, and even my haircut marked me as a kid from the sticks, and I was called "country boy." I think I had my first fight on my first day of school.

But I was lucky, too: Kim Il's mother ran a popular restaurant with the most delicious Korean barbecue for a hundred miles. Whenever Kim Il and I got hungry, we'd head there. His mom would see me and smile and instantly prepare my favorite dish, white rice with pork side dishes and white rice. Kim Il's parents had only one child, and they treated me as their second son. In North Korea, sharing food means more than it does in the West, especially in those hard times. It means, You are one of us. I was very touched by this.

Kim Il and I spent whole days together, exploring and talking and doing dares. By that time, we were tired of playing spies. Spies weren't fun anymore; we were too old for that and wanted to do something involving real danger. So we played a game, *yeon chee gee,* using some sort of mystery metal that we found lying around our houses that we could form into different shapes, like stars or animals. We'd put our metal fish or wolf in the middle of the main road. We'd do a quick round of rock-paper-scissors, and the loser had to dash into the street and grab the fish, dodging the speeding cars going by.

I was becoming stronger and more daring. I don't know if this was inside me all along or if I just wanted to survive.

It's hard to overestimate how much movies sustained North Korea during these hard times. They were all we had to look forward to. North Koreans are addicted to motion pictures; even Americans can't compete with our unslakable thirst for them. Even the most remote towns had a movie theater, and everyone knew someone with a TV. When feature film time, 8:45 p.m., rolled around, the streets would empty. All cooking, tinkering, idle conversation, hoeing of weeds, stopped. We watched the same movies over and over again. Later, we would listen to the neighborhood storytellers recount the plots, despite having seen the films with our own eyes.

Movies were our fantasy and our drug. I never really absorbed much government propaganda through the radio or from newspapers. The main indoctrination tools in Manyang were ten-foot concrete billboards with slogans carved into them. They were specifically designed for a country that often lost power. Even if the electricity went out and there was no radio or TV, the billboards would always be there to remind you to be grateful to the state. The mottos carved in the concrete were a way to tell what was happening in the capital.

One said, "I will protect my leader even if I have to sacrifice my life!"

Another read, "In order to succeed, you must run ten times faster than the others." This one dated from just after the Korean War, when the whole country had been devastated. The world didn't believe that poor North Korea could catch up to the more advanced countries in Europe and elsewhere. This motto meant that if an American capitalist worked one hour, we would work ten. It was a way of saying that North Koreans can do anything.

I'd always liked that saying, but when the famine came I bitterly resented those billboards and public monuments. That's because to build their statues, the government would ask starving families to donate copper or iron or cement. You had to sacrifice your pots and pans for the glory of Kim Jong Il, and if you didn't have any, you had to spend precious time looking for scrap metal when you could be hunting frogs. You might even have to trade food or valuables so you would have something to give the government collectors when they came around. I often saw people scrounging in the garbage dumps on the outskirts of town, pawing through mounds of scrap paper and filth, trying to find a bit of metal to fill their quota. Meanwhile, their children were back home, half starved to death. When I saw these poor people, I would ball my fists in helpless fury.

But movies? I surrendered myself to them utterly.

Many of my favorite films were set during the Japanese occupation of Korea. They showed how some rich North Korean families treated their servants like dogs and even helped the Japanese when they oppressed Korea, while Kim Il Sung and the peasants fought to drive the foreigners from our country. The movies showed why our social system was correct: the rich had earned their terrible treatment by betraying the nation. The peasants had fought like crazy to give us our freedom. It made sense that they should now reap the rewards.

One animated film in particular stays in my mind. In it, a rich landowner suddenly has a hankering for strawberries. He asks his loyal servant to go to the mountains to pick him a few. It's late winter and the servant knows there are no strawberries in the mountains, but he goes anyway, and spends all day climbing and looking for fruit to take back to his master. There isn't a single plant to be found, however, and the servant returns at night with empty hands. His furious master then beats and whips him to death. The next day, the servant's young daughter is sent to the mountains to find strawberries. And there, in the middle of winter, she does find a plant, with one ripe strawberry hanging off of it, so red against the bright white glare of the snow that it shines like a ruby. She brings the strawberry home to the man who killed her father.

This was a popular legend of North Korea, and it was supposed to teach us two things. First, that the desires of the rich are cruel and unrealistic, so unrealistic that they demand summer fruit in the middle of winter. Second, that a child's devotion to her parent, if strong enough, can work miracles. The bond between North Korean parents and children, we believed, was stronger than in the corrupt West, where the young dumped their aging parents in old-age homes like so much rotted firewood.

Because of movies like those, I felt lucky to live in North Korea. More than that, I was ready to die for my country. Despite the struggles we faced, we were still better off than the feral people who lived in South Korea.

This patriotic faith was soon to be tested. Our new house didn't bring good luck. The famine was unrelenting, and we soon had to do the same thing in Manyang that we'd done in July 8th. In 1998, we sold half our house. This time, since our home was much closer to the city center, we got enough food in payment to last a month. We moved our belongings into the remaining two rooms, and considered ourselves lucky.

We thought this was how the rest of our lives would be: living hand to mouth, only half nourished, often dizzy, too weak to really flourish. But we were alive.

My family had survived the first onslaught of the famine.

CHAPTER FIFTEEN

The year 2000 turned out to be "the good year," at least in comparison to what came before and after. More crops appeared in the market. Prices came down. My family gradually knit itself back together. The famine, at least for us, receded.

My father had found a new job, working as an accountant in a service company that fixed televisions and other consumer products. We bought things slowly: new clothes, pots and pans. I heard fewer stories about bodies appearing outside our neighbors' doors in the morning, and the electrical outages didn't happen as frequently. Most important from my point of view, we bought a television. This was one of the most joyful moments of my boyhood.

Every evening, some families from the neighborhood came to my house to watch TV. They'd start arriving at around 8:15, to get a good seat and gossip about what might happen on their favorite shows. By 8:45, when the popular dramas began — either a movie or a Chinese soap opera — some of my schoolmates had arrived. I was a bit of a tyrant: if a boy or girl wasn't nice to me that day, I would say, "Yejoon, don't come over to watch the movie tonight." What a terrible penalty! They would pout and beg but I always remained firm. The next day, you can be sure, they were as sweet as could be.

My family now ate tofu and corn with a bit of white rice thrown in, as well as rabbit — rabbits were easy to raise and bred like crazy. My corn pancakes reappeared on our table. I was grateful; the first time my mother served them again, I swore I had never tasted anything so good.

Hunger no longer tormented my family, and so everything should have been good with us. We'd survived a disaster that had carried off hundreds of thousands of people and nearly destroyed the country. But life isn't that way; when a problem disappears — even death! — a new one hurries to take its place. And soon one arrived in the house in Manyang: my grades.

In North Korea, grades range from 1 (failing horribly) to 5 (perfect). I routinely got 1's and 2's in school, except for phys ed, where I was always at the top of the class. I was just a terrible student. I can't really explain my lack of motivation. During the past few years, academics had seemed pointless, but I don't know how much of my awfulness at school had to do with the famine. A bit, certainly. The past few years had shortened my focus to the next twenty-four hours: what was I going to eat for my next meal?

I had also missed a lot of school during the famine years, pulled out of class to scavenge for food or to help plant an emergency garden. But I can't blame all my 1's and 2's on hunger. It was more and more in my nature to be rebellious. The famine only accelerated this tendency.

Instead of school, I was concerned with other things: gaining respect by fighting stronger boys, for example, who picked on me for being a country bumpkin. I was often forced to defend myself more than once a day, scrapping in the dust of the schoolyard while my classmates — connoisseurs of the art — watched how I took a punch and what I gave back. Everyone at the school had been together since first grade except for me. I wanted to be accepted, to be popular. Good grades weren't going to get me those things.

There was one boy in particular who tormented me that year. His name was Jung Choon Hyuk. He wasn't much taller than me, but he was a dangerous, sneaky fighter. Choon Hyuk wasn't very popular when I arrived; I think he saw his chance to rise in the rankings and to have some fun being mean to the country boy. *If I whip the new kid,* he must have thought, *maybe more people will like me.*

And he did whip me. We fought twenty times that fall and winter, and he beat me every time. This was a terrible disappointment to me, but it was worse for my few friends, who cheered me on fervently, only to find me lying spread-eagled in the dust every time. They were nasty fights, with Choon Hyuk trying to scratch my eyes out and cutting my cheeks. I would rake his face with my fingers, too, and by the end we'd both be bloody and dirty. But no matter how hard I tried, and no matter the technical advice my friends gave me — *Hit him with your forearm, not your fist! Kick him in the privates!* — I never walked away the winner.

So I dreaded going to school. It was a bore, and Choon Hyuk was always lurking, hoping to rack up another win. I didn't want to be there.

This broke my father's heart. As a boy, he had survived an epidemic that nearly wiped out his family. He lost almost all his brothers and sisters. But instead of being defeated by this tragedy, he'd studied intensely and gradually worked his way out of rural poverty, rising to become a respectable man.

My father tried again and again to get me to read my textbooks, but I refused. As far as he was concerned, I was failing him. I was his only son. He wanted me to use his own life as a foundation for bigger things. He would say to me, "Oh, Kwang Jin, I can't wait until the day you pull up in your big car and I come out the door and you give me a big bag of fish." Only important, powerful people in North Korea had cars, and fish was a delicacy in the North, far beyond our means. This was how he saw me in twenty years: as an important man in the government, an army general, or a diplomat. I'm sure the famine had only intensified his desire for me to become a member of the elite, someone who need never fear starvation.

But as I saw it, my father had served the state for so many years — a Party member at twenty-four! — and what had it gotten him? A dead family, nearly. When the famine had come, the government had abandoned him, its most loyal servant.

I was failing him. But in 2000, I began succeeding on my own terms. I grew a few inches and put on ten or so pounds, and I could hit. I began training for my fights with Choon Hyuk, getting up early in the morning to run for miles while the sun was just breaking over the hilltops. I bribed an older boy named Lee Hyeon Chul to teach me martial arts. He was two or three years older than me, the smartest boy in his grade as well as the best fighter. I bribed him by fixing the ski poles we used to propel our sleds down the hillsides in deep winter. In return, Hyeon Chul showed me his martial arts moves (he was famous for throwing his opponents over his head during the initial tug-of-war that started every fight) and taught me how to kick my enemy even when I was lying on the ground. The two of us soon became friends, and a rumor went around our school that we were in fact cousins, a rumor I did nothing to discourage. This meant no one could intervene in my fights, because Hyeon Chul would beat them up.

But being a sidekick also meant new threats. One day my friends and I went swimming in a nearby river. Afterward, as we walked home along the packed-dirt road, laughing and daydreaming of our dinners, one of Hyeon Chul's biggest enemies suddenly appeared, coming from the other direction. When he reached us, he picked me up as if I were a sack of rice and body-slammed me on the ground, then continued walking as if nothing had happened.

Despite that painful setback, my status was rising. But nothing helped like the time I finally beat Choon Hyuk.

It was another dirty, nasty fight. By fifteen minutes in, my ribs felt like they were broken and poking into my lungs. My mouth was filled with dust, and blood ran into my eyes. At thirty minutes, I stood up after a wild bit of wrestling and found that Choon Hyuk had stayed down. More than that, he was crying. My arms felt like lead weights as my friends came and pumped them in the air. I only felt relief, but my friends were transported with happiness. Their long investment in me as a fighter had paid off.

This was a rare good day at school. I didn't realize it, but the training I was getting in those schoolyard brawls would be worth far more to me than the little geometry I learned. It was far better preparation for what lay ahead.

CHAPTER SIXTEEN

FIGHTING WASN'T MY only vice. I had other bad habits that tormented my father. I liked to gamble, for example. There was a game at school where the other boys and I wagered with house nails. One day I came home with my pockets full of them. I'd had an amazing run of luck and couldn't wait to show my father as soon as he walked through the door. He gave me a stern look. "You shouldn't gamble," he said, but he, too, grew excited as I poured my winnings into his broad hands. He flashed a smile and his eyes turned warm as they ran over the heap of black nails. "But look how well you've done! With these we can start to build an addition on our house. Put them in my toolbox, and when the time comes, those will be the first nails I use."

It was always about houses with my father. They were his greatest achievement. His one and only son? I didn't come close.

I grew so excited by my father's newfound pride in me that day that of course I went back to school and kept gambling, against his strict orders. And of course I lost, and of course I borrowed nails from other boys to keep going, hoping to get enough for the addition my father dreamed of. And of course my losing streak went on and on, and I couldn't win a single round, and then one night I crept back home very much in debt. It was such a small amount, a matter of twenty or thirty cents perhaps, that it appears ridiculous to me today. But that night, when no one was around, I went to my father's toolbox, filled with his hammers and wrenches, and stole the nails I'd given him. I did so without a thought of what would happen if he found out.

When he noticed the nails were gone, he didn't scream at me or beat me; in fact, he never beat me at all, unlike many North Korean dads. But the look on his face made me wish he had. It was one of bewilderment and deep, deep sorrow. His eyes said, *What have I done to deserve a son such as this?*

My biggest mistake that year was taking a loan from one of my schoolmates who, unknown to me, was really stingy. One day, two of my good friends were going to the snack store. I was flat broke, but I wanted to go. So I found this older boy I didn't know well and he gave me five *won*. I had no idea he was a maniac when it came to being paid back right away. I learned later that he didn't have a father and was known for being very rude; sadly, I was to learn this the hard way.

When I didn't give the money lender the cash back the next day, he showed up at my house, yelling, "Joseph's father, give me ten *won*." He had added one hundred percent interest to the loan in twenty-four hours! And he wouldn't go away, screaming for everyone to hear that I owed him money.

I was out playing somewhere. My father went outside to shut the boy up and they got into a tussle, fighting there in our front yard. Finally the lender left without his money. But my father was humiliated by the whole experience.

When I came home that day, he said to me, "You are no longer my son."

Those words! How they stung me! I didn't know what to say. I retreated to my sleeping mat, where I cried until I fell asleep. The next morning on the way to school, the words spooled over and over again in my mind. "No longer my son . . . no longer my son . . . no longer . . ." It was something he could never take back. I felt like an orphan, misunderstood and unwanted.

Despite my father's disappointment and shame, I still didn't find the motivation to study or stop gambling. Maybe I improved for a week or two, poring over my books at night so that he would see me, but there was no lasting change. I just didn't see the point of it, and my father's insistence that I get good grades only made me more defiant. I was going to be a soldier fighting for North Korea—why did I need to know trigonometry? The bad grades continued.

Thank God my parents had Bong Sook. She was a good student, very organized and detail-oriented. Bong Sook never once caused my parents any trouble. Even in the worst times she was cheerful. Other teenagers were rebellious. They would say things like, "Why do I have to go to the farm instead of hanging out with my friends?" My sister was never that way. In a house filled with three headstrong people, she was the one who accepted what life gave her.

I think back and wonder about what was going on behind that kind, pretty face. What were her dreams of life? What did she want to be? (My guess is a teacher, but it's only a guess—we never talked about it.) Did she have a crush on a certain boy in school? Whom did she like? Who liked her? It haunts me to this day that I know nothing about these things.

I didn't even know the name of Bong Sook's favorite book. She had very few to choose from; most of the titles in our house were about the North Korean Communist Party. Like every family we knew, we had a copy of Kim Il Sung's memoirs. They came in an eight-volume set, and Bong Sook liked the one in which the Great Leader described fighting the Japanese in Manchuria. There were many action scenes and battles, and illustrations of Kim Il Sung and his brethren bayonetting the enemy. It's a very good book. Whether it's true or not is another story.

Bong Sook would read to me from one of the volumes. I spent many nights curled up in her lap on the heated floor of our house, listening to her soft voice. Kim Il Sung's story was full of dramatic and vivid scenes, and I asked her to read our favorite chapters over and over again. At one point, as the Japanese crackdown on Korean rebels intensifies, Kim Il Sung is forced to flee into China:

> Avoiding the watchful eyes of police, I walked away from the ferry pier to Jul-mok. The river Yalu was frozen there and I would be able to walk across. The Yalu was less than ten feet wide at that point . . . My feet refused to get on the ice because I might not feel the soil of Korea again. I turned around and picked up a small pebble and held it tightly in my hand. I wanted to take a piece of Korea with me . . . That moment at the Yalu bank was one of the most heart-wrenching of my life.

I was thrilled by scenes such as these. But now I ask myself: Were these really Bong Sook's favorite chapters too? Or did she read these passages just because I liked them?

I don't know where my sister's love for me ended and the real Bong Sook began. I depended on her as grass depends on the sun.

I wish I hadn't been so selfish with Bong Sook. It never occurred to me to ask myself, "Does she really want to wash my socks today?" or "Why is Bong Sook giving me her food?" I was the boy. It was simply her role to serve me, or so I thought.

Our only entertainment on these long nights was my father's stories. He was a wonderful storyteller. He would begin his tales when the lights flickered and went out at night and there was nothing to do but lie on our mats and stare at the painted white ceiling above us. My father had a light baritone voice, and for an hour it would take us away from our worries, bring us to places far from Manyang.

One of my favorite stories was about Kim Il Sung's return from a visit to Moscow. It was the Great Leader's habit to circle an airport three times before landing, to make sure everything was OK with the approach. When he flew back to Pyongyang one afternoon, assassins had planned to shoot down his plane with some kind of missile. As he neared the city, Kim Il Sung, sitting in the back of the plane, ordered the pilot to circle only twice. The assassins, waiting for his third loop, missed their chance, and the Great Leader landed safely.

"How did he *know?*" I asked my father. He just smiled at me and raised his eyebrows. The Great Leader was an extraordinary person who'd saved North Korea from slavery; tricking some assassins was all in a day's work for him. But he was gone now, I reminded myself. Such miracles were in the past.

My favorite stories of all were about my dad's time in the Special Forces of North Korea. He told us how, as an eighteen-year-old, he and his fellow soldiers were ordered to cut a hole in the ice of a frozen river. They then stripped off their uniforms, dived into the numbing water, and swam a certain distance before breaking another hole in the ice with their rifles — this time from underneath! Another time, during parachute training, his instructors told him that if his parachute got tangled with another recruit's, one of the two should cut his own lines and fall to his death to save his comrade. "The things we had to do were very hard," my dad said. "During our training, one piece of candy had to sustain me on a twenty-five-mile march!" A few years into his ten-year service, he lost his hearing in one ear during an ocean dive and had to leave the army.

My father signed a paper when he left the military, promising he would never use the skills he'd learned there in civilian life. He took that oath so seriously that he would never teach me how to fight. His only piece of advice in this area was "Never close your eyes," because that shows you're scared and also hampers the accuracy of your punches. I always remembered that.

When my dad told his tales, we were transported aloft to a North Korean air force plane, or we joined a mountain march where men stumbled through the darkness, nearly asleep on their feet. His stories gave us courage; we were no longer sick and hungry creatures, but comrades of these dashing men. When I heard my father's voice in our dark house, it would feel as if his arms were around me again and all was right with my country.

I would soon come to miss those nights very much.

CHAPTER SEVENTEEN

In the fall of 2000, our "good year" — really, it was just six months — came to a sudden end. Inflation shot up again, and a kilogram of rice that had once cost forty or fifty *won* now cost two hundred. The rest of the country was recovering, but my father had become sick. Hunger had taken a hard toll on his health, and he had contracted cirrhosis of the liver (though he'd never been much of a drinker).

We went back to our "farm" in the country, two and a half hours away on foot. By then, we'd realized why the government had given the land away — it was at the base of a mountain where the trees had been cleared by burning, and the soil wasn't very good. Year after year, our plot yielded fewer and fewer vegetables. We ate string beans and the first corn, which came in around August 15, Korean Independence Day. But soon we were back in Manyang, starving and worried. The famine returned to our home, and it was like an animal that had grown up and gotten stronger. It began to devour us.

Home was bleaker than ever. My mom took out loans and was unable to pay them back. There was no more rice or grain. We subsisted on weeds and wild grasses, scavenged from the fields that bordered the mountains. My father warned us about mushrooms. He was worried we would be so hungry that we'd be unable to wait to bring the mushrooms home for him to identify and mistakenly eat a poisonous one. We'd heard whispers that entire families had been found sprawled around their dinner pots, where the bad mushrooms still sat in lukewarm water.

Hunger sucked away our energy. We entered a kind of brownout, a time of slow starvation. Your mind is partially numbed but your stomach is racked with pain, and each day is lived on the wire between the two: when it glows hot, the scraping in your stomach is almost unbearable and you want to scream. Your mind turns against you, flashing images of lavish meals in front of your eyes. When the connection grows dim, you slip into a half slumber. You feel irritable. Your heartbeat is shallow and fast.

As the weeks went by, Bong Sook looked weaker and weaker. She would sit unsteadily on her sleeping mat, as if she was going to topple over. One day, my mother asked Bong Sook to pass a plate of cabbage leaves so that she could dump them in the cooking pot and boil them. The leaves sat on a table five feet from Bong Sook. She turned to get up, but her limbs wouldn't support her and she collapsed back on the mat after rising only an inch or two. Then she attempted to crawl, but again her body betrayed her: the left arm buckled and she sank down on the mat like a building that had partially imploded. Once Bong Sook was tilted over, she didn't have the strength to straighten up, so she stayed there, slumped at a steep angle.

It was the first time I ever saw terror in my sister's eyes. Bong Sook looked at me, then at my mother and father. Her eyes were loud with fear. *What's happening?* they cried. *Why is my body doing these strange things? What does it mean?*

My parents struggled to their feet and pulled her up straight. I couldn't move. It felt like I was watching through the kind of haze a fire throws off. *This is how it happens,* I thought. *How families are found dead.* If my parents didn't have that last reserve of strength, we would have watched each other topple into unconsciousness, barely realizing it was real and not a dream. We were close to the precipice.

My mother's pellagra returned in full force, and my father grew more ill as the weeks went by. Hunger caused his stomach to swell, and the cirrhosis darkened his skin and caused intense, jabbing pain. The skin above the liver became hot and painful as the organ swelled and scarred. We had no money for a doctor, so beyond the initial diagnosis, my father was never really treated, and we never found out what caused the disease. But the fact that both my parents were weakened by their illnesses worried them terribly. They dreaded Bong Sook and I becoming *Kkotjebi*.

One day my father came home from work looking excited. "We should go to the river," he said. "My colleague told me there are small snails there that you can boil and eat. The river is full of them!"

We'd never considered snails as food before. But the thought of having meat, which we hadn't seen in months, was too tempting to resist. We all began dreaming of this exotic new food, how it might taste — like miniature shrimp, firm-fleshed and delicious, or like ocean fish, briny and bracing?

That weekend, my father and I walked to the river carrying empty buckets. I hadn't thought of what he meant when he said "the river." It was the same place my friends and I went swimming. It was summertime, and they were sure to be at our favorite spot. I hoped they wouldn't see me. That would be embarrassing.

I needn't have worried. My father led me to another section of the river that was shallower than our swimming hole. And we found that his colleague had been speaking the truth. There were snails everywhere, clinging to the rocks and small boulders that lined the bottom of the river. We began to gather them. I felt along the mossy rocks until I found a shell under my fingertip. I plucked it off and tossed it in the bucket. Soon the dark gray things were making that rich clicking sound of shell on shell. I thought of the feast that awaited us.

At about four o'clock, we headed home with our haul. My mother met us at the door and took the bucket. While my father and I washed up, she rinsed off the snails and poured them into a pot of water already near boiling on the fire. She stoked the flames underneath, and soon the snails appeared at the little cave of their shells, trying to escape the heat. I looked at my father. He nodded, so I picked up a shell. It was so small. Holding it between my index finger and thumb, I sucked the snail out of its home.

"Father!" I cried. "It tastes awful!" And it did—slimy and eel-like.

My father looked at me sternly.

"Eat it anyway."

I closed my eyes and swallowed miserably. "Do we have salt at least?"

My mother shook her head. Salt was a luxury far above our station. The disappointment of the snails soon gave way to simple ravenousness and we ate the meat. I thought, *No wonder my father's friend told us about these things. They're disgusting.* But I ate them until I thought I would throw up.

Dogs began to disappear from the streets. Before the famine, you would see them on leashes outside the homes in Hoeryong, with their own tiny houses by the front door. They ate scraps and guarded the property. Really, their lives were pretty bad. But when the famine came, you never saw dogs walking the streets anymore.

Rats were next. Before we got hungry, perhaps one in a hundred families had ever tasted rat. I remember one girl, Oon Hwa, whose father used to trap rats in the market and take them home for dinner. We would laugh at her, saying, "Her father eats rats! She probably does too!" But now the rodents became sought after, though my friends never admitted they'd tasted rat meat.

By the spring of 2001, it seemed that even the lowliest sources of food were drying up, leaving nothing remaining. My father left his job, which meant we had no more government farm to supply our food. My parents argued often now, and my father would sometimes kick my mom out of the house, usually after she admitted she'd lost the latest loan he'd arranged for her. One day, after I hadn't seen her for a week, I was walking to school when I saw my mother by the side of the road. She motioned me over, her face strained and her eyes filled with sadness. "Kwang Jin," she said, "take these." She had somehow found enough money for a new pair of shoes, which she stuffed in my school bag, and ten candies. I gobbled up two of them and put the rest in my pocket. My mother embraced me and I walked away, leaving her crying by the roadside.

My heart was torn with childish grief in those days. I didn't understand why my mother couldn't live with us.

Mothers and sons have a powerful bond in Korean culture. My father used to tell me this fable: In famine times hundreds of years ago, there was a son who could no longer afford to feed his mother, so he put her on his back and made his way to a mountain, where he planned to abandon her to die. She knew what he was doing but said nothing until they got close to the mountain, when she finally spoke: "Son," she said calmly, "I have been snapping branches from the trees and dropping them behind us. After you leave me, follow them home and you won't get lost."

Finally, that spring, my mother left Hoeryong for the house of one of her friends in the north. I think she was glad to get away from my father and the constant tension.

I wonder now what my parents' marriage would have been like without the famine, without the stress of having nothing to feed their children. Would they have made it? Would they have been happy? Were the cracks that split them apart geographical ones — the result of living in North Korea? Or were they fault lines that lay deep inside their love affair all along?

When summer came, the three of us remaining in Manyang hoped that the harvests would bring us relief. But instead the famine grew more intense. With no job, my father had no money to buy food. His concern deepened. Would we survive until the fall harvest from our little farm? Alone, without my mother, the responsibility for saving us weighed on him even more.

Bong Sook and I spent our days in the mountains, leaving home in the predawn darkness. Alongside us on the road, barely seen, were other figures with bags hanging from their hands. They were villagers headed to the same hills, hoping to forage their evening meal. To make the journey easier, Bong Sook would tell me stories or we'd talk about the good days when we could buy snacks anytime we felt like it, about the Sundays when the TV channel started broadcasting at 9 a.m. and we'd stay home all day eating corn cakes and watching movies. It made us feel happier for a moment or two.

We worked all morning, then took a break around noon and munched on anything we brought with us — root vegetables or leftovers from the night before, if there were any. Any edible weeds we found we put in a plastic bag. We usually managed to fill the bag after a ten-hour day. It would be near midnight before we headed home to collapse on our sleeping mats.

One day, as we were walking to the mountains just after dawn, we saw a peasant woman walking ahead of us, an infant tied to her back. (This way, the woman would be able to pick weeds without putting the child down on the ground.) I noticed something in the toddler's hands: corn chips. *Where on earth did she get them?* I wondered. Instantly I felt a wild desire to steal the treats out of the baby's hands and devour them.

Hunger is humiliation. But hunger is also evil.

Finally, after a few months, the mountains had nothing left to give. When we told my father, he nodded slowly. He looked like he was aging: his face was lined, his back no longer as straight as it had once been. His skin was yellow from the cirrhosis and his belly had swollen like a pregnant woman's.

There was nothing left to do, nothing left to sell. The heat pressed through the ceiling and there seemed to be no oxygen in the house.

I spent the days in and out of a delirium I didn't want to wake from. The weaker we grew, the less terrifying death seemed.

CHAPTER EIGHTEEN

As our family sank further and further, old people from the neighborhood stopped me on the street and told me: "You have a wonderful sister. You should be thankful for her!" I must have toughened up by this point, because I remember the old people waiting for me to heartily agree, but I just stared at them, a frown slashed across my face. *Why don't they mind their own business? What concern is it of theirs if my sister is good or not? Aren't we almost starving, Bong Sook or no Bong Sook?* Perhaps I was feeling a bit guilty about all she was doing for us, and about my tiny contribution to the household.

I couldn't trap animals. I was useless at business. My brain produced no ideas for new sources of food. It was mostly dormant, shuttered for lack of nutrients. I was just a stomach.

The reason the old people were so impressed with Bong Sook was that she had come up with a way to save us. She took up where my mother left off, buying and selling noodles to help us survive. And at least in the beginning, she proved a much better businesswoman than my mom. The old people were always running into her on the streets as she bicycled this way and that in pursuit of food to feed our family.

Every night, Bong Sook would take my father's old bicycle and head off to the local market to get corn. She bought twenty pounds and took it to a nearby factory, where she laboriously ground the kernels into flour to make noodles. Part of that process involved adding water, so her twenty pounds of corn resulted in twenty-five pounds of noodles, which she stuffed into plastic bags to keep them moist. The next morning, she got up, dressed, washed her face, and loaded the noodles onto the rickety black bike parked outside. She pedaled for about two hours, until she was in the farthest depths of rural North Korea. Then she would knock on farmhouse doors, asking, "Any corn noodles for you today?"

The country people had less access to fresh noodles and would pay her a few *won* for a handful. Sometimes the farmers had no cash and would pay her in corn instead. She would give them a pound of noodles, and they'd give her a pound and three ounces of loose corn.

Her profit was minuscule. And the whole enterprise, as my mother had learned to her chagrin, was risky. If you didn't sell the noodles the first day, they began to lose moisture, which meant she had to give the buyers more noodles in each pound. The longer the noodles remained unsold, the drier they got, and the slimmer Bong Sook's profit.

The trip out to the rural districts had its dangers, too. Noodle girls were often accosted. I remember one girl was hit on the head with a rock and woke up to find her noodles gone. Another was raped near Hoeryong, and I'd heard stories of girls being beaten when they refused to hand over their goods. There were few police far out in the country, and discharged soldiers, dressed in their old uniforms, unable to find work, had turned to robbery. How could girls like my sister hope to defend themselves in those distant places where no one even knew their names?

That winter, I woke one morning and saw Bong Sook's big brown eyes staring at me in the gray gloom. The wind howled outside. Sometimes it sounded extra-cold; it seemed as though its edges were sawing away at the door, trying to get in. I put my cheek down on the mat and felt the heat flow through my face.

"Kwang Jin?" she said.

"Yes?"

"I will go in ten more minutes."

I nodded and we stared at each other, saying nothing. It was enough to be warm and with Bong Sook and not to be going to school. I thought of the long day ahead, spent inside, doing nothing. I didn't have the strength to go out and play.

"I wish I didn't have to go," Bong Sook said.

I stared at her silently. It was so unusual for her to say such a thing, to admit that her life was hard. I was stumped for a response. *Don't go,* I wanted to say. *Stay here with me and we'll talk about old times.* But if she didn't go, we would end up eating the noodles, and Bong Sook would have nothing to sell.

The ten minutes was up. Her eyes were sad. I knew that as we spoke, the noodles were beginning to dry out.

"Five more minutes," she said.

"Five more minutes," I repeated. I didn't know how to comfort my sister. I wasn't good at such things. I kept wishing I had a secret cache of money that I could use to buy a month's worth of corn — I imagined being a rich trader with thousands of *won* in his pocket. More and more, my daydreams of being a spy or a heroic soldier were giving way to ones where I surprised my family with truckloads of food. That way, I could keep Bong Sook with me and retrieve my mother from her journeys.

Five minutes later, Bong Sook lifted herself off the floor, wincing at the joint pain that seemed always to go with long bouts of hunger, and got dressed. Soon she was gone, and from my mat I could hear the sound of the old bike clattering down the road. I pictured her pedaling along the roads, the baskets of noodles bouncing on either side of the back wheel. I hoped she would come home soon with a pouch full of corn.

CHAPTER NINETEEN

My FATHER KEPT telling us his wonderful stories, even in the darkest days of the famine. Kim Il Sung and his battles against the Japanese. My father's adventures as a soldier in training. But in the late spring of 2001, the subject of his stories began to change. The adventures of Kim Il Sung disappeared, never to return. Now my father would take me aside at night, even when the electricity was still on, and tell me about the rituals of North Korean funerals.

Mourning in North Korea is complicated, and everyone must play his part precisely in order for the dead person to be sent on to the next world without losing honor. The oldest son is very important in all of this. He is the *sangju*, what you might call in the West the master of ceremonies. The *sangju* must take the lead in all of the rituals, or the spirit of the dead parent will feel alone at the moment he or she is leaving for the afterlife.

My father stressed each step in the grieving process, repeating himself on successive nights. "First, the body is laid out in a straight line," he would say. "You must cover it in a white sheet. If you can find something to screen the body from people entering the house, that is good." In front of this screen the *sangju* stands with a photograph of the dead person as incense burns on a table next to him. In the old days, he would dress in the traditional Korean costume, with each region having its own style — in Andong, for example, a long, belted coat made of the finest hemp, called a *top'o* — but such things were impossible to obtain in 2001. Any black coat would do, along with a black ribbon or armband. The *sangju* isn't allowed to leave the side of his loved one except to use the bathroom. He is the dead person's guard; he cannot depart. It is a special feature of Korean culture that the *sangju* is there not only to protect the dead person, but also to atone for letting his parent die.

"This is the first day," my father said. I listened, finding nothing strange in his telling me these things. The transition from the escapades of North Korean soldiers to the arrangement of incense sticks was seamless. There was no need to worry: it was just another plain subject that my father would turn into something wonderful.

"The second day, the body is cleaned and dressed and put into a coffin." (He went on to describe the intricate procedure. I forget some of the instructions he gave me; they did go on forever.) The *sangju* must supervise every detail of this process, of course. Then he drapes a black ribbon across the photograph of the dead person and sits next to the coffin on a mat made of coarse material. The roughness of the mat he sits on — this I remember — is part of his penance.

Now the visitors come. They bow to the photo, then bow to the *sangju*, who bows back. In the old tradition, the *sangju* would say nothing throughout the entire second day — he has sinned, the body in the casket is evidence of his sin, and he must atone for it — but in modern times he is allowed to thank the visitors for paying their respects. In earlier years, the mourners would leave an envelope filled with cash. But nowadays few people had money to spare even for the living.

On the third day, the casket is carried to the burial ground, led by the *sangju*, still holding the picture of the deceased. At the gravesite, the *sangju* recites the life story of his mother or father, and mourners, if they wish, can offer memories of the person's integrity or goodness of heart. When the casket is being lowered into the ground, the *sangju* throws three handfuls of dirt on top of it. The grave is filled in and a low mound of earth left atop it, with a small stone on it telling everyone who is buried there.

It used to be that for three years after his loved one's death the *sangju* had to withdraw from normal life, not get married or have sex, to atone for his horrible error in allowing his loved one to die. Now, after only a few days, he may rejoin the world.

It's obvious to me now that my father was preparing me for his own death, charging me with the knowledge of what I must do afterward. I admit I didn't realize it then, however. As I said, my dad could make anything sound magical: his voice drew you in. But I was a poor student, missing the essential lesson as always. It was one reason I had disappointed him so consistently.

My father also told me how to tell if a person was really dead. When a living person lies on the floor, he said, if you put your hand under the small of his back, there is space there — you can slip your open hand in, palm down. But if a person is dead, there is no space to fit your hand. It was an odd fact, but my father was always passing on bits of strange information to me.

I wonder now if he found comfort in envisioning his death in painstaking detail. Perhaps it was like attending his own funeral, which must have had its appeal — to know that even in a time of famine, when so much of what he treasured had disappeared, the old ways would survive. I suspect he was being so precise because I was not the most focused child. Deep down, he was telling me: Son, forget your usual wild nature and do me this last service. Observe the rituals that my grandfather taught my father and that my father taught me. Kwang Jin, don't let me down.

My mother returned to the house with the money she'd accumulated from her business ventures. She'd made some friends in Sambong, a city north of Hoeryong, and was doing business there, but her profits fluctuated widely. She wasn't making enough to feed her family consistently.

By the fall of 2001, we'd exhausted all our options for staying alive. We'd collected wood in the mountains above our house and taken it to the market, but fewer and fewer people had money to buy it. We had no harvest from the farm. We'd bartered away almost everything we owned. To have to sell your household belongings is a terrible loss of face for a North Korean man, an admission that you can't support your family, and it took a lot of courage for my father to walk out the door carrying the cooking pots. But he did it, and returned with enough noodles to last a day or two.

The beloved black-and-white television that had made me a prince of the neighborhood went next. My father told Bong Sook and me, who were distraught over loosing it, that he was selling the TV only to buy a bigger one. The bigger one, of course, never appeared. Most of the clothes followed, then our clay bowls and our furniture. Then the clock on the wall, which my father took down one day and sold to a merchant in the Hoeryong city market. Finally there was nothing left.

Around this time, we learned that my maternal grandmother had died of starvation. A friend who'd journeyed from my grandmother's village came to our house and told us the news.

I was devastated when I heard this. Grandmother's life had been painful. When I thought of her, the cold expression on her face came back to me, the expression of a woman who expects nothing good in life. I tried to remember her smiling, but couldn't. Still, I recalled those spoonfuls of rice she gave me while she told her stories. *She loved you, Kwang Jin*, I told myself. There is no greater sign of love than a spoonful of rice.

My mother was shocked by the news. Her dark energy filled the house, but this time we contributed to it, our thoughts of Grandma starving, with us unable to help. Soon Mother told us she would be leaving again — not for a relative's house (who would have taken her in?), but for China.

Escaping to China was dangerous. If you were caught on either side of the Tumen River, which lay a few miles away and bordered China, you'd be imprisoned. (Though people in Hoeryong, many of whom had relatives across the border, sometimes got reprieves if they stayed in nearby Chinese towns and didn't proceed to the interior.) But we'd all heard stories of North Koreans going to China and getting fabulously rich, returning with enough money to buy a new house and living off their earnings for years. This had an obvious appeal for my mother. She would go across the border and work or trade — the details were murky — then return to us flush with cash.

When my mom left, I didn't cry. I had no idea she was going to China; I thought it was just another trip to her relatives in the south, which she'd taken many times before. I didn't even hug her, just whispered, "Goodbye."

Weeks after she left, there was no food in the house and no prospect of getting any. It was time for last measures.

My father had a distant relative, a second or third cousin, who lived three hours away by foot. She was an ordinary farmer, far below my father in social rank. We'd heard that she'd had a big harvest that season, producing more than enough to feed her family. If my father waited any longer to seek her help, he might be too weak to ask. My father feared going to see his cousin and dying on the way, alone by the roadside, leaving us to starve without ever knowing his fate.

If he was going to go, he had to do it now. After much deliberation, we decided that forty pounds of cornmeal was the least we could ask for and still be able to survive the coming winter. In the spring of 2002, my father would pay her back. How, he didn't know. But his reputation preceded him. My father was a small legend, a man who'd succeeded young and risen far above his station. Of course he would pay his cousin back.

I remember him leaving the house. He was hopeful. His back was straight and he had that air of strength and purpose I always associated with him. He simply said goodbye and was off at eight o'clock in the morning. Bong Sook and I lazed around that day, barely moving, with that luxuriant feeling of waiting for a meal so full and bountiful that it will stretch your stomach to its limit and send you off into a snoring, happy sleep. We were sure of his success.

That evening, we heard footsteps coming up the path to our house. I sat up, hoping I'd see my father push the door open with his feet, a heavy bag of corn clutched in each of his hands, a big smile on his face. But he slipped in quietly. He couldn't bear to tell us what his relative had said to him. (Bong Sook and I would spend hours theorizing about the precise form our cousin's cruelty took. "Are you out of your mind?" is what I imagined her shouting at my father, standing forlorn in her doorway. "What kind of world do you think you live in?" was Bong Sook's guess. That, or "Go home, you idiot!") My father staggered into the house, the right side of his face rigid and the right eye staring blindly, as if he'd suffered a stroke.

"Father, what's wrong?" my sister cried out. He collapsed into her arms and I rushed over. Together we lowered him to the mat.

My father seemed to be undergoing some kind of rapid aging process. He couldn't speak. He couldn't move his hands, which he held out in front of him as if they'd been scalded. His condition seemed to worsen in the few seconds since he'd come through the door. The symptoms stabilized that night, but he was practically catatonic by the next day. And three days later, the screaming began.

Bong Sook and I didn't know what was wrong with our father. We could recognize the signs of starvation, but then there was his yellowed skin and the terrible pain — not the usual symptoms of hunger. To us, something had entered his body and was slowly eating him from the inside, hollowing out his belly. Something far worse than disease.

A loss of dignity. Hot shame.

I imagine my father's state of mind that night as he approached our house empty-handed, humiliated by his own flesh and blood. He believed he was going to watch Bong Sook and me die in front of him. This is his deepest fear; it has been with him for many years, and now, as soon as he opens the door, the process will unfold in scenes that cannot be altered or stopped or slowed even for a moment. This is what he is seeing in his mind: flashes of the near future, starving bodies, dead brown eyes. I believe it was fear, as much as anything else, that paralyzed my father's body. As he takes hold of the doorknob (perhaps it happened earlier, on the road into town, or as he passed the accordion houses to our left), he sees that his children will not survive.

Can one will oneself to fall into a coma, to unsee what is before one's eyes? I don't know. I think my father's heart was in turmoil, and he was overcome by a kind of prescient horror. Whether he willed himself to die or his body and mind simply gave way, it's hard to say. To me, they are almost the same thing.

That night, my father began to disappear.

CHAPTER TWENTY

THE SHAME OF my father's long walk to seek the help of his distant cousin seemed to release all the toxins in his body to a free-for-all in his poor belly. He suffered agonizing stomach pains. He screamed continuously. His belly swelled further, its surface horribly distended and shiny, like smooth scar tissue. We didn't know what was killing him. The lack of food over the years had weakened him so much that it seemed there was a race to see what would finish him off, starvation or cirrhosis.

In a way, it didn't matter, because there was no medicine for either of his conditions. If you took your loved one to the hospital, the doctors would tell you, We have no medicine, take him home, let him die in a place he knows. The doctors had sold the government-provided medicines to profiteers in the market. They did this to survive. So when you went to the hospital, they would say, Go to the market and talk to this seller or that one. They knew exactly whom they'd sold the medicine to. But when you went to the market, the drugs would cost a fortune.

The father I'd known was gone. Only a body remained, a wretched, writhing, foul-smelling body so bone-thin it pained me to touch him. My father would often scream through the night, then lapse into unconsciousness, terribly still. But even when he was awake, he was no longer the stern but secretly loving man I'd always known. He was a raving thing that pain twisted and turned at all hours. Sometimes I worried the strain would snap his back.

On those nights when I could no longer take my father's yelling, I would go outside and walk, just to hear the crickets and the sigh of the grass by the roadside. The night sky was my only consolation in those days, the stars so beautiful and clear that it felt as if I could reach my hand up and scorch my fingertips on the light.

I wandered by the accordion houses that lined the streets. If the moon was out, I would look up at it as I made my way along the road. Behind the dark windows of the nearby houses, I sensed my neighbors were awake. Surely no one could sleep through my father's howls.

Sometimes I walked so far that it seemed physically impossible for me to hear the screams. Two hundred yards. Three. But they were always there, coming over the rooftops of orange Chinese tile. Perhaps the sound had become inaudible after only a few blocks and what I was hearing was something that began in my own mind. An echo of my father's suffering. The voice of guilt mixed with sadness and the desire, deep down, for it to be over, one way or the other.

I loved my father deeply despite our fights, but sometimes I wished he would suffer in silence, like others were doing. I knew that all across North Korea there were people who were as close to death as my father. And there were others who wouldn't even live through the night. Those families would bring their loved ones' bodies out in the morning, and young boys — sad-faced and bewildered *sangjus* — would stay with them while the others went to the casket factory. It's strange to say that I envied those boys their corpses, but in a way I did. Their anguish was private, dignified. Ours had entangled the whole neighborhood in its course, like some too-loud soap opera that began every night around ten o'clock. They could tell the nights when my father slept and those when the pain turned unbearable. And when, exhausted, he at last sank into unconsciousness, they could take to their beds and get a good night's rest.

Most nights, I headed to the mini-mart that was owned by Kim Il's grandmother. In order to feed her family, she had opened a store inside her home. You could go up to the small glass window in the front of the house and look inside. The entire contents of the store — tubes of toothpaste, a few handfuls of corn, some candies — were visible in that little square, lit by a single bulb. If you didn't see what you needed, you moved on. If you didn't see it, Kim Il's grandmother didn't have it.

When I knocked, I could hear someone stirring. As the famine had worsened, honest people had turned to stealing, as I had in the fields. If you didn't keep constant watch over your goods, these people, driven mad with hunger, would smash the window of your shop, scoop up a handful of corn, and stuff it in their mouths. So Kim Il's grandmother slept on the floor of the store on a thin mat. Soon the door latch clicked and the door opened.

The grandmother smiled at me. She knew what I wanted. She could hear my father's screaming, a little softer now but never losing its hoarse, animal-like bellow. She knew that a bit of food or a sedative, injected by Bong Sook, would soothe him for an hour or two, until the pain woke him again. I gave her what little money we had left — provided by an old friend of my father's — and took the vial of sedative. My pace was faster now as I thought of the peace the medicine would bring and of my bed on the warm floor.

I would hand Bong Sook the vial and she would take out the needle. In a few minutes, we'd be able to sleep until the first cry of the next day woke us again.

The two and a half months it took my father to slowly pass away were the strangest of my life. A friend of my father's was giving us small amounts of money from time to time, but my poor sister still had to work herself to the bone: going to the factory to buy noodles, bicycling to the rural districts, then coming home to care for my father, washing my socks, barely sleeping four or five hours. I didn't work and I'd stopped going to school, so I was with my father constantly, often staring at him as he lay in a coma, unable to speak. I was paralyzed by a shapeless feeling that often turned into childish rage or apathy. I couldn't tell my father how much I missed him.

My sister and I were the only ones caring for him during this time. As for relatives, there were no phones to call them, and besides, we'd already tasted the bitterness of their charity.

One of my father's relations did visit once or twice. He was my father's uncle, but we always called him Small Grandfather. He would bring kimchi or a few side dishes from his place, twenty minutes from my house. He would sit next to my father and say, "How could you do this to me? How can you leave now?" In our culture, it's considered almost rude for a son to die before his father, or a nephew before his uncle. Small Grandfather didn't mean to chastise my father; this was his way of expressing sorrow.

A nurse who lived thirty minutes away came for a few weeks, but when she saw our situation, she ended up crying more than my sister. In North Korea, you must give nurses or doctors a meal when they treat your loved one, and we had nothing to spare, so eventually she stopped knocking on our door. Before she left for the last time, she showed my sister the proper way to give the sedative injections. She saw me watching her, and she came up to me and put her hands on my shoulders. "I know this is hard," she told me, "but you have to grow up and be a man."

I did neither. If I grew up, it would mean my father was gone. I wanted him to wake up and be my dad again, and for my family to magically knit itself back together into what we'd been during the good year of 2000.

Instead, as I sat in our house, my mind wandered to the past. Sometimes I thought of silly things, like imagining what was happening on a North Korean TV series we used to watch. Or I pretended to be a secret agent. In my mind, I was battling enemy aggressors, America and Japan, capturing their agents and plugging them — *pow!* — with my gleaming black pistol. I had played that game many times as a child in the hills behind our house in July 8th.

But other times I would try to untangle the mystery of why my father and I had drifted apart. What had caused me to hate him at times, and for him to disown me. Most of all, I asked my father to come back to me.

One bright, warm day a few weeks after the nurse had visited for the last time, I was sitting in our room watching the sunlight play in the dust motes that rose from the floor, daydreaming as usual. I'd had nothing for breakfast, and Bong Sook was off on the bicycle in the countryside, trying to make enough money for dinner. If she didn't come home with something, the hunger pangs in my belly would spread to my bones. Hunger informs you that your skeleton really is hollow.

Suddenly I heard my father's voice, for the first time in many weeks. "I'd like a cigarette," he said calmly. I sat up straight. It was as if a ghost had spoken. I looked over and saw his figure sitting up, too, a light smile on his face, his eyes clear and unworried.

I was speechless. What was going on? I felt like my mind was playing me for a fool, that my desire to see my father as he'd once been was so strong that I'd willed this mirage into being. He hadn't been coherent in over two months, and now he was sitting up and talking to me as if nothing had happened.

My father met my stare, his brown eyes confident and serene. Hope flared inside me. He was real. Magically restored! So many possibilities arose in my mind. The things we would do together now.

But first, the cigarette. I ran out into the street. If I had scraped together all the money we had, I could have gotten him a real, factory-made cigarette. We had enough money for that, just barely. But my brain rattled along in the ruts of old instincts — *survive, survive, only survive* — and so I walked through the streets of the town, studying the gutters and the fringe of grass near the road, looking for discarded cigarette butts. When I had four or five, I raced home and watched as my father, weak as he was, gently tore the papers open and shook out the tobacco until he had enough for a smoke. He wrapped the tobacco in the least torn of the papers and lit up. He smiled at me, though I knew that this patched-together thing must have tasted awful.

If I had known what was to come, I would have bought him a quality cigarette. This torments me to this day, every time I pass a store with Marlboros and Camels and Lucky Strikes. Why didn't I take our little bit of money and get him a fresh, Chinese-made product? He would have enjoyed it. He might even have sensed that I had watched over him all those weeks, praying for his recovery, that night after night I had run to get him medicine and racked my brain for a solution to his mystery illness.

My father said, "Son, come help me outside."

I helped him to the door and we pushed it open. It was clear, the sky blue and cloudless. A fine spring day. We stood in the doorway, my body pressed against the warmth of his. I thought, *He's going to be fine. All that worrying for nothing. Stupid boy.* I felt as light as a leaf carried along by the breeze.

He didn't scream that afternoon. Or that night.

The next day, my father made a gurgling sound and dark liquid came rushing out of his nose and mouth. I was terrified. He was staring up at the ceiling, his eyes bulging.

"What should we do?" I cried to Bong Sook.

"Run to Small Grandfather's house," Bong Sook said. "Hurry!"

I took off out the door as Bong Sook knelt by Father's head, cradling it in her lap. As I ran, my mind repeated the words *Not yet, not yet, not yet.* When I reached Small Grandfather's, my uncle, the soldier, had just arrived. I blurted out that something was happening to my father. They looked at me with stricken faces and we hurried back to our house.

When I opened the door, I could sense that my father was dead. His face was clean; there was nothing coming out of his nose or mouth. But his skin had already collapsed a bit on the bones, as if something had departed.

Bong Sook was staring at the floor. "He stopped breathing five minutes ago," she said quietly.

I had never seen my uncle cry. He was always a calm and sweet-natured man. But now he began to weep. "Brother, why couldn't you wait five minutes more," he wailed. "I just arrived and now you're gone!" Then he apologized to my father for being so late. Small Grandfather nodded but said nothing.

My sister and I performed the test our father had told us about: we tried to slide a hand under the small of his back. But there was no room.

I didn't know what to do or how to feel. So much pain was over for my father, but now I had to live without him.

CHAPTER TWENTY-ONE

I KNOW WITH ONE hundred percent certainty that my father was an excellent *sangju* in his time. I can see him, his back ramrod-straight, holding the picture of his father without letting it shake so much as a millimeter. He would have been exacting and knowledgeable in every detail, and the black-clad women would have spoken about him in admiring whispers. He would have honestly felt the guilt that the ritual was supposed to absolve. Believe me, if you wanted an eldest son to send you on your way, you could hardly do better than my father. Perhaps he even wore a hemp coat.

I, on the other hand, was a second-rate, famine *sangju*. There was no ceremony for my father, no first or second day. Many people did come, perhaps a hundred. My mother returned the day after my father died. She'd been arrested in China, but since it was her first offense, she was released from jail and allowed to join the mourning party.

I did my best as eldest son, but I couldn't scrounge up a black outfit and instead wore my school uniform, which hung loosely on my emaciated body. I brushed it and made it as presentable as I could.

I held my father's picture and bowed to the people as they entered our house. They didn't stay long, just dipped their head toward the body, then stood against the wall for a while before making their escape. To go to the funeral of a man who starved to death and expect to be fed is its own contradiction.

A *sangju* isn't supposed to cry, but there was one moment when I couldn't control myself any longer. It was when two officials from the local Communist Party arrived to confiscate my father's documents. For my entire childhood, the papers had sat underneath the portrait of Kim Il Sung, our little North Korean shrine. They were kept in a thin booklet, stamped with the Party's seal. That magic number — a Party member at only twenty-four! — was confirmed in black typewritten letters. My father had treasured those documents.

The officials entered our house, and the more senior one took the booklet down and read aloud what was typed there. The crowd listened, hushed, eyes cast down at the floor. When the official finished reading, he nodded and tucked the booklet into his chest pocket. It was then I let out a yelping sob. Tears streamed from my eyes. It was only at that moment that my father really ceased to be alive for me. Why had I not believed my eyes when I looked at his corpse? Maybe I believed in the state more than I thought I did. Nature was variable; it changed its mind all the time. But the Party? Never. I knew then my father was not coming back.

My sister and I couldn't afford to transport the body to the graveyard. Luckily, the bosses at one of the companies my father had worked for years earlier sent a car. My military uncle was good enough to pay for the coffin.

On the way to the casket factory, my uncle looked down at me. His eyes were unreadable, but there were multiple sorrows in them, I felt, instead of just the one sorrow inside me. "Poor Kwang Jin," he said. "You shouldn't have left your father's side, today of all days." He said this with what we call *hansoom* — a deep, troubled sigh. "Poverty makes you mature," he said in his next breath. It was a North Korean saying: even as life hurts you, it prepares you to accept the next bit of pain. You're growing up too fast, he meant to say. You should just be a boy, but life isn't letting you.

I thought of my father's lessons on North Korean funerals. He must have known we wouldn't be able to honor him in those ways, which were from another time. He was thinking of his father's and his grandfather's funerals and not his own. Was he sad that he wouldn't have the same rituals? My father never complained about his fate, but I think he would have liked those last things to have been done, to have a dignified farewell.

Instead, it was all I could do to find a piece of wood at the casket factory to mark his grave. We couldn't afford stone. We carved his name on the plank and shoved it deep into the dirt on the side of the mound.

My period of mourning lasted only a day or two. Then I had to go back to surviving.

CHAPTER TWENTY-TWO

SMALL GRANDFATHER — my father's uncle — had been a big man in North Korea. An economist, he'd been higly placed in an important ministry in Pyongyang. But he'd lost that job for mysterious reasons, and soon went to work at a government agency with much less prestige. Despite his demotion, Small Grandfather was what I suppose you could call a government loyalist. He was tall, with swept-back gray hair and penetrating eyes, eyes that told you he expected to be obeyed. He had a diplomat's charm and could talk most people into anything. He once told me that when he visited the Soviet Union as a government representative, he got the Russians to raise their glasses and cheer for Kim Il Sung — the first time that had ever happened at an official dinner.

I had seen Small Grandfather often as a boy. We would go to his house for holidays and his birthday, and I would sing out my little good wishes before running off to watch his TV. (It was the first set in our family.) The reason my father moved from Undok to our pigeon coop apartment in Hoeryong was to be near Small Grandfather and, he hoped, share in his success. Small Grandfather was super-smart. He had graduated from eighth grade but couldn't afford high school. Instead, he'd waited until he was eighteen, then joined the army and fought in the Korean War. He was so smart that, when the war ended, he skipped high school and went straight to college. I never heard of another person doing that.

As a boy, I loved Small Grandfather. Or at least I think I did. He was part of a childhood that I remembered fondly, before the famine came, and so he was surrounded by the warm feelings I had for that time. But I always found his deep voice to be scary. I would jump a little whenever I heard it.

Smart and coldhearted — that describes my small grandfather. And proud of his frosty reserve. He once told me, "In normal life, you can be a romantic. But in economics, you must keep a cold heart." He liked the saying so much, he sometimes forgot the "economics" part and applied the lesson to all of life.

After my father's funeral, my mother, Bong Sook, and I had to move out of our house. My father's friend, who had given us small amounts of money when my father could no longer work, informed us he was taking the space as reimbursement. Mother and Bong Sook thought this was cruel, but I didn't blame the man. He'd spent cash on us, and now he was getting it back. I was thankful that he had lent us the money, so we could afford aspirin and a little food to make my father's final days comfortable.

We spent our last few days in the house trying to think where we could go. It was during this time that Small Grandfather came to see us.

"You can live with me," he told my mother. We were surprised and a little mystified by the offer, but very grateful. We took our belongings — they fit in a small bag — and followed him to his big house in Hoeryong, in a nice part of town with widely spaced unattached houses. We had gotten lucky, we thought; a place like this in a time of hardship. It was the best house we had ever lived in.

The memory of my father lingered. I would be playing in the front yard of Small Grandfather's house and for a moment I'd forget that he was dead, and then some memory of him would prick my heart, and I would remember, *Oh, yes, he's gone,* and want to cry again.

Small Grandfather and his wife had adult children, so none of them lived in the big house. He'd retired almost a decade before, and had put away enough money to survive ten years. Or so he thought. Now the rampant inflation that had doomed so many families was eating into his savings. Still, we had food, and so we began to relax. Small Grandfather was nice to me; he even let me ride his bicycle, which was a big deal in those days. We had long ago sold our family one.

But after we'd been living with Small Grandfather only a few days, he grew concerned about his shrinking savings.

"What are you going to do now?" he asked my mother one morning. "Do you have a plan to support yourself?"

My mother was taken aback. What could she do? There were no jobs, and no one had money. People were abandoning their children because they couldn't feed them.

"I don't know, Small Grandfather."

His brow furrowed. "Listen, I have an idea," he said, not unkindly. "You should take Bong Sook to China and live there."

Though my mother had her own mind and opinions, we were living in Small Grandfather's house. I'm sure she thought that she couldn't defy him. She stood there, her head bowed, and nodded slightly.

"You must be thinking about Kwang Jin," Small Grandfather said, seeing her hesitation. "Don't worry about that. I will take care of him. Just make sure to send us money every month—once you get settled, of course. Money is easy to make in China."

I didn't know it, but this was the moment that determined the rest of my life. This, far more than my father's death. My father wasn't able to protect us; the famine had taken him as it had thousands and thousands of others. And *his* brothers and sisters could offer us no protection. An epidemic had killed his siblings when he was just a boy, which meant that there were no paternal relatives nearby to save us now. Small Grandfather and my uncle were the only ones. It's strange to think that your fate was written before you were born, in a tiny virus that swept through a village where your father had lived as a child.

The deal was quickly done. If we ran out of money, my mother would take Bong Sook to China. They would earn money there, sending back a small portion of their earnings to pay for my keep in Hoeryong. When they had enough money to set up a household, they would return. I didn't think of what my mother and sister would do to make all this cash. To me, China was a land where no one was ever hungry and where people had everything they needed. I wasn't completely naïve; I didn't believe the streets were paved with gold or that cash fell out of the sky. But I believed there was money there, more than we had ever seen in our lives.

When the time came to leave, my mother and sister would make their way two hours north to Sambong, where they would hire a broker. The broker knew some of the soldiers who regularly patrolled the Tumen River and would bribe one to let them cross. Their journey would still be scary and dangerous. There were many other soldiers who might challenge them and even fire on them. But this was the safest option.

In the meantime, to support us my mother got involved in fish smuggling. Many Chinese believed that fish from across the border tasted better. So North Korean fish were a popular commodity in Chinese towns. My mother began buying fish in the Hoeryong market, then smuggled them across the river. She even snuck into the border towns to arrange the transactions. "China isn't like the government says," she told us when she came back, and I felt hope rising in her. "The Chinese are much richer than North Koreans, and they'll pay for delicacies."

My mother was making good money. We ate white rice every day, and she thought of buying me a bicycle — a Japanese bicycle! — so that I wouldn't have to use Small Grandfather's all the time. My mother was always happy to spend money, unlike my late father, who was very cautious.

We were doing well, so the move to China was put off for the moment. Our fears receded. My frame filled out again and I put on weight. I hoped Mother had finally learned how to succeed, and that she wouldn't have to take Bong Sook away. The longer it went without her leaving, the more hopeful I was.

But always inside me there lingered the fear that the only real family left to me would be taken away.

CHAPTER TWENTY-THREE

IT WAS AROUND this time that I discovered three things in rapid succession: smoking, girls, and fashion. Smoking was easy to pick up in North Korea, where people rarely worry about living into old age and so light up every chance they get. My friends and I thought it was an adult thing to do. We bought cheap North Korean cigarettes one at a time, smoking them until the ash singed our fingers. When the smoke hit our lungs, we coughed as though we'd been doing this for years.

Fashion and girls came next. Those discoveries were intimately related to each other. One day I announced to my mother that I wanted a new school coat, a black one that was of better quality than the one the school had provided. A black coat would disguise the mud that vehicles splashed on me as I walked the unpaved roads of Hoeryong. I would look cleaner, sharper, more like one of the boys from rich families who bought their clothes in China, even if they were knockoffs. I begged my mother incessantly. I desperately wanted new shoes, too—I'd always loved having a clean, new pair, so much so that when my father would buy me shoes as a boy, I'd tell him, "I don't have to have dinner tonight, this is enough!"—but the coat was all-important.

I needed to look good to impress the kids at school, like Hyang Mi, the smartest girl in my class, with a round face I found irresistible. When I looked at Hyang Mi, I felt a longing to be with her, to make her laugh. A decent outfit was, in my mind, the first requirement in getting her attention.

My mother bought me the wool coat and I wore it to school proudly. I began to brush my one pair of trousers and clean my only pair of dress shoes before leaving for class every day. I was becoming a typical teenager, I suppose.

A few weeks later, after my transformation, Hyang Mi whispered to me that she wanted to give me something. The next day she slipped a small object into my hand, cold and smooth. I looked down. It was a plastic figurine, brightly colored, a toy of some kind. She must have stolen it from her little brother. I didn't need a new toy, but the figurine meant a great deal to me because it was from Hyang Mi. I gripped it tightly in my hand on the way home.

From that day on, I felt proud getting ready for school, putting on my new black coat and the school uniform that my mother had bought in the market. Knowing that Hyang Mi was getting dressed too, and thinking of me, made my head feel light. The pain of my father's death receded slightly.

Of course, this being my mother, the good times couldn't last. I suspect she overreached again and got stuck with goods she couldn't sell. Within four months, my mother had no more money. This time my father wasn't there to cover her debts. She wore the clay mask of false confidence again, and I grew depressed, knowing that bad times lay ahead.

Small Grandfather? There was no chance of help there. My mother was too afraid to ask him for a loan. She went to him in his room and told him she would be taking Bong Sook to China. They set the departure date for the early fall. On September 12, the day when it is traditional to visit the graves of your loved ones, Mother, Bong Sook, and I went to my father's. We were all feeling melancholy, and Bong Sook sobbed so much at the graveside that her body shook. I thought she was still grieving over my dad.

Why didn't my mood sensor, which I was so proud of, tell me the true reason for her tears? I felt nothing strange, but clearly Bong Sook was thinking about her future. She was in torment, and I knew nothing about it. This has always bothered me, these signs that I missed again and again.

After the visit to the grave, we went to Sambong, a two-hour train trip north of Hoeryong, where the broker lived. We stayed at her house while my mother prepared for her crossing into China. There is a hill in Sambong that is the highest point for miles around. When you climb to the top and look southwest across the Tumen River, you can see another hill on the Chinese side. Just beyond it, visible only from this one spot, you can see a small Chinese city, Kai San. The day before she and Bong Sook were scheduled to leave, my mother took my sister and me for a walk to the top of the hill.

My mother scanned the horizon, shading her eyes. Finally she found what she was looking for and pointed. "Look, do you see that house?"

The air was clear in Sambong. There was no industry to pollute it. You could pick out individual streets, the shapes of the bigger houses, even the kind of tile used on the roofs.

"Where?" I said.

"That one, two stories, light stone, dark orange tile."

"Yes!" I said. "Who lives there? Do you know them?"

"In this house live two men," my mother said. "One is eighty years old, the other only fifty. I know them well; I've stayed at their house. If anything happens to me, they will know where I am."

I looked at it in wonder. I had no idea that my mother had made friends across the river. (I later learned that the fifty-year-old was the partner of the North Korean broker, and sold everything she brought to him from our side of the border.) To have a Chinese friend is a big deal — both a big risk and a big opportunity. I had a new respect for my mother: she had waded across the cold river that flowed at our feet and made contacts in a foreign city. It was impressive.

"And behind this house lives a very good woman," my mother said. "Her name is Cho Hee. To me, she's like a second mother. I even call her that." She had cleaned Cho Hee's house and listened to her stories. The old woman's daughter was working in a faraway city, so Cho Hee had practically adopted my mother.

Like my father with his stories of the *sangju,* my mother had a reason for taking me to the top of that hill, but it wouldn't be clear until later. Then I would understand the motive behind that leisurely afternoon walk.

My mother and Bong Sook got ready to leave the next evening. I watched them pack, thinking this was just another trip, one of many my family had made to survive. When it came time to say goodbye, we stood in the foyer of the broker's house. Bong Sook was wearing a dark red sweater, and her hair was tied up in a ponytail. I can't recall what my mother was wearing.

"Goodbye, Kwang Jin," Bong Sook said.

I thought I would be seeing her again in a few weeks, two months at the most. She would go to China and earn lots of money and come back. I was calm and unemotional.

"Bye," I said.

I remember the moment before she turned and walked away. In my mind, her face is dark and the air around her head is dark, too, as if someone smudged the space behind her with a thick pencil. I can't make out her features; everything except the shape of her head is obscured. I can't tell you what her face looked like, if there were tears in her eyes. Did she know the truth of what was happening?

My memory is infused with a feeling of foreboding and sadness, but at the time, my mood sensor was turned off. I had said goodbye to my family members many times, and this was no different.

I wished my mother a safe journey and turned away.

CHAPTER TWENTY-FOUR

I STAYED IN SAMBONG for two weeks, until my mom sent her first batch of money. It was six hundred *yuan;* after the broker took her fee, I set off for Hoeryong with four hundred in my pocket. I'd never held so much money at once; it was enough to buy basic supplies for four months. When I got to Small Grandfather's house, I gave him the notes. He was satisfied.

Small Grandfather left me alone for the most part. I went back to school and played with my friends. I brushed my dark coat every time mud splashed on it and did the best I could with my old shoes. I had crushes on girls and resumed my love affair with movies.

I was twelve now, almost a teenager. My life was my friends. I tried not to think too much about my mother or Bong Sook, dreading the unhappiness that would cloud my heart. *I'm doing better than most,* I told myself. *I mustn't complain.* One day, I stopped by one of the two rivers that run past Hoeryong (not the Tumen, which bordered China and was off-limits to civilians), sat on the rocks, and dangled my feet in the water. I stared at a distant hill on the Chinese side and thought of my family. On the top of the hill was a Japanese-style pagoda, a familiar landmark to me since I was small. *Somewhere over there are Bong Sook and Mom,* I thought. *I wonder what they're doing right now.*

My youthful innocence came to an abrupt end when my mother was arrested by the Chinese authorities and sent back to Hoeryong. I found this out when a friend ran up to me as I was walking near the market: she'd seen a group of defectors being marched through the streets, their hands tied together. (The police did this not so much to humiliate the escapees; they simply had no cars to transport them.)

"Your mother has been caught!" the friend told me.

Conflicting emotions surged through me—shame at my mother's embarrassment, eagerness to see her, hope that she had earned enough money to buy us all some nice things in the market. But most of all, I was desperate to ask about Bong Sook.

We had to wait twenty days for my mother to be released from custody. Since she hadn't gone to the interior of China, she was regarded as a trader. The North Korean government had let her off with a warning. But if it happened again, she would go to prison for many years.

I returned home from school one day and found my mother at Small Grandfather's. She was sitting on the floor eating a bowl of steaming soup when I arrived. I was shocked at her appearance. Her hair was matted and her cheekbones protruded from her flesh. Her clothes were stained and smelled of sweat. My mother had been tortured in jail, forced to sit cross-legged for hours, and beaten if she moved so much as an inch. When I sat down next to her, she didn't even notice I was there. She continued hungrily slurping the soup out of the bowl.

Bong Sook was nowhere to be seen.

She's starving, I thought. I'd always looked on my mother as a kind of god—all children do, I think. She was bigger than me and stronger, and I always feared her moods. It never occurred to me that the world could hurt her. But here she was, so famished that she couldn't speak.

I took some soup from Small Grandmother—my great-aunt—but I could hardly eat. I felt my sorrow deepen with every passing moment. My mother didn't acknowledge me, let alone turn to hug me. She looked unnerved, wizened, and poor. The food in North Korean prisons was known to be rancid.

As I watched her eat, my small grandfather arrived, having heard the news. He was furious, as angry as I had ever seen him. He knew the dream of surviving on Mother's wages was over. He slammed his hand on the table.

"I don't know this person!" he shouted. "Who are you? I know no widow of my nephew!"

I looked at him in shock. He was disowning my mother, freeing himself of all claims to help her.

"Small Grandfather, how can you say this?" I wanted to yell. But I was frightened of him and said nothing. I had so many questions for my mother — What had happened? Where was Bong Sook? — but before I had a chance to ask them, Small Grandfather had thrown everything into confusion.

"You've dishonored this family!" he continued shouting. "You must leave this house. And take your good-for-nothing son with you."

I stood up, shifting from foot to foot. Small Grandfather was so commanding, but I felt my fists clench with rage. "But you told her to go to China in the first place," I wanted to scream. "You lived off the money she sent you!"

Small Grandfather stormed away, tossing angry words back over his shoulder.

It was then I realized why Small Grandfather had sent my mother and sister to China: he didn't want to work. That was all. He had retired from the government many years before but his savings had run out. He didn't want to go out and do something else, like work in the fields. Small Grandfather needed to eat, of course, and he wanted to stay in his big house. Many people in Hoeryong did the same, living off relatives who had gone to China and sent back money.

Small Grandfather may have cared for us, but for him, my father's death was primarily a business opportunity. And now our business with him was over.

After that outburst, my great-aunt came in carrying something. Her face was filled with pain and sympathy. She was very different from Small Grandfather, a kind and quiet person.

"Here," she told us. "Take this."

It was a small plastic bag with two looping handles. Inside was food:

some cooked rice, green vegetables, corn. My great-aunt looked from my mother to me. Her eyes said, *I wish I could do more.* But they didn't say, *Forgive him.* Or *Let me fix this.* We had to leave their house.

This was the way things were in North Korea. Kinship melted away in the face of hunger. Why didn't I see that after so many times? Why did I expect each new episode to end differently?

My mother and I left Small Grandfather's house, our heads bowed, our minds swimming. What would become of us?

CHAPTER TWENTY-FIVE

WE WALKED TOWARD the center of town, trying to formulate a plan for our lives. I finally had a chance to ask my mother where Bong Sook was.

"She's still in China," she said. "She's living with a man."

I nodded, not comprehending. Had she found a husband?

Later I would realize that my mother hadn't taken my sister to China to find work. She had taken her to China to sell her.

The Chinese towns and villages near the North Korean border have lost many of their young women to the factories in Shanghai and other industrial cities, and many farmers and small businessmen are looking for wives. Not wives in the Western sense — these are not romantic relationships. The woman is there to cook and clean and have sex. These are the "bride slaves" of North Korea, sold for about 1,500 *yuan* (around $240). Seven out of ten refugees who leave for China are females; eighty percent of them become bride slaves.

It's a sad fate, but not uncommon. My mother, who had no money to feed Bong Sook, must have felt she had no other choice. Perhaps she was trying to save me by letting go of my sister. And being a bride slave is not the worst thing that can happen to North Korean girls. Others cross the border, led by Chinese or North Korean guides, and become sex slaves.

The guides tell the girls they're going to earn good wages in a factory in the interior, where there will be plenty of food and money to spend.

Instead, they're sold to brothels and forced to become prostitutes. Often their introduction to China is to be beaten for days and left in a room with no toilet, until they're broken. Then they are raped repeatedly and violently. When they go out into town, a minder watches over them at all times.

I didn't know—and I still don't know—which of these lives Bong Sook was living. I asked my mother, but all she would tell me was "We will talk about it later." With my small grandfather forcing us out on the street, and my mother so ashamed and depressed, it wasn't a good time to delve deeper. But it was also that North Korean attitude: the world is going to hurt you eventually. There's no one to blame but life itself.

I always thought we would sit down one day and she would tell me everything I wanted to know about my sister. But that time never came. The truth is, my mother didn't know where Bong Sook was. She'd had to turn her over to the broker, the fifty-year-old Chinese man in Kai San who had paid her way across the border. She didn't know where her daughter had ended up.

Bong Sook was gone. That was all there was to say.

My mother decided to take me to her younger sister's house in Un-dok—the same "small aunt" who had gone to the humiliating birthday party with us years before. We got a ride in a truck, and two and a half hours later we found the house. I knocked on my aunt's door around dusk. She answered and said my name with concern. Then she saw my mother and invited us in.

At first my aunt was sympathetic. She found old sleeping mats we could use and fed us her simple dishes. We were safe for the time being.

As the days progressed, the relationship between my aunt and me became kind of like that of high school sweethearts: one day we'd be super-close, gossiping and laughing, and the next she'd be angry with me, for what reason I didn't know. She would shoot me angry glances and refuse to speak to me. Food was at the bottom of this, of course. The family was rich now, by North Korean standards. My uncle had gotten a visa to visit relatives in China, and he'd come back with televisions, clothing, and other consumer goods and sold them at a great profit. I could see that my aunt wanted to take care of my mother and me, but as a survivor of famine, the fear of hunger never left her. Often she compromised by splitting the available food, which just meant that none of us got enough. My stomach bloated with malnutrition, and the overstretched, shiny skin became painful to the touch.

I, too, was facing a dilemma: Should I steal some of my aunt's white rice and risk her wrath? Or should I accept what I was given and hope it got me through? I had no real loyalty to my cousins; they were merely competitors for food. That's how I felt. The same heartlessness that my relatives had shown to me I now felt for them.

Eventually the urge to eat became too much. One day while my aunt was away gathering firewood, I stole an uncooked turnip from the bag where she kept her vegetables. I estimated that I had a good hour to eat the whole thing. I bit into it hungrily, ignoring the bits of dirt clinging to the skin.

But five minutes after I took that first bitter bite, my aunt suddenly pushed in the door. I quickly hid the turnip behind my back. We stared at each other.

My aunt's eyes filled with tears. "Kwang Jin!" she cried out. "You're my nephew! You should have just asked me."

I handed the turnip to her, my eyes cast down. I felt shame, and anger at my shame. At least Auntie still had a human side. As for me, I was like a starving rat; my hunger controlled me. I felt brutal and nasty.

I didn't have the advantage of long experience with people in normal times. The idea that most people are good if you give them enough to eat and a warm place to sleep was foreign to me. I had mostly seen people's evil, jealous sides. I tried to tell myself: *It's just the famine talking. She really is a good person.* But I'm not sure I believed it.

I hated it when people were selfish. When I was selfish it was even worse, but it's hard to act like a human being when no one you see is doing the same. You feel like a dupe. Your good heart will take your life.

I didn't want to die. I was determined not to. I really was different from my father, who had been too honorable to steal.

CHAPTER TWENTY-SIX

MY AUNT'S HUSBAND was a miner. For years he had held down a job in a state-run company until the economy collapsed. The electricity at his work site had stopped one day, and the workers were forced to go all over the countryside and dig random holes in the ground, straight down, which only a North Korean would call a mine. They used equipment they'd scavenged from their old jobs. Despite the money he'd earned trading Chinese goods, he still worked at the mines to support his family.

After a few weeks, my aunt suggested I go along and work in the coal shafts, to pay for my keep. "At least do *something*," she said. I agreed immediately. I'd never had a real job, and the thought of having money for snacks and other things was exciting.

The job of a miner is the lowest in North Korea. Even *Kkotjebi* who are in the last stages of starvation will refuse to go down into the tunnels. "I'll wait just one more day," they'll say, "maybe I'll get lucky begging at the market," when they hadn't found a thing to eat there in a week. There was something final about the mines. Dying there is ugly. Many men are caught by cave-ins in the tunnels, where few beams hold up the ceilings. When their bodies are pulled up, their mouths are so tightly packed with dirt it seems like some underground monster did it out of malice. The mines are the last stop before the graveyard.

We walked two hours to the head of the tunnel, where about a dozen men were gathered around, preparing to go down. My uncle and I approached the miners and he told them I wanted to work with them. The men studied me carefully. I remember those looks very well: horror, but a kind of wonder, too. "This child," one miner said, turning to the others, "has come to *us*?" The black-faced men said I'd made a mistake. They told my uncle to take me away. When I stood my ground, they tried chasing me off, but I always returned. My uncle didn't intervene: if I wasn't tough enough to get into the mine, I wasn't tough enough to do the work.

When the miners realized I wouldn't give up, they waved their hands at me in exasperation. If you want to kill yourself, their expressions said, be our guest.

I climbed into a large metal bucket and a man at a hand-operated winch began lowering us into the earth. I was very afraid the first time I went down. The shaft was so narrow, I could reach out and touch the soil as I was lowered, and the air around me turned black and ferociously hot even before I reached the bottom. Once the bucket knocked against solid earth, about one hundred yards down, I got out with my tool, a heavy iron crowbar. I stooped down, following the other miners into a horizontal passageway cut into the earth. When the man in front of me stopped, I heard the ringing of iron against the walls. I turned and began to slam my crowbar into the coal seam.

There were no lights in the mine, only the small lamps attached to our plastic hard hats, the kind with a strap that went under your chin. There were no beams or supports along the passageway that I could see. I didn't want to think of what would happen if the earth gave way and came down around my ears.

I pounded at the coal flashing in the little beam of my light, and I didn't stop for twelve hours, except for a short lunch break, noodles and a small cornmeal cake. The good thing about risking your neck in the mines was that the work was so hard they were forced to give you a decent helping of food.

By the end of the day, I couldn't feel my arms or upper body. When the man next to me tapped me on the shoulder, I bent down and gathered up the coal I'd chipped away, put it into a large bucket, and carried it to the light that shone down from above. It felt like my spirit was walking alongside my body, so complete was my exhaustion. When I got to the surface, I saw that my pile of coal was tiny compared to those of the men around me. My wage was the lunch I had eaten, plus a small share of the coal in my bucket. I took my portion back to my aunt's house and saved it. Every day I added another bucket to the pile, dreaming of the morning I would go to the market, sell the coal, and buy an armful of food for my mother, along with several delicious snacks for myself. I lingered over those fantasies for hours at a time, especially while sweating and laboring deep in the mine pit. I felt I was working toward a little bit of happiness.

But it wasn't to be. After a few months, my aunt came to me and asked if I could contribute the coal to the family's budget. My dream was crushed. The money she would make would be insignificant, yet she wanted it anyway. I had to press the bitterness down into my heart and say nothing, but for days I was upset and close to tears.

The miners, most of them, were kind to me. They knew there was nowhere beneath this place, nowhere else to fall to. After a few weeks of my pitiful hauls, they found me an easier job. I was shown how to work the oxygen pump, which was a converted bicycle wheel attached to a pipe that carried air down to the men in the tunnels. I spun and spun the wheel for hours, until I could no longer feel my right arm. All sensation ended at the shoulder. At around two o'clock on my first day at the wheel, I unconsciously slowed the spinning. It felt like I was on the edge of blacking out.

Suddenly the metal pipe attached to the contraption began to chatter. The miners down in the shaft were shaking it to let me know that I wasn't pumping enough air. If I didn't wake up and spin the wheel faster, they would die. I fought off the blackness in my mind and picked up my pace. As the sun began to sink in the west, the bucket rose from the shaft and the miners gathered around. I could see they were angry, but when they saw me — God knows what I looked like by the end of the day—their eyes softened. "Try to pump a little harder tomorrow," my uncle said. I nodded yes.

What I remember most about those days were the candles. Every morning, we would light one and drip some wax onto the bottom of an iron bucket and set the candle there, so it wouldn't tip over. Then the miners tied the bucket handle to an old rope and lowered the bucket into the mine. Bit by bit the flame grew smaller in the blackness. If there was no oxygen, then there was no work. If there was no work, the miners' families would go hungry. Many of the men had children at home who were so malnourished that a few days without food would kill them.

When the candle remained lit, the miners would gather their tools and descend. Other times, though, the flame would flicker and disappear, and we knew that no one could survive down there, even with me pumping what little oxygen I could through the pipe. A feeling of desolation would go through us, and we'd pull the bucket up in silence. No one spoke. Being a young boy, I was fascinated to discover that fire needed oxygen to burn, but the others were thinking only of their loved ones.

That image comes back to me when I try to explain my homeland to people who've never been there. The basic ingredients of life had disappeared. My schoolmates, my beloved television, my house and family, all had vanished like the candle flame, swallowed up by darkness. If we'd been capable of it, the miners and I would have laughed at the thought that even the oxygen had disappeared from North Korea. What was next, water? Sunshine?

I'd witnessed this kind of thing once before, on the train to my uncle's town with my father and Bong Sook at the start of the famine. One morning on that endless journey, I was half awake and daydreaming when I saw a North Korean soldier stirring from sleep. He cried out. During the night, someone had stolen his jacket. A few of us passengers watched him closely as he looked around wildly for the missing uniform. But it was gone.

In normal times, stealing a soldier's jacket would have been not only illegal but unthinkable. Your brain wouldn't even form the thought, *Boy, that army jacket looks good. What if I . . .* As we watched the soldier, we worried about what he might do—perhaps he'd call the police and accuse us of stealing. Perhaps he'd beat us and leave us by the tracks to become food for wild dogs. Passengers began to edge away from the man.

But instead of anger, a look of what I can only describe as hilarity appeared on the soldier's young face. He began to laugh, a total-body laugh. More people woke up and stared at him. We didn't know what to make of his reaction, and the strangeness of it has stayed with me over the years.

It was only when I was working in the mines that I realized what the soldier was feeling at that moment. The reality he'd known since he was a baby had disappeared. Food was gone. Authority, too. Many hundreds of people were piled onto a train to nowhere. And people were stealing the uniforms off the backs of the Korean People's Army. His laughter seemed to say: *No, this can't be real. I refuse to believe it! What mad world is this I've found myself in?*

This is what people don't understand about North Korea in those days. We didn't "give up" hope or "lose" it. We grasped it tightly with every bit of strength we had. What was missing were the few molecules of air that hope nourished itself on. Those were sucked away by the strange place we happened to inhabit, by the unseen powers we never met or spoke to. The candle went out and blackness flooded in.

Under those conditions, hope was a superhuman effort. I began to have more sympathy for my father, who had been broken by this country. I know now I was too hard on him. How can you be expected to breathe when there's no air?

After my mother and I had lived with my aunt for some months, she asked us to leave her house. So another connection to our family was cut. As we gathered our things, my mother again talked about going to China to make money.

I could see that I was soon to be alone.

CHAPTER TWENTY-SEVEN

By the spring of 2003, we were back in Hoeryong. My mother went to stay with a friend as she prepared for another trip to China. It was best we separated. She couldn't care for me, so she told me to find my way to Small Grandfather's house.

I still couldn't comprehend that Bong Sook was gone and that her fate was so dark. I clung to the hope that she was married to a kind person who was treating her well. Many nights, I'd have imaginary conversations with this Chinese man. *Please take care of Bong Sook. She deserves so much better than what she got in life.* The old people in Manyang were right: Bong Sook wasn't an ordinary sister. I realized that only when I had lost her.

As I wandered Hoeryong those first few hours after we returned, what I thought about the most was the last time I saw my sister, that lackluster "Bye" that I gave Bong Sook when she must have known the truth. Why didn't she rush to me and give me a hug? Why didn't I embrace her?

I had no idea our goodbye was for the last time. It's haunted me ever since.

Someday, Bong Sook, I said to myself, *I will find you.*

I wasn't prepared for life on the street. We had arrived in Hoeryong without extra clothing or money. I was dressed in the black coat I'd asked my mother for the year before, the one inspired by my crush on Hyang Mi.

I no longer had the figurine Hyang Mi had given me. I no longer had anything from that life. All I'd managed to save was the coat, and it was so torn and stained it was hardly fashionable anymore. But I was thirteen and there was something exciting about being on my own. I was free for the first time in my life.

I walked three or four miles in and around Hoeryong looking for something to eat, but found nothing. I had no idea where to look for food or how to go about asking for it.

That night I walked toward Small Grandfather's house. Just beyond its walls was a cornfield where I'd often listened to the stalks waving in the wind, making that dry rustling sound that corn makes. I had the strangest feeling passing by the path that led to the front door of his house. My mind made a right turn at the gate and walked up the path as I had done so many times before, even as my body walked on toward the rows of green corn. My mind slipped through the front door and made its way to the right where my room was. It drank in the warmth of the room wafting up from the floorboards. It prepared for sleep.

But I didn't knock on Small Grandfather's door—I was afraid to. Soon I was in the field next to his house, hidden deep in the cornrows, looking for a place to bed down for the night.

The stars were out by the time I found the right spot. It was in one of the furrows of dry dirt that were angled up on each side, leaving a narrow valley in the middle, perfectly sized for my thin shoulders. I lay down and looked up at the sky through the husks just beginning to sprout the light brown tassels that show the corn is getting ripe. The plants moved above me as gusts of warm wind came sweeping down the rows. I was snug against the warm earth.

Small Grandfather's house was five hundred feet away. I imagined him and his wife settling down for the night, talking in low voices. Were they wondering where I was? Did they know I was back in the city? Did they worry I'd had nothing to eat that night, or had thoughts of me passed from their minds months ago? Small Grandfather had probably erased me from his memory the moment I'd left his home. He wasn't one for remorse.

But I wasn't unhappy. I thought, *This is better than my old sleeping mat!* I could see the beautiful stars, the universal consolation for North Koreans who had no roof over their heads. I was pleasantly tired and soon fell asleep, my furrow of earth holding me in its snug embrace.

The first enemy of someone sleeping rough comes at about one in the morning. You feel a chill. You're aware in your dreams that something is stealing over you. Your skin becomes aware, even if your mind is still asleep. Then the cold dew wakes you up. From being warm and dry, you're now miserable. I opened my eyes at about two. The rows of corn were black now, with just the fringes edged with moonlight. My good mood had disappeared. This was my first true moment of being homeless.

I tossed and turned, trying to fall back to sleep, but the dew had mixed with the dirt and turned its topmost layer muddy, and my clothes were getting dirty and matted. Eventually I stood up, my sleep over for the night. My skin was covered with a thin film of soil. I was famished. At three or four in the morning, I started walking to the Hoeryong city market.

When I got there half an hour later, the lane where the sellers stood in their little stalls was deserted. A sense of loneliness came over me. It felt as if I was the only one awake in Hoeryong and no one knew or cared that I was hungry.

When the sun rose over the hills people began to stream in, sellers who set up their humble stands or stood by the side of the road holding their products: combs, sunglasses, clocks, onions, cucumbers, cornmeal. The soup makers came with their pots filled near to the brim and placed them carefully on the ground. *Kkotjebi* arrived, tiny black-faced figures in oily, ragged clothing, begging for a bit of food or watching for their moment to steal. Nobody gave me so much as a second glance.

I hung around the market that day from dawn until dusk, unable to speak. Other homeless children came and stood beside me. It was a hot day. We smelled like rotten fruit.

Some of the homeless kids cried out to the customers, "Can I have the last of your soup?" In North Korea, you didn't beg for a full meal. You asked for the leavings of a bowl of soup, one swallow of cloudy water at the bottom of the wooden cup. A few of the *Kkotjebi* found people willing to give them the dregs from their bowls. Not much, only a few calories to last an hour or two. The rest of us watched them drink, our Adam's apples bobbing as they swallowed, as if we were eating too. But I said nothing, rooted to the ground in a peculiar fear, feeling my hunger pangs grow sharper.

If I asked for soup, I thought, my condition would somehow become permanent. I feared the words would act as a spell, turning me from a normal boy into a *Kkotjebi*. Unlike some of the other children here, who'd been abandoned when they were four or five, I had been cherished by my parents until I was a teenager. I had plenty of happy memories, and this gave me hope.

But it also made it harder to believe I was truly homeless. And so I was silent. *If you keep this up,* I told myself, *you surely will starve.*

That evening, when the sellers had all gone, I went to a friend's house. He let me sleep there for one night. I didn't even ask about staying longer—more than that, I knew, and you became a burden. Before the famine, if you arrived at a friend's place at lunchtime, your hosts always invited you to eat. But now it was considered rude to show up unannounced. You were asking to be fed. That you could not do.

The second day, I was back at the market, but still unable to force any words past my lips.

I slept in the cornfield and returned to the market on the third day, telling myself, *Say something. Ask for the soup and maybe you'll eat.* But still my mouth stayed shut. I felt embarrassed by what I'd become. Layers of dirt and coal soot coated my face, giving it a shiny patina that made me look like a scary doll. My filthy toes, crusted with mud from the road, stuck out through the holes in my shoes, which had begun to decompose in the rain and slop. My eyes appeared bigger because hunger had stretched the skin around them, and lice had made a home in my ragged, foul-smelling clothes.

I hadn't bathed in a week or two. My last bite of food had been three days before. Yet I still thought like a teenager from a fairly well-off home who went to school and had crushes on girls. Like a boy who had a father to protect him and a sister who gave him her rice and claimed to be full. But I wasn't that boy any longer. I had to accept it.

As the afternoon of the third day wore on and the customers began to grow scarce, the hunger pains were like knives scraping down my rib cage from top to bottom. I walked to the far end of the market, away from the path that my classmates would take home from our school. I feared seeing someone I knew. That first look of recognition when they spotted me among the *Kkotjebi*. The beautiful Hyang Mi staring at me with a look that said, *You are not human anymore, and I am sorry for you.*

Around me, the other *Kkotjebi* called out, "Can I have the last of your soup?"

The merchants who were selling soup and corn noodles and rice looked at me angrily as I stood, swaying slightly, at the side of the road, trying not to pitch forward into the mud. They knew that just the sight of me, let alone the smell, robbed their potential customers of their appetite. They used the same bowl for all their customers, and if one of them saw it being touched by a *Kkotjebi,* they might turn away and go to the next vendor.

Was it just our uncleanness or that they feared our condition would rub off on them? I didn't know. I didn't have room in my brain for such questions.

We were called *Kkotjebi,* "wandering sparrows," because of the way we would bend over and look for grains of rice or kernels of corn on the ground. And we did look like birds, I suppose, but not sparrows. More like crows or ragged vultures, descending on our next victim, crying out the same thing.

"Can I— Can I— Can I—"

I didn't feel human anymore. A human being has many thoughts running through his mind, many emotions, some happy, some sad. The wandering sparrow has only one thought—*food*—and one emotion, which can be summed up as *I don't want to die.* This causes you to lose any gracefulness you once had. Hunger makes your voice sound odd. Your eyes become glassy and depthless. Your arms snap out at customers in the market, frightening them. You can't help yourself.

Finally I couldn't stand it any longer. If I didn't get something to eat, I thought I might not make it back to the market the next day. I scanned the crowd for someone who might have a bit of kindness left in him after the long years of famine. I spotted a man who looked like a traveler. He was older than my parents, clearly from the country, not rich, with something sympathetic about his face. *This man knows what it is to struggle,* I thought. *He's the one.* I rushed over to him and called out, "Can I have the last . . . ," my voice high and nervous. But he looked at me with a bored expression and passed me by.

After you've done it once, it gets easier. I got two swallows of soup that day. I could feel the lukewarm liquid whip into my bloodstream, like a power surge that brightens the lights in a house before fading.

Even when they handed you their bowls, most people would snap, "Take it and get away." They would shove the bowl at you so hard that some of the soup would slop over the edge and fall to the ground, which defeated the purpose. When the buyers had gone home, I went to the Hoeryong train station and slept on one of the long wooden benches, my belly nearly empty. Later, I would move to an abandoned steam-engine train, rusting on a sidetrack. Its heavy iron absorbed the heat of the sun all day and kept me warm at night.

I was grateful for the food. I felt I had won a victory. But I knew two sips of soup a day wasn't going to keep me alive for very long. I needed to become smarter if I hoped to survive.

CHAPTER TWENTY-EIGHT

I WENT TO THE market faithfully every day, arriving just after dawn. I was usually one of the first *Kkotjebi* there, but soon others would swarm the lane. When I wasn't crying out to customers, I studied the most successful beggars, the ones whose eyes were clearest and who had the most energy. I saw that they always targeted certain types of people. They had a strategy.

Soldiers were the best. The ones who came to the market were mostly officers, and some of them made extra money from bribes paid by those crossing into China. They were young, still idealistic, still proud of North Korea, like my father. Only about half the soldiers offered me a bit of food, but this was far more than I got from the average citizen. A young officer would give me the last swallow of his soup and say, "You poor boy, take it." If I saw a soldier walking along the lane, I made sure to be the first to run up to him.

Next best were the grandmothers. They usually came to the market to shop for their families during the late morning. They would look on as you noisily slurped down the last mouthful of soup, and even if they didn't say anything, their eyes were soft and filled with sympathy. Maybe they had grandchildren like me. Sometimes I wondered if they gave me the soup they needed for themselves.

But I never refused it. That was unthinkable.

After a few weeks in the market, I could tell you who the most likely givers were. People from the countryside were better than city people.

Women were better than men (except for soldiers). The rich were useless. By carefully choosing my targets, I increased my daily intake to four sips of soup.

But I still wasn't getting enough nutrition. And there were times I couldn't persuade a single person to give me the dregs of their meal. Those days I felt panic rising in me. *This isn't working. I'm not going to make it.*

Sometimes I would watch new *Kkotjebi* come to the market and stand just like I did at first, afraid to speak, afraid to cross over into the unknown. Or perhaps they imagined that all they had to do was sit by the side of the road with a miserable look on their face and some passerby would take pity and offer them something to eat. They didn't know that this never happened, not once. You had to ask or you would die.

By the second week, the smart beginners would steal something from a cart. By the third or fourth week, they would form alliances with other *Kkotjebi* and become part of a small gang. (Being homeless at the market was like being at school: in your first few days there, you bonded with the other new *Kkotjebi* who'd showed up at the same time. These "classmates" often stayed together for years.) One orphan would distract the seller or cause a ruckus while the others plundered his cart. Knowledge was exchanged, techniques were honed.

How quickly we all changed! I was astonished by this. We readily took the step from innocent children to tough boys who plotted to deceive good people. And the ones who didn't change simply disappeared. These were the boys and girls whose bodies you would smell in the tall grass as night fell and you went looking for a place to sleep.

There are only two things you really need as a homeless person: food and heat. Heat keeps you alive at night, when the temperature falls below freezing. On those nights you have to be inside or you will die. Occasionally, *Kkotjebi* found electrical transformers on the street and huddled against them for warmth, but these units were badly serviced and their wires frayed over time. Some orphans were electrocuted on cold nights.

I never did this, but I was always on the lookout for ashes. House-wives would throw out the coals that heated the floors of most North Korean homes onto a pile in the back of their houses. Sometimes the ashes were still warm. If I saw a pile of fresh coal ash, I would lie on top of it and press my cheek against the surface, absorbing the heat. It was soothing and smelled like my old house in the July 8th neighborhood. I slept and dreamt of a time when I had a roof above my head and people who loved me. The only downside was that the coal ash would stick to you. That's how many of the *Kkotjebi* acquired their black faces.

Heat you needed for only a few hours a night. If you got desperate, you could gather some of the increasingly hard-to-find tree branches and start a fire. But food you thought about constantly. How to get it, how much there will be, what it will taste like when you do get it.

I became a different person when I became homeless. For one thing, I was shocked to learn that I was a better thief than I was a beggar.

It happened very naturally. It was almost as if my body knew what to do when the hunger reached a certain point. I don't remember any moral debate about whether stealing was wrong.

The sellers who lined the road approaching the Hoeryong city mar-ket were my first victims, but they were crafty, thanks to many other *Kkotjebi* who had tried to steal their goods. To prevent people like me from sneaking up behind them and swiping their cakes, the merchants would sit close to the cinderblock wall that lined the market street and place their baskets in front of them. I could approach these sellers only from the front, and when I did so, their faces would turn ugly and they would scream at me to go away. They had families to support, I sup-pose. But I didn't think about that. I just saw the cakes and buns in their baskets and heard the hateful way they yelled at me. I didn't let their snarls scare me away.

I observed these sellers for a long time. I noticed that first thing in the morning, many of them stood hypervigilant over their baskets, their eyes darting at the approach of anyone who looked suspect. (I looked very suspect.) But few customers had enough money to buy a bun, so the merchants would end up staring at their baskets for long periods without a break. This became boring after a while. As I watched the sellers' eyes hour after hour, I realized they'd turned dreamy. To test their reaction, I would walk in front of their baskets to see if they noticed me. Sometimes they didn't. The sellers had hypnotized themselves. They were thinking about their children or remembering a movie they'd seen. This meant I could sneak up next to one of them, reach down, slip a bun from his basket without his noticing, and walk away as if nothing had happened. The first time I did it, my heart pounded in triumph. I sauntered down the lane, munching on the bun like I was a rich boy.

Stolen buns taste sweeter than bought ones. This is something else I learned.

My trick worked only occasionally, however; most of the time the sellers were alert. So I developed a new technique. Some sellers would sit on the raised bank of the Hoeryong River where pedestrians passed on their way to the city center. The river was six feet below, bordered by concrete walls built to contain high waters during flooding. I would walk to another part of the river, jump into the shallow water, then double back along the water's edge until I came to the sellers, whose backs were turned toward me, just above the top of the wall. I grasped the edge of the concrete and pulled myself up until I could see the merchants' baskets a foot or two away. Then I quickly reached my hand out and grabbed a biscuit or bun. Focused on the people walking by, the sellers had no idea I was there.

I felt rather proud of my cleverness. But pedestrians, startled to see a boy's hand appear out of nowhere, eventually alerted the sellers that something was going on. That brought an end to my bun snatching.

My new profession was exciting. For the first time, I saw hope — not for a life as I'd once imagined, but for survival.

My testing, as it turned out, had only begun.

CHAPTER TWENTY-NINE

AFTER A FEW months of being on my own, I was growing weaker. The more experienced merchants had learned my tricks, and there were few new ones showing up with food to sell. The number of *Kkotjebi* grew day by day. Everyone was eating less. Often I went to bed in the old, broken-down train at the railroad station and was unable to sleep because of hunger. Sometimes I would go for one or two days without a single bite of anything.

I decided to devote myself to thievery.

There were three places where thieves operated in North Korea. One was at railway stations. In the early 2000s, the government was importing basic supplies from China. Corn and fertilizer were transported on long trains of closed cars that were closely watched by guards. Major railway stations in North Korea tended to be far apart, so when a train pulled into one of them, the crew often needed to take a break. A few of them wandered off to use the bathroom or buy a meal from a roadside stand outside the station. That's when the thieves struck. They ran to the tracks and stooped underneath the railcars in search of something to steal, and later to sell.

All kinds of people did this: grandmothers, fathers, pregnant women, old men, and orphaned kids. They would swarm beneath the platforms and scour the ground between the rails and just to the side for corn that had fallen through the cracks of the cars. The train would be there for an hour or two, and in that time you might gather half a handful of yellow corn, mixed in with the cinders and dirt. I joined the station people once or twice. I can still remember the surge in my bloodstream when I saw the kernels spread across the shadows. It was like a spray of gold nuggets. You had to move fast, because the corn would be gone in seconds, and it might be days before another train came through.

The fertilizer trains were tougher to steal from. Chemical fertilizer in North Korea is very sought after and expensive, so if you can get hold of a cupful you can make enough for two good meals. A full bag of the stuff is a jackpot, but you have to take your life in your hands to get it. If the guards catch you, they'll crack your head open with their truncheons and leave you on the tracks to be squashed by the next train. I saw people clamber up to the tops of fertilizer cars and try to break open the locks, only to be batted down by security men. The thieves fell to the tracks with a heavy thud.

The second good place to steal is at the market and the lanes leading up to it. Here pickpockets and snatch-thieves thrive. The market is dominated by the *Kkotjebi*. It's like a syndicate. You have to ask for the permission of the group that controls the market if you want to graduate from, say, ordinary thief to pickpocket. If you just show up one day and snatch a few *won* from a peasant's pocket, the other *Kkotjebi* will shout and warn your intended target, who will likely give you a beating. If your intended victim doesn't attack you, the *Kkotjebi* will box your ears and run you off. The market was the only place in North Korea that belonged to the homeless, and they guarded it jealously. You began by stealing a head of garlic or a single pepper from a vegetable merchant and trading that for a bit of noodles in the food court. (This worked at least for a while, because the merchants never expected us to steal raw vegetables, and the food sellers always needed fresh ingredients for their dishes.) Then you slowly worked your way up.

The third place to steal is from people's homes. A stack of firewood on an apartment balcony. A row of green onions at midnight. A bicycle. This is what I took up after leaving the market. I began with sewer grates.

I was so hungry that I needed to steal something readily available, so I could fill my belly immediately. I recalled that once I had seen lots of scrap iron near the train station, so I walked there, but by then, of course, it had disappeared, scavenged by other hungry people and sold off. My thoughts turned to the sewer covers that dot the roads of Hoeryong. I knew that iron dealers were always eager to have scrap, which they would sell to Chinese foundries. Why not the heavy sewer grates? Here was metal just lying, literally, in the street. I decided to wait up one night and see if I could steal one.

There are two kinds of manhole covers in North Korea: one weighs about fifty pounds; the other, massive ones the size of a large bicycle wheel, a hundred pounds. I probably weighed about ninety pounds at the time, so my only chance was to steal the smaller size. One night, I waited along a main road until it was clear in both directions, then ran into the street and pounced. By pulling at the small gaps in the cover, I got it out of its hole and rolled it to the bushes at the side of the road.

But now that I had the thing, what was I going to do with it?

The reason there were any manhole covers left in Hoeryong at all was that they were state property, and the penalty for stealing even one was public execution. (Also, they weren't worth that much, which made them less attractive to thieves.) If the police caught you stealing someone's vegetables, they might beat you for not giving them a bribe, but for state-owned items, you faced death in front of a firing squad.

The iron dealers wouldn't buy manhole covers; if they were caught with one, they too would be executed. You had to break the covers down into pieces in order to get rid of them. So once I had the cover out of its hole, I rolled it to a back alley where no one was walking, hoisted it as far as I could into the air, and dropped it on the ground, where it shattered into dozens of pieces. The covers were made of a low-grade iron that couldn't withstand much stress if you dropped them on their ends. I then crushed the larger pieces with a rock until I was left with chunks of iron about the size of a big marble. These I swept up, placed in a cloth bag, and took to the scrap dealer.

This man studied the iron carefully and gave me a suspicious look. I knew that he knew the stuff came from a sewer grate, but he could always mix my pieces with iron from other sources. He handed me 250 *won,* less than half what the iron was worth. I immediately ran to the market and bought two pounds of noodles. It was enough to live on for a day or so.

I was happy. I went out the next night and stole another grate, smashing it to the ground under a thin sliver of moon.

Over time I branched out, stealing anything that could help me survive. Peppers were expensive, and you could trade them at the market for cornmeal or noodles. If you could fill up your shirt with the shiny green vegetables, that was a good night. But stealing peppers is also more dangerous, because the farmers watch their fields closely and the plants only come up to your waist. You can't go running into a field and start picking off peppers like you can with corn. Anyone standing guard can spot you, outlined by moonlight, and give you a severe beating. Even if he doesn't spot you right off, you have to be careful not to jerk the peppers off their stalks, because that causes the whole plant to shake, giving away your position. Stealth is very important.

What you have to do is crawl in at the edge of the field, never poking your head above the level of the tallest leaves. You slide along on your knees and elbows, pushing yourself down the rows until the plants hide you from the road. You feel in the darkness — if there's no moon — for a ripe pepper; you don't want to waste your time cutting leaves. When you touch the cool, smooth skin, you feel for where the stem is attached to the plant. One swift twist and the pepper drops into your hand. If you do it right, a man watching the tops of the plants won't see even the slightest shiver from the plant.

Snatching corn isn't easy either. You have only so much room inside your shirt or in the bag you carry, and corn in its husk is bulky. What you really want is the ear itself, but peeling off the husk makes a lot of noise. So you crouch down and slice the ear off, then cut away the husk, letting the leaves fall to the ground. But there is a price to this method: an ear of corn without its husk marks you as a thief at the market, and the plant is less valuable because it holds its sweetness for a shorter time. When you're alone in the cornfield, you have to think like a trader.

I began sleeping in abandoned trains during the day and stealing at night. Hoeryong is a small city. After a week or two, everyone knew I'd become a thief. They could have easily deduced this from my clothes, from the fact that my family was gone, and from the fact that I was still alive. Without a family, either you lived with rich relatives or you stole, or you died. Really, those were your only options. Begging alone kept just a few *Kkotjebi* alive.

One day, I decided to look up Kim Il, who had been my best friend in Manyang. When you are all alone, your heart feels empty and you get these sudden whims: *Hey, whatever happened to so-and-so?* I suppose by going to see my old friends I was convincing myself I was still a person who had a past. My life had changed so much that sometimes I had to go and touch my memories to make sure they were real.

I knew where to look for Kim Il: at his mother's restaurant. It was the only place in the area that served Korean barbecue and was still thriving. I walked the half mile to the restaurant and, sure enough, there he was, tall and commanding, leaning against the cinderblock front of the building.

I hadn't seen Kim Il in several years. He seemed happy to see me, and we started talking about old times and old friends. It was pleasant; I felt the emptiness in my heart fill up a little. And yet things weren't the same as they once were. Whenever we'd met as boys, Kim Il would invite me to the restaurant so that his mother could say hi and we could eat. But now the minutes ticked by and there was no invitation to eat.

After ten minutes, I took out a cigarette. "Do you have a lighter?"

I knew Kim Il didn't smoke. He was a good boy. But if he didn't have a lighter, I hoped he would invite me inside to get one, where I could greet his mother and perhaps have a meal. It was an obvious ploy on my part, but it was all I had.

Kim Il looked at me. "Wait here," he said, and went into the restaurant.

Oh, how clever you are, Kim Il, I thought. He'd handled the situation so well! I was a known thief, and so he'd kept me from entering while at the same time appearing not to offend me. I understood his reasoning: Who knows how far I'd fallen since I'd seen him last? Maybe I was desperate enough to swipe something valuable from my friend's mother's restaurant — a fancy lighter, money set aside for bills. I respected Kim Il for being a man about such things. The probability that I would have actually stolen something was very low — I can't say zero, because when you become a thief, it's hard to stop. But quite low. Still, Kim Il hadn't taken the chance.

Sadness came over me and I wished I had never sought out my old friend. Why had our lives changed so drastically? Why couldn't we still be buddies?

But Kim Il's life hadn't changed; mine had. I felt a surge of bitterness. At that moment, I hated the world for what it had done to my family and me.

Kim Il came out with a lighter and bent toward me and lit my cigarette. I nodded my thanks. I knew I would never see him again. This reunion had turned out to be more painful than I had expected.

I felt my heart begin to shrivel and harden. *Is friendship really nothing?* I wondered. *Will I never have another pal?*

CHAPTER THIRTY

As a thief, it wasn't the police I was afraid of. They mostly ignored the *Kkotjebi*. And when they weren't ignoring us, they were helping us steal. Criminals would give the local police chief a carton of cigarettes or some money at the end of the year for not arresting them.

No, what I was most afraid of was the Saro-cheong.

The Saro-cheong was the North Korean Department of Youth, which was in charge of young adults between the ages of fourteen and twenty-eight—their welfare, their schooling, their behavior. In every major city you went to, there would be a large building, usually made of brick, four or five stories high. This was the Saro-cheong building. Even if you went into the army at age eighteen, you still "belonged" to this organization; it was just lending you out for a certain number of years. The Saro-cheong was your real master.

You can imagine what a disaster the *Kkotjebi* were for the Saro-cheong administrators. The department was supposed to control the youth of the nation and mold them into fine and dependable citizens. But here were thousands of young people who had no family, no job, no loyalty to the state, and no love for the Saro-cheong. We were dirty, thieving affronts to the department.

Every so often, the Saro-cheong's officials would conduct a roundup of us orphans. They would sweep the streets clear of the *Kkotjebi* and herd us into abandoned apartment buildings, where they would feed and watch over us.

You might think this would be a blessing. Free housing and food! But the meals at a Saro-cheong facility were awful: watery soup or maggoty cornmeal, and not enough of either. Many times, kids weren't given enough to survive and, trapped behind boarded-up windows, faded away to nothing. You weren't allowed to leave the apartment to go and look for extra food at the market. You were restricted to however many calories the Saro-cheong gave you. What the government promoted as saving the youth of North Korea was really enforced starvation. They wanted you to die out of sight of everyone else.

At least on the streets you had a chance. So when you saw a Saro-cheong official coming, you ran.

The other part of the department's program was to send you to a regular school. This the orphans hated much more than the food. By the time you're officially a *Kkotjebi,* you've descended into an awful state. Your clothes are ragged and smelly. Your face is unwashed. Your hair is dirty and clumped with twigs and dirt. If you walk into a school, the normal kids will treat you like an alien.

I knew this because when I was in fourth grade, before my father got seriously ill, a *Kkotjebi* kid had come to our school. We treated him terribly. No one spoke to him. No one invited him to play games with us. The worst times for him were the four "sports and activities" events. On those days, days that kids looked forward to all year, there were all kinds of contests and races and games to play. You wore the closest thing to athletic gear you could scrounge up; North Korean mothers put aside a little money throughout the year so their kids would have decent clothes for these all-important social events. And the moms made goodies and treats for their kids to bring and share with their friends, or they bought snacks at the local shops.

The *Kkotjebi* boy showed up at the first "sports and activities" day with his old ragged clothes on. He had no food to share, so each of us had to take a spoonful of ours and put it on a plate for him. He looked down at the ground as his plate made its way around our class, all of us begrudgingly spooning out a portion for the boy. It sounds like nothing, but most North Korean kids would rather risk starvation than go through that embarrassment.

We knew our lives were disasters. But we didn't want to be pitied.

The Saro-cheong in Hoeryong didn't operate out of the goodness of its heart. Its "humanitarian" mission was actually a cover for a much less innocent activity: a labor racket. Its officials made money by the use of free work. Ours.

If you were too old to go to school, or even if you weren't, the managers at the Saro-cheong house sent you out on work crews. Sometimes you'd be assigned to fix up the department's headquarters. (If you ever have a chance to see the building in Hoeryong, some of the exterior is my handiwork. I once spent many days hauling concrete and helping to patch up holes in the front of that horrible place.) But mostly you were sent out to work for a friend or a cousin of the local Saro-cheong boss. Instead of hiring real laborers, who expect a real wage, the friend tells his contact, "Send over ten *Kkotjebi*." At the end of the week, the official, not the *Kkotjebi*, gets paid, and the friend has a new addition to his house.

We knew we were being exploited, but really, the term "exploited" doesn't exist in North Korea. It's simply the way things are. If you were unlucky enough to be caught in a Saro-cheong raid, the "friend" jobs were the ones you wanted to go out on. If you were sent to a school or a government factory, you went in a large group watched over by five or six guards. Escape was nearly impossible. But if you were part of a small, black market work gang, you'd go to the site with maybe one guy watching you. Your chances of running away were much greater. And if you decided to actually work, the food at the black market jobs was much better. You might get a full meal: a bit of meat, some rice, and a vegetable, depending on how rich and generous your employer was. The government lunch was always the same: half a handful of corn noodles or some soup that was three-quarters water.

So we were eager to be exploited.

Sometimes our residences were on the upper floors of old hotels that the Saro-cheong rented to house homeless kids. I was told that *Kkotjebi* often tried to escape by tying together bed sheets and shinning down from their windows. I knew of one boy who jumped from a high window and broke both his legs attempting to flee, and I'd heard stories of other boys and girls dying in escape attempts from higher floors. These made us street *Kkotjebi* even more determined never to go to a Saro-cheong house.

On the third or fourth night of my manhole-cover spree, I was lurking by the side of the road on the outskirts of Hoeryong, waiting for the last people to get off the street so I could steal a cover I'd had my eye on for a couple of hours. My belly was aching, rumbling like long, rolling peals of thunder sweeping through. I was impatient, but the thought of the firing squad kept me from being too eager. There was a half-moon out.

Finally the street was empty from one end to the other. I stepped out of the darkness, ran to the sewer cover, and grabbed the edge of it. It was then that I noticed a shape at the far end of the road. It was a cluster of young men, not striding home purposefully, but loitering like me. My throat tightened. I didn't like what I saw. The boys looked like me. Thieves. Gangsters. Normal kids with parents wouldn't be out at one in the morning.

The boys were going nowhere, and my stomach was burbling with its demand for food. I decided to wait them out. After a few minutes, one of them spotted me and said something to the others. They all began walking my way.

Dirty faces, shirts with many holes poking through. Surely this was a gang. I knew they were going to ask me for a cigarette. I didn't have any. Which meant they would probably beat me up or steal my shoes. The problem with getting beaten up when you're starving is that not only is it humiliating, it's dangerous as well. One broken bone can end your burglary career for a week, which is plenty of time to begin a descent into starvation.

They came closer. I let go of the sewer cover and it rocked back into the hole with a loud noise. I stood up, brushing some of the mud from my hands.

A short one, a tall one, and one with a stupid face. Their eyes were cool, contemptuous.

"Hey, brother, you got a cigarette?" one of them said.

"No, I'm afraid not," I said.

"You don't have a cigarette?" They moved closer. "Or you don't want to give us one?"

"I don't have one."

Silence. There was a choreography to these things. It was almost as if the lines were written somewhere in a gang handbook. I couldn't run. I waited for the first blow to fall.

Their faces turned harder. But as I watched the tall one, something about him struck me. He didn't look familiar, but his voice nagged at me.

"Hyo Sung?" I said finally. "Is that you?"

He was startled, but then his expression warmed.

"Kwang Jin?"

"Yes!" I said. It was my childhood friend, the sly one, from July 8th.

I felt so relieved. The other two looked on, wondering what was up.

Hyo Sung seemed very different from my childhood memories of him. His hair was long, curly, and unkempt; it looked like it hadn't been washed or cut in months. His clothes were almost identical to mine —holes in his shirt the size of pennies, the hems of his pants in ragged strings from being dragged along the road. But he obviously had some other scheme going on in his life. I'd never seen him begging at the market or sleeping rough at the train station or anywhere else. He at least had a place to stay.

He asked what I was doing, and I said stealing manhole covers.

"Are you some kind of idiot?" he blurted out.

My face crumpled. I thought I'd found a friend, and here he was chastising me in front of the others.

"I know, I know."

"They'll execute you," Hyo Sung said loudly. He wasn't angry that I'd become a thief, but at how stupid a thief I'd turned out to be.

"I have no choice!"

Hyo Sung said nothing, just gazed at me and nodded. We were standing in the street, staring at each other while the other two gaped at us.

"This is dumb, Kwang Jin," he said finally. "You're risking your life."

"What else can I do, Hyo Sung?"

He shrugged. "Well, you could join us."

I didn't know who "us" was, but secretly the thought of belonging to a group of friends thrilled me. I looked at the other two. Their faces were hardly welcoming, but they didn't argue with Hyo Sung. They were obviously not impressed by my sewer-grate idea, but they'd allowed their friend to make the call.

And that's how I became part of the Association for Redistributing Wealth in Hoeryong.

CHAPTER THIRTY-ONE

THE ASSOCIATION WAS a brotherhood of thieves. They'd started out stealing on their own, mostly from what passed for rich people in Hoeryong—that is, anyone who had more than enough to eat. But that presented a problem. A poor person's house you could pretty much bust into with your bare hands. Rich homes had better locks, higher walls, bigger dogs. Often you needed help if you were going to get inside the place of someone who had things worth stealing. So the three of them had banded together under the noble motto "Making things balanced." They told themselves they were improving life in Hoeryong by stealing from the rich and giving to the poor—themselves.

The famine had made normal people into bandits. I soon found out that even Hyo Sung's mother was part of the Association.

I thought about Hyo Sung's offer. I was a little scared about what it involved. Maybe the Association was into evil things: kidnapping homeless kids or robbing merchants and beating them up. How should I know? When you met people you hadn't seen in a long time, you could be fairly certain the famine had done bad things to their character. I'm sure that's how Kim Il's brain was working when he saw me. He'd just assumed I was a criminal.

So I hesitated. But what choice did I have, really? Hyo Sung was right. I was probably one or two sewer grates away from a firing squad.

"OK," I said.

Hyo Sung nodded and we began walking toward town, talking all the way.

The three members took me back to the apartment where they stayed. I greeted Hyo Sung's mother as I walked through the door. She was about four feet tall and talked a mile a minute, just as I remembered. I wasn't too surprised that she had become a den mother to the Association. What else was she supposed to do?

When we'd settled down with some soup, Hyo Sung told me his story. His father, the giant man who'd been our family friend in July 8th, had died of starvation, just like mine. And there were more similarities between our lives. Amazingly, his sister had also gone to China under mysterious circumstances that I knew not to ask about. He hadn't heard from her since. I told him about Bong Sook and his face took on a mournful expression.

Hyo Sung introduced the others to me. There was Moon Ho, who was maybe eighteen or nineteen years old, shorter than me, with big, widely spaced eyes. His shirt had more holes than it had material and his face was dirty. But I noticed something about Moon Ho immediately: he had presence. He looked capable; he had that calm that men who know what they're doing in life have. I sensed that he was the brains of the Association. *This man is cunning,* I said to myself.

The other guy was named Dae Ho. He'd been abandoned at five years of age and nearly died of exposure while sleeping on the street his first spring as a *Kkotjebi*. He had curly hair and, like the others, an unwashed face, which usually wore a kind but dumb expression. He often served as the butt of our jokes and never interrupted when the rest of us were arguing about something.

I got along with Moon Ho quite well. I felt he had things to teach me. I could tell that he'd traveled around more than Hyo Sung. He told me he'd been left on his own at an early age — maybe ten or eleven — and I realized we had things in common. Hyo Sung always had his mother, and that made him a little softer than Moon Ho and me. If we didn't make it on our own, no one was going to rescue us.

The next day, we went to the market, which I knew was controlled by a group of older homeless teens known as "the gangster brothers." They ran the place. They decided when you could graduate from begging to pickpocketing. They decided who could steal where. Some orphans were restricted to the vegetable market. Others could work only in the household goods section. You might get away with wandering outside your assigned zone once or twice. You could always say, "I was following a guy and he walked from one area to another. What am I supposed to do, give him up because he wanted a bite to eat?" That might work a few times, but if you did it too often, the gangster brothers would hurt you in front of everyone.

In Hoeryong, to be a gangster brother meant you were at the top of the heap. They had each earned their spot: either they had beaten three guys at once in a fight or they had refused to give up while getting pummeled. The first result meant you were uncommonly strong, the second that you were stubborn. Both were very good qualities.

When we went to the market to buy things, the people there saw Moon Ho and nodded respectfully at him. I noticed the gangster brothers, who were always so aggressive, avoided any kind of confrontation with Moon Ho. I'd never seen that happen before.

"Why are they avoiding him?" I asked Hyo Sung.

"Have you seen Moon Ho fight?"

I shook my head.

"He's really fast," he said. "And really crazy."

I had been around the market a lot but had never seen Moon Ho in action. Perhaps he never really fought at all. Perhaps it was how he looked that got him his reputation. This is the ultimate power, I thought: to earn respect just by the fierce expression on your face.

We began to go out at night, the four of us, stealing. We picked locks in apartments and stole the entire contents, cleaning out the places of pottery, food, and firewood. If we couldn't pick the lock, we smashed it open. My first night out, we hopped a fence and plundered a field planted with ripe onions. Dae Ho kept a lookout for the owner while the rest of us ripped the onions out of the ground and stuffed them in a bag. In fifteen minutes, we filled our bags. I immediately saw the advantages of being with the Association. If the owner burst out of the house, we'd each have only a twenty-five percent chance of getting caught.

After we filled up our bags, we hopped the fence and headed back to the fifth-floor apartment where the Association members lived. Here I met the Association's manager, a thin, elegant man in his thirties named Yoon Chul, who had been away the afternoon I arrived. The group handed over all of their takings to Yoon Chul, and in return he provided food, shelter, and alcohol.

Hyo Sung detailed my qualifications for Yoon Chul: I knew a lot of people in the market, I was big for my age, and I'd been on my own for many months. Also, I had gotten as far as sixth grade in school, further than most orphans. I was, all in all, an above-average recruit. My qualifications and Hyo Sung's word were enough for Yoon Chul to accept me into the Association.

Every day we would lounge around the apartment, singing songs and drinking. We played round after round of cards, hooting and laughing. The loser would have to go out and buy North Korean moonshine, very bitter and strong. How terrible that stuff was! I'd never really been a drinker before, but it was like a rite of passage with the Association. When Yoon Chul handed you the glass, you had to gulp it down in one swallow. If you tried to sip it, he would fill the glass to the top again and hand it back with a smile. To be a thief was a man's job.

We had to watch out for three groups: the owners of the homes we raided, the police, and soldiers. Thieves with a lot of money (unlike us) could buy off the police with a bribe, but the soldiers were different. Growing up, I had always wanted to be one, and I'd seriously considered joining the army before realizing that, with my family background — a sister missing in China, a mother known to be a smuggler — I would never be able to become an officer and make good money. My childhood dream of being a spy and fighting the Yankees had ended. I felt a trace of sadness over that.

But by this time, the reputation of North Korean troops, once so high, had begun to suffer. I knew soldiers assigned to poor rural areas who were malnourished and frail (while those in Pyongyang and along the border with China often lived very well). This was shocking to me, having grown up believing the slogan I saw on the cement billboards: "Soldiers first!" Now I heard stories of troops whose eyes bulged from their sunken faces; even though the government wasn't feeding them, they were expected to march and burn calories as if they were still living in the glory days.

When soldiers came out of the army, they began robbing ordinary people. There was nothing anyone could do. You saw them in the mountains or on the roads that connected one small city to another. They set up roadblocks and shook down everyone who came by. If you didn't have money, they beat you. We stopped going to the mountains after nightfall because you didn't want to walk the roads by yourself.

Even real soldiers could turn dangerous. These young men were mostly eighteen or nineteen years old, and the collars of their uniforms hung loose on their scrawny necks. In normal life, they would have been pathetic—I could have beaten one to a pulp. But with soldiers, the fight is never the end. If you beat up a soldier, he would come back with his squad and attack your whole family. It was once a glorious thing to wear the olive-green uniform with the bright red collar. But during the famine, we had a name for those uniforms: "tiger skins."

The soldiers were insatiable. We learned to avoid them. But staying free in North Korea was easier said than done.

CHAPTER THIRTY-TWO

I WAS HAPPIER THAN at any time since I became homeless. Depending on how successful we'd been that day, I had food and drink. I had somewhere to sleep every night. I had my childhood friend Hyo Sung and the cunning Moon Ho to teach me how to be a better thief, and I had Yoon Chul, who showed me something else: how to be an optimist. "If your mind is strong," he told me, "you can survive anything." I was luckier than ninety-five percent of the *Kkotjebi*. I didn't aspire to anything higher, and never thought of leaving North Korea.

Being in the Association was like having a full-time job, with assigned hours. Our day would begin at about 8 p.m. We had to be in position by 8:45, at the house we'd scouted the night before. That was the hour when North Korean television broadcasts the dramas and homemade tearjerkers that the whole country watched. Movies and TV series had become even more important for those people still affected by the famine. When you spent all day hunting for food, bent over in the mountains or crouched in supplication in the market, this was the only time you could sit down and have a rest. Really, the entire nation shut down at 8:45 for at least an hour. If you ever wanted to invade North Korea, that would be the time to do it, because half the country would be at a neighbor's house waiting for a show to begin.

The third night I went out stealing with the Association, we waited for the sound of a soap opera's opening theme before breaking into someone's accordion house. After a few hard smacks, the lock snapped open and we were inside. We found a bag of uncooked rice and a few small vegetables. There was also some cooked rice that had just been prepared. Perhaps it was for the next night's dinner, but in any case we descended on it like wolves. I took a spoon and bent over my plate — we were so confident that the occupants wouldn't be back, we decided to eat the rice right there in the house — but as soon as I dug into the food my hand began to shake. I relaxed my fingers, then gripped the spoon again. But it was no good. My hand was shaking so violently the rice wouldn't stay on. I had to drop it back onto the pile.

The others were watching me and shook their heads. They must have wondered whether I had what it took to be a member of the Association.

Was it nerves? I suppose so. I had never been inside someone's house before as a robber. It seemed so intimate to steal the rice still warm from their pot.

We returned to our base and turned everything over to Yoon Chul.

I was doubtful at first about his role in the Association. Here he was, sitting in his apartment while we were out stealing things and risking getting caught by the authorities. What risks did he take? But slowly I learned to respect him. His wife had left him when the famine struck, unable to deal with caring for their two children, a three-year-old boy and a six-year-old girl. This wasn't shocking. It was actually more shocking that Yoon Chul had kept his kids rather than run away himself. So many Kkotjebi had living parents who had dumped them at the market one day, unable to feed them and unwilling to watch them starve. Yoon Chul's attitude was different: "My children are going to make it, whatever I have to do." I admired him for that.

Yoon Chul never told me what he did before becoming a manager of thieves. But he was very good at his new position. The four of us decided what to steal, because so much depended on opportunity on the particular night we were out working — who had left his bike with only a skimpy lock on it, whose field was coming ripe. But Yoon Chul was a wizard at getting a good price for our stolen goods. His connections were unbeatable.

We told ourselves we were the men who balanced out the world. If you had too much, we would come to your house and relieve you of the surplus. It might seem cynical, but we really believed this. If you had called us criminals, we would have fought you. But the reality of our work never matched our illusions, because the rich had taller fences and stronger locks to keep us out. We ended up stealing from ordinary people.

Once, when we stole a bicycle, I went to see my father's friend who'd lent us money when my dad was dying. This man's job was repairing bicycles, a very lucrative trade because transportation was so important and the roads were so bad. I found him in his shop, which smelled pleasantly of rubber and oil. "Some of my friends stole a bike," I said, "and I'm getting a commission to sell it. Can you help me?" I didn't want to admit I'd become a thief myself.

My father's friend looked at me and saw the shame in my eyes. He shook his head. "Kwang Jin, in these times you may die of starvation, or a beating, or freezing. Death is everywhere, so you must be ready to do *anything* to survive. Why do you go out and steal too?"

I nodded. But deep down, I still didn't feel right about what I was doing. It was hard to get rid of that emotion, planted in me by my father so many years ago.

My father's friend didn't end up buying the bike. Despite his concern for me, he offered me only half what it was really worth.

CHAPTER THIRTY-THREE

IN MY FIRST few weeks as a member of the Association, Moon Ho and I became close. We were always talking, telling stories about how we survived in Hoeryong. And soon I realized that the Association wasn't as tight as I thought. Moon Ho was scheming.

"Why should we give Yoon Chul a hundred percent of everything we get?" he said to Hyo Sung and me one day as we walked home from another night of thieving. "Shouldn't we be able to keep ten percent for ourselves? Is that so wrong? I'd like to buy some snacks, maybe save up for a new pair of shoes. But Yoon Chul takes everything! Why should it be that way?"

The Association was divided. Moon Ho wanted a bigger cut. Hyo Sung wanted to be loyal; his mother, after all, was a manager. "We gave our word," he said. "Yoon Chul takes care of us. We can't go behind his back."

I thought it best to stay neutral. I was new to the Association, and I valued Moon Ho's friendship. I couldn't afford to make enemies. The deciding vote fell to Dae Ho, and dreaming of those snacks he remembered from childhood — chips and homemade sour candy — he voted with Moon Ho.

Soon we were going to the street vendors once or twice a week, spending our ten percent on schoolboy things. Even as he stuffed his mouth, Hyo Sung would mutter, "This isn't right." We ignored him. I decided one day to plunk everything down for a piece of chocolate. I had never tasted chocolate in my life. It was a small piece, the size of my thumb, wrapped in an old piece of waxy paper. I paid the woman twenty *won* and popped the chocolate into my mouth.

"Oh, boy," I mumbled as I chewed the delicious stuff. The chocolate seemed to pour through my veins, coating them in that sugary warmth. I wanted more.

Yoon Chul soon figured out something was wrong. I'm not sure if Hyo Sung had said something to his mother, but a few days later Yoon Chul tapped me on the shoulder.

"I have to go see a friend in Manyang. You know that area, right?"

"Yes," I said.

"Come with me, then. It'll be good to have someone to walk with."

Manyang was about a forty-minute walk from the city center, but we weren't on the road for more than five minutes before Yoon Chul asked me something odd.

"What do you think of Moon Ho?"

My chemical sensor buzzed a warning. This was not a normal question. Yoon Chul was the boss. Why should he care what two of his workers thought about each other? I was immediately on guard.

"What do you mean?"

"I've been watching him," Yoon Chul said. "He's very smart, you know? But also very sly. I think he wants to do things for himself."

My nerves began to jangle. If I sided with Yoon Chul, the other boys would consider me a snitch. If I sided with Moon Ho, Yoon Chul might consider it a betrayal and throw me out of the Association. Or worse.

I didn't want to sell out my friend, so I simply said, "I'm a new member, and I want us all to do well. Whatever he's thinking, Moon Ho is still our friend. If we kick him out, who's going to take his place? If he's doing jobs behind your back, that can be fixed."

This was what Yoon Chul had taught me. Be optimistic. Look for the positive way forward. I was admitting that, OK, we've been a little bad. All of us are taking a bit for ourselves. But it's not the end of the world. We can work it out.

Yoon Chul said nothing more, and we walked to his friend's house in Manyang in silence. But I could see he was thinking about what I'd said. I believe he respected the fact that I hadn't snitched on Moon Ho. I hadn't told him what he wanted to hear.

He never brought up Moon Ho again. That was a lesson I learned that day. Even if life has made you a criminal, you can be true to yourself. In fact, you *have* to be true to yourself.

Joining the Association was the luckiest day of my life up until then. It gave me shelter and taught me many things. My one source of sorrow was the memories of my family. When we came back to the apartment after a long night of stealing, Hyo Sung's mother would fuss over her son and they would talk and laugh. I saw the affection between them and missed my mother even more. Before bedtime, I would daydream of becoming a millionaire and buying my uncle's house — the fanciest one I'd ever seen. I would send agents to find my mother and my sister and reunite my family in the grand house. We would eat whatever we wanted and watch movies from China all day long. Or my mother and Bong Sook would return to me and I would go to school, dressed in new clothes and carrying a fresh black book bag.

Every night, I fell asleep thinking of Bong Sook. *We'll all be together again,* I told myself. *Kwang Jin, you must find her.*

CHAPTER THIRTY-FOUR

THERE WERE GOOD and bad days with the Association. Sometimes we came home with nothing to eat or sell and so went hungry until the next night. But still, I was eating more than I had in months. I put on a little weight, rising from ninety pounds to close to one hundred. My clothes fit snugly instead of hanging loosely off my bony shoulders. My face filled out and my ribs retreated back underneath my skin.

I felt stronger. My mind was streamlined: food, sleep, and work were all I allowed myself to think about, besides the memory of Bong Sook.

My mother returned to Hoeryong without my knowing it and began looking for me. She'd been in Sambong, trying to find a broker to take her to China, but no one had agreed to arrange her escape. Finally, one day in the Hoeryong market, she ran into Hyo Sung's mother and returned with her to our apartment. She decided to stay with us, which made me happy. At last I could support her and repay her for the many years of struggling to feed me. Hyo Sung's mother welcomed my mother and the two became fast friends again. My life was almost complete. Only my sister was missing.

One afternoon, I went to the market to get some snacks before our work began. When I returned to the apartment, I found my mother standing at the door, her eyes were wide and frightened.

"They came for the boys," she told me.

I looked past her into the apartment. It was empty. "Who came?"

"The police!" Her voice was frantic. "Kwang Jin, we have to leave now or they will return for you."

I couldn't believe it. The Association had been arrested, each for his own crimes. I found out later that someone had turned us in, probably one of our neighbors. Having so many *Kkotjebi* teenagers living next to them had caused them to fear for their own property.

I turned and walked quickly down the hallway, my mother hurrying along beside me. We clattered down the stairs, my heart fluttering. How did the police know? Did we make some mistake? Were more police waiting for me on the street? But most of all I wondered if the others had told the police that there was a fourth member of the Association — me.

When we walked out the door into the mild sunlight, everything looked normal. Peddlers, pedestrians, a few *Kkotjebi* on their way to the market. I saw no policemen lurking nearby. My heartbeat decelerated slightly. It turned out that Moon Ho and the others never spoke my name to the police, something I've been grateful for ever since.

We turned right and made our way to the main road.

"Where will we go?" I asked my mother.

She looked at me, then away.

"To a place near the train station. I know a man there who will take us in."

I could barely process the words. She "knew" a man? What did that mean?

When, an hour or so later, we reached the streets bordering the train station — a nice neighborhood whose apartment buildings were covered with yellow or blue tiles — my mother finally admitted that she had met a man. And they had an understanding: if one of them was ever in trouble, the other would help.

It was what we called "convenience love." There was no love in it, but this man was effectively my mom's new husband.

I felt a wave of heat across my face. I was suddenly furious with my mother. How could she find a man so soon after my father's death?

Did he mean that little to her? I knew that during the famine people got together for many reasons: food, shelter, protection. I don't believe romantic love really existed in North Korea during this time. But why did my mother have to pair off with someone new?

I felt bitter and cynical. *I hope she's found a rich man,* I thought as we walked down the well-kept streets. *He can buy me new clothes and support me like a true stepfather.* I marched along, rage simmering in me. But after a few minutes, my anger gave way to faint hope. Even if he wasn't rich, maybe Mother had found a good person to be with and we could all live together in the same house. Bong Sook was still missing, but I had to begin somewhere in reuniting my family.

When we arrived at the apartment, my new stepfather opened the door; he was very tall and broad-shouldered and his face looked stern. I nodded and entered, and my mother told me to sit down. I couldn't bear to look at her.

Haven't you learned your lesson from your father, Kwang Jin? I told myself. *It's not her, it's the famine, it's everything. You mustn't judge your mother.* But I couldn't look at her next to her new husband and not taste bitterness in my mouth.

I saw immediately that my mother's was truly a famine marriage. They had no official certificate; there had been no ceremony, let alone a celebration. There were no signs of affection between them, no touches, no smiling looks. Still, I felt angry. Was this the best my mother could do? The tall man—I wouldn't even use his name—wasn't a very good prospect. He had no job, and he had a crippled, dark-haired daughter who lay on her sleeping mat the whole day. She was about my age, but small and fragile and unable to walk. Her hair hung low on her face, pasted sweatily to her forehead. I stared at her in pity and frustration.

My new stepfather was saying something to me.

"What?" I said irritably.

"What are you going to do?" he said in a commanding voice. "You have to go out and find us some food."

I met my mother's eyes, which were filled with pleading. I could see that she had the same hope I did — that someone was going to take care of all her needs. Namely, me. She expected me to provide for her, the tall man, and the crippled girl as well.

I felt so hopeless I wanted to cry. But what could I do? The Association was finished. That night, I went out stealing on my own.

CHAPTER THIRTY-FIVE

I WAS ALONE NOW, without lookouts or partners. I was more and more afraid of getting caught. Everything was still scarce: soap, clothes, shoes. Some *Kkotjebi* would sleep with their sneakers in their arms, tucked under their chins, to prevent their competitors from snatching them. But I saw fewer and fewer homeless kids doing this; their shoes were so torn and dirty no one wanted them. That was true of all of North Korea. People took fewer precautions against thieves, because what was there left to steal?

That first night at my stepfather's place, I was walking a few blocks from the train station, looking for something to steal, when I saw an apartment building behind an eight-foot cinderblock wall. It was shortly after midnight. I had been out for several hours, searching without success. My veins seemed to burn with the need for food. My mother and her new husband were waiting for me, famished. The crippled girl was hungry too, and for her — maybe only for her — I felt real sympathy.

I looked around. No one on the streets, just wind blowing the electrical wires and moonlight above.

Go on, Kwang Jin, I said to myself, *you have to find something.*

I found a big rock next to the foot of the wall and climbed up on it. I put my hands on the top of the cinderblocks, took a breath, and hoisted myself up. Trying not to make much noise, I stood on the wall's narrow ledge and looked up at the nearest balcony. It had about three armfuls of firewood stacked on its raw concrete. But there was a six-foot gap between the wall and the balcony, and a big drop if I missed the jump, enough to break bones.

I ran along the wall, trying not to stumble off. When I was close to the balcony, I launched my feet toward it. I grabbed the edge of the balcony and pulled myself up.

Immediately I knew something was wrong.

"What are you doing there?" A voice from below.

I crouched on the balcony, saying nothing.

Louder now. "Hey, you, what are you doing? Do you want me to call the police? Come down here."

Damn it. Damn these interfering people. It wasn't even the owner, just a tough guy passing by. Maybe he'd been robbed before and wanted to take revenge. If I didn't talk to him, he would wake up the whole building and I would have real trouble.

"OK," I said, standing up. I jumped down, landing next to the tough guy. He was thirty-five or forty years old, squat, a face squeezed up in anger and confusion.

"What's going on?" he huffed.

I mumbled something. I was frightened.

"What?"

"Forgive me this once and I won't do it again," I said. There was no point in lying. I could feel the desire for violence coming off him like the smell of sweat.

"So you *are* a thief!" He struck me in the face, hard. I felt a trickle of blood like a hot spurt against my skin, but that warm feeling was lost in pain from the rest of my body. The man seemed to be hitting me everywhere at once. I tumbled to the ground. That turned out to be a mistake, as he began kicking me with his dirty boots. I thought he would kick my head off.

"Please!" I yelled. "Please don't!" I couldn't get to my feet. He was so strong, I wondered where he got the energy. I felt my right eye swelling, my lips ballooning. I was bleeding from two or three places, mostly around my face. My ribs were aching from his kicks, and my breath came in short bursts.

He beat me for what seemed like a good ten minutes, grunting and sucking in breath. By the end, I didn't have the strength to cover my head anymore, and he kicked it freely.

Finally he leaned over and shouted, "Don't ever try this again."

I curled up, waiting for the next kick. But he was gone, stomping off down the street, having expended all his rage on me.

I pulled myself up bit by bit. Blood slid from my mouth onto the dirt. I spit more out. I felt hot licks of pain up and down my side. I thought he'd broken some ribs.

I managed to get on my feet and staggered off to my stepfather's apartment. I felt that if I fell, I would black out.

When I knocked on the apartment door, my stepfather swung it open. I thought he would say "What happened?" or "Are you OK?" Instead, he stared at me and said in shock, "Why have you come back empty-handed?"

I tried to explain. An apartment, a stranger, a beating. But I was mumbling, my lips too thick to make sense.

He slapped me sharply across the face. "How dare you come back with nothing," he said. He stalked away and left me standing at the open door.

Tears spilled from my swollen eyelids. Why did he hit me? Wasn't I out stealing for him and his daughter?

I'm sure my mother heard his outburst and felt terrible for me, but still, I felt a suffocating sense of persecution. Was anyone ever so unloved and misunderstood? My belly ached with emptiness, and each part of my body contributed its screaming to the din. I crawled to my mat and tried to sleep. My tears dripped onto the wooden mat.

That night I gave in to despair. To be cut off from the ones you loved was one thing. To be oppressed by their companions was worse.

I have to do something, I thought. *I have to find a new way to live.*

CHAPTER THIRTY-SIX

THE NEXT DAY, I left the apartment early. I wanted to scout out places farther from the train station where perhaps thieves hadn't hit yet. It seemed like a normal day, except there were no kids on the streets. This was one of the early-summer weeks when the schools emptied and sent all their students to the fields outside Hoeryong to weed the corn and soybean fields. Since I hadn't been in school for three years, I hadn't gone to the countryside.

What I didn't realize was that this work made the Saro-cheong's job much easier. Instead of having to figure out who was going to school and who wasn't, the officials knew, by process of elimination, that any kid found on the streets wasn't going to school and was therefore a *Kkotjebi*.

A man in a suit came up to me as I walked. His face was calm, almost bored. I knew immediately: Saro-cheong. He blocked my path, and I saw another man over my right shoulder, blocking my retreat.

"Why aren't you in school?" the calm man asked.

"I'm sick," I said, thinking on my feet.

"OK, then tell me who's the Saro-cheong master for your school."

Every schoolchild knew the master's name. But I'd been absent from class for years, and my mind was a blank.

"It's . . ."

I could picture the master's face but couldn't remember his name.

I stammered out breath, but no words. One of the men grabbed my arm.

"You don't go to school. You are delinquent!"

What the hell, I wanted to yell. It's not that I didn't want to go. I couldn't go!

The Saro-cheong men dragged me down the street past startled pedestrians. They took me to the headquarters—a squat brick building—then shipped me off with some other kids to a rural area near rice fields.

I found myself at an old school that had been turned into a detention center. It wasn't only for *Kkotjebi* but also for other youths who'd broken the law. You could be sent there for as little as three days (for not wearing your Kim Il Sung badge, say) or a week (for fighting in the streets). Wearing your hair long like a South Korean pop star would get you seven days. My sentence was more severe: three months.

The building was about three hundred feet long by one hundred feet wide and held about one hundred fifty boys and girls at any given time. I knew the place when it was the Song Chun School, one of the best arts academies in Hoeryong, but that was a long time ago. As I walked in, I could see the length of the central hall. It looked like it had been through a tank battle: there were huge holes punched through the walls and broken cement everywhere. Shouting and screaming echoed from the inner rooms. *This place is full of evil.* I was afraid.

An inmate came over to me and started barking questions—what was my name, where was I from, what was I doing before I got arrested? Then the other new prisoners and I were ordered to change. We couldn't wear our street clothes inside, because it would make it easier to run away. I had on a nice shirt and cotton pants that my mom had gotten me, but the team leader, an inmate in his early twenties, snatched them away. He would either keep them for himself or barter them for a bottle of moonshine. In return, I was given some old clothes they found in a corner, a dirty school uniform that was way too big for me, including a ragged blue jacket with four buttons that covered my body down to the knees.

The Saro-cheong Detention Center was a brutal place. The first day I was there, I saw a group of men surround a thin teenager, just as Hyo Sung and the Association had surrounded me, except these men were taller and more muscular. The teenager's face was frozen in an expression of animal fear. One of the men shouted, "Are you stupid?"

"Yes," the teenager said. "I'm stupid."

He'd been in detention for some time, I realized later. He knew how to answer properly. But the men only came closer to him.

"Why are you so stupid?"

"Because—"

Fists holding bricks and stones descended on him. I heard a sharp crack—was it a bone breaking?—and the teenager fell to the floor, his figure lost behind a blur of sleeves and legs. He was beaten unmercifully. No one tried to help. I stared in disbelief. I'd never seen anyone attacked like that before. It was a competition to see who could hit him hardest. The boy's skull was their favorite target. They smashed at it with all their might, and I saw a smudge of scarlet blooming on the cement floor near his face. I turned away. I didn't want to see the blood and brains on the floor.

If that boy survives, I thought, *he'll never be normal again.*

The guards stood by and watched this happen. I soon learned that they didn't run the prison; the older inmates did. There was a group of inmates in their late twenties who dealt out punishments and made money off the younger ones.

The boys were held in one room and the girls in another, larger room, where everyone ate their meals and sang songs at night. The boys slept side by side on the wood floor with no space between them. Everyone lived and ate together.

During the day we worked hard. We were sent to a factory where huge rocks were piled in front, and we had to break those rocks into smaller ones, and those into smaller ones still, until we had a pile of pebbles the size of corn kernels. Or we were sent to the fields for fourteen hours a day to tend the rice crop.

Within a day or two, the gangster brothers knew your story. They would see if any family members came to save you, and if not, they knew you had no place to go and no one to protect you. Such orphans became their first victims; we had no one to stand up for us or to complain if we disappeared. Later I learned that on my second day at the detention center, my mother had come to find me, but she went to the building in the city center and not the one where I was, out in the country. The guards had told her there was no boy of that name there. I had lost my chance for a quick release.

The kids in the detention center outnumbered the gangsters five to one. We should have banded together and fought them. But the kids from normal families were terrified of their fellow inmates, and the rest of us, the *Kkotjebi*, had been street people for too long. *Kkotjebi* were used to surviving on our own; we didn't trust anyone, not even our partners in crime. So to bond with a bunch of strangers was impossible. The gangster brothers knew this. They knew that thieves would not join in common cause.

The good part of being at the rural detention center was the fresh air and the fact that I could ask for more soup or noodles and usually received them. Sometimes the Saro-cheong hired a local family to provide food for us, and these good people allowed some of us to have extra portions. This gave me hope for tomorrow.

But at night, Bong Sook's face came to me again and again. I missed her so much that the pain of losing her was stronger than my hunger. In my Association days, I'd seen her face only when I dreamed, but now I thought about her constantly. And perhaps this was why: her love was unconditional, completely different from what I saw inside the detention center.

I felt a deep despair, like I was slowly sinking into black water. *I want to save my family,* I thought, *but I can't even save myself.*

CHAPTER THIRTY-SEVEN

THE DAYS BEGAN at 5:30 a.m. with the guards shouting at us to get up. We would go out into the field in front of the building and sing for fifteen minutes. Since the gangster brothers ran everything, you could forget about political tunes. Instead, we sang old songs that the kids had been taught in high school. Having been a *Kkotjebi* in the market and having spent my time drinking with the Association, I'd never really learned the songs, so I moved my lips silently while trying to pick up the lyrics. I was afraid if I messed up, I'd be beaten. But honestly, the gangsters didn't need that excuse.

After the singing, we'd walk to the nearby river and wash our faces and hands. Arriving back at the center around 6:30, we'd eat a meal of corn mush and soup, which consisted mostly of water and salt. At 7:00 we'd go out to work and not come back until well after dark—around 9:30 p.m. We'd eat our dinner and gather in the girls' room for a round of *orak heh*, or musical performances. We sat in a big circle, and one boy or girl would get up and sing while a few others would shuffle around in a dance. Like everyone else, the performers were so exhausted they could barely stand, and they had to catch themselves from collapsing on the floor. Anyone who stopped the *orak heh* was set upon by the gangster brothers and thrashed.

The first night, I desperately wanted to sleep. Blackness kept stealing over my brain. If I slept, though, I was afraid I wouldn't wake up. We had to keep singing for the team leaders, who wanted to show that their members had spirit. But most of all, the older inmates wanted to demonstrate that they owned us. So they had us perform these ridiculous songs.

I was shy and apprehensive. I willed the brothers not to pick me to perform. Of course, I was the first one chosen that day. I stood up, my hands shaking, my throat hot and dry. I didn't know any cheerful songs and instead began croaking out the first thing that came into my head, a mournful dirge about a son and his dying mother. I'm not a very good singer, and I watched the faces of the gangster brothers as I forced out the words. They looked confused at first, their mouths hanging open, but this confusion quickly turned to anger.

"What the hell is that?" one of them yelled. "We don't sing songs like that here. Sit down!"

I sat down, my skin burning with embarrassment. It turned out that sad songs were forbidden at the detention center because they "disturbed the good atmosphere." That is, they made everyone depressed.

I was never chosen to perform at *orak heh* again, which was fine with me.

Things got worse. The next day, the guard with the hoe handle, the boy who'd fallen so far in the world, attacked me when I couldn't find my shoe. After that, whenever he saw me, he'd give me a hard slap or a blow with his stick. There was no rhyme or reason to the violence. It was sudden and completely irrational.

That night, as I lay on the floor, afraid to sleep, I heard a commotion. It was the gangsters again. This time they were walking through the crowd. A cold fear gripped my insides as I realized they were grabbing people like me — new arrivals.

I heard the gangsters yelling: "Where is your money? Don't show me your pockets — where've you hidden your cash?" They demanded cash from each new inmate. We had come in off the streets, so we should have something on us, a few *won* at the very least. If you didn't have money, you were knocked down and kicked in the face. When they came to me, I could see their teeth and eyes in the darkness. Their breath smelled of alcohol. *Where are they getting liquor in here?* I wondered.

"Give us your money," one of the men said, sounding bored.

I reached into my pocket. I had a few *won* I was going to spend on snacks. A hand snatched the money out of my palm.

"Is this all?"

"Yes, everything."

I sensed their massed shapes in front of me. I feared a hand or a brick might smash me out of the darkness. I bowed my head, thinking, *Pass me by. Pass me by.*

I felt the men move on.

Nothing made sense. Another night early in my stay, I woke up at around two or three in the morning. I got up off my mat and saw the night guard watching the sleeping prisoners.

I stepped over several boys and made my way to him. I bowed.

"May I use the bathroom, please?"

He turned to look at me. "No," he said calmly.

I was stunned by this answer. My bladder was painfully swollen. What objection could he have to letting an inmate relieve himself? But I couldn't risk asking why. I lay back down and stayed awake until morning, the pressure in my bladder growing until I was sure it would explode like an infected appendix.

If I am ever a guard, I thought, *I will let every boy pee when he needs to.*

I had no peace at the center. Even when I was out of sight, I worried that the guard with the stick was sneaking up on me, ready for another round of humiliation. I seethed with a violent hatred, but what could I do?

I was trapped, like the other inmates.

CHAPTER THIRTY-EIGHT

Three weeks into my sentence, I fought the hated guard and won. Now it was my job to interview all the new arrivals. "What's your name?" I would ask them. "Where are you from? What's your crime?" I tried not to be too intimidating. If it was their first time in detention, many boys shook with fear. I wrote all the details down in a book. The team leaders read it through and estimated how much they could extract from the newbies. It was their price for survival.

My other duty, of course, was to watch the prisoners at night, keep order, and make sure no one escaped. I had to stay awake most of the day, snatching twenty minutes of sleep when I could, then remain vigilant through the dark hours. The leaders didn't want this job — they were too eager to sleep. But I was grateful for it. Even though I barely closed my eyes, it often kept me from getting beaten up. I wasn't a leader, but I was an employee. My status had risen.

I won't lie: it felt good to have power. I had boys older than me approach where I stood and bow deeply. "How did you sleep, *hyung?*" they'd ask (*hyung* means "older brother"). Most of the time I wouldn't answer them; it didn't pay for me to become too friendly with the inmates. They would ask permission to use the bathroom and I usually said yes — I was still traumatized by the memory of my own experience — but I couldn't be seen as a pushover. Every so often I would bark, "No! Lie down!" and the inmate would walk away, crestfallen. If I were seen as soft, the gang members would start victimizing me. I had to make an example of some boys.

The leaders abused me despite my new position. Often at night around eleven, they would send me to the local store to get snacks or drinks for them. When I returned, they would look at me as if they'd never seen me before and begin slapping my face. There was one brother in particular, Small Pig was his nickname, who liked to attack me. He had a round face and very short hair. His face was such a perfect circle it was mesmerizing. Whenever he saw me, he would smile and come toward me. I would bow, but as soon as I rose to full height, he would shout, "Your back is not straight!" and slap me hard across the face.

When the mood in the detention center was dark, more people joined in the beatings, until one time four or five people tried to kick my head in. The trick was to fall to the floor and protect your skull. When several people were attacking you, there wasn't much room, and they eventually got tired of wrestling with one another to land a good shot. You can't ask why you're being beaten, because then you'd suffer more. The rest of the night, my torso and shoulders throbbed and my cuts festered, oozing blood.

I stood guard until dawn, staring at the moonlight as it came through the holes in the roof or cast its glow on the yard outside, which appeared lunar and peaceful. My eyelids would begin to droop, and it seemed someone was singing in my ear: *Sleep, sleep.* But if the leaders found me napping, or if one of the boys escaped, I would get a severe beating meant to maim me. I might also lose my position and be forced to work in the fields again. Two or three o'clock in the morning was the worst time. There was no coffee to help you stay awake. I was barely able to stand up.

Often on those nights I heard screams, terrible high-pitched screams. It could only mean one thing: an inmate was being raped in one of the other rooms, forced to be the sex toy of this or that older man. (The victims were always girls; I never heard of a boy being sexually abused at the detention center.) I wanted to stop my ears, but I knew the sound would still penetrate. I closed my eyes and dreamt of escaping.

The only time I could be alone was while bathing in the nearby river. It was just a creek, really, maybe ten or twelve feet across. On a hot day the water was clean and fresh on our faces. There was no soap or shampoo, but when I felt the first shock of coolness, I had a sudden urge to live longer. Nothing else gave me that feeling. Even food. If I had enough of food, I would eat uncontrollably and it would hurt my shrunken stomach. But river water was like the promise of another kind of life.

One day, a young boy, ten or eleven years old, was brought to the detention center. I heard he was from Undok, where my mother was born, and this gave me a feeling of kinship. I saw how frail the boy was, his ribs visible through a torn green shirt. I didn't think he would survive very long. It seemed that he couldn't stand up to even the most casual beating.

I took him aside and questioned him gently. His parents had abandoned him when he was six or seven, and he'd been floating around ever since. Every day he'd get on the train in Undok, beg for food, and hop off. But one time the train left the station before he could get off. He had to stay on until Hoeryong, and he was arrested there.

I kind of adopted the boy. I made sure that he had a good sleeping spot near me and enough to eat. The center's cook, a twenty-three-year-old woman who was an employee, not an inmate, had taken a liking to me. She was very pretty; I and the other night guard, Kook Cheol, would often watch her and marvel at her beauty. Kook Cheol was nineteen, a former leader of the beggars in the marketplace and a typical *Kkotjebi*: energetic, smart, and very bitter toward life. When he was eleven, his mother had taken him to the market and asked him to wait while she went to the food court to get his favorite snack. He stayed there for hours, but she never returned. Eventually he became a beggar and a pickpocket. His hatred of his mother was something to see. "That bitch is probably in China living the good life with some man," he'd tell me. Like many orphans who'd been abandoned, he had a recurring fantasy: he'd become rich and buy a mansion in Hoeryong and one day his mother would come begging at his door. "And I will take a heaping bowl of white rice and eat it, all of it, six inches from her face, as she watches." I had the same fantasy, not about my mother but about Small Grandfather.

(Ironically, Kook Cheol's mother showed up one day, months later. But instead of tormenting her or turning her away, Kook Cheol took her in and supported her by pickpocketing for many months afterward. His fantasies, like many of the *Kkotjebi*'s, were really a masked appeal for love.)

Whenever the beautiful cook smiled at me, Kook Cheol would glare angrily and I would laugh. But I wasn't looking for romance; what I wanted was food. So I asked the cook, with all the charm I could muster, for extra rations. She smiled slyly, and at the next meal there was a heaping portion of corn mush on my plate. I shared it with the boy. I started giving him snacks in the evening and allowed him to use the latrine whenever he wanted.

One night, one of the team leaders ordered me to take some wood and coal to his parents' house. It was about three in the morning when I left with a wooden cart; the little boy and two other inmates came with me. On the way, we got so tired we had to stop. I told the others we'd rest for half an hour, and we lay down in the middle of a municipal garden and fell asleep. The grass felt so good underneath my head. For me, the garden was like a five-star hotel.

When I woke, the sun was up. It was at least six in the morning. The little boy was awake, happily watching the early-morning pedestrians walk by.

I looked around. One inmate was still asleep, curled up on the grass.

"Where's the other one?" I asked the little boy, sitting up quickly.

"He ran away."

The ingrate, I thought. *I'll suffer for that.*

I looked at the boy. He was regarding me calmly. "Why didn't you run, too?" I asked.

The boy's eyes registered shock. "But that would mean you'd be in trouble! How could I?"

I laughed. We got up, roused the other boy, and resumed pulling the cart to our destination. It was hard work, but I felt glad that, out of all this horror, I'd found friendship with at least one other human being.

It was the first time I'd ever taken care of someone else. I protected the little boy because, if I didn't, I felt I would drown in wickedness.

I will not become one of them, I told myself, *any more than necessary.* I didn't know I would have to sink much lower before my chance at redemption appeared.

CHAPTER THIRTY-NINE

THE BOY ESCAPED a few weeks later. One day, he ran away from his work group and I never saw him again. I felt sad that I didn't get to say goodbye, but at least he was free.

But I sank further into cruelty. Being the night guard was harder than I thought it would be. If someone disobeyed and I didn't punish him, I would be beaten and replaced—the team leaders made this clear. So I beat those who refused my orders; I beat them with my fists as they looked at me with hatred. Once I took a leather jacket off the back of a new boy and kept it as my own. I took it because I wanted it; that's what the streets of Hoeryong had taught me.

The leaders had another scheme for making money, one that I shared in. The children who had no survival skills were sent to farms or construction sites to work, but those like me were employed in our old jobs, as thieves. Instead of staying at the detention center during the day, Kook Cheol and I were sent to the market to steal. The gangster brothers gave us a quota we had to meet each day—say, five hundred *won*—which we turned over to them when we returned. The rest we kept for ourselves.

I now became a pickpocket. Kook Cheol and his *Kkotjebi* friends were my teachers.

At first I served as a spotter. When we went to the market in the afternoon, I began to look for anyone who appeared out of place. Farmers were easy to pick out: they wore heavy, ankle-high work boots. Meanwhile, the teenagers from the country would dress up like they were going to a party, which market day was for them. They tended to look around slowly, as if there was a video camera in their head recording everything for the folks back home, and they studied even the small buildings with real interest.

Once I found a mark, I would watch him. What is he interested in? Is he shopping for a new cooking pot, a television, a radio? If he wants a radio, is he looking at the more expensive models (good news) or the cheapest ones (bad)? You have to know what your target is interested in, because you have to anticipate where he's going to be in two or three minutes, so you can position your friends to rob him. Is he going to talk to that seller who's got a set of bowls in his hands? Is he just browsing? A bumpkin who is negotiating a price is a distracted bumpkin, and that was good for us pickpockets.

Most important, I had to figure out where the mark kept his money. When I knew where the cash was, I would tap that place on my body so the pickpockets had the right spot. Some people stashed their money in their back pocket, but they were a rarity; even someone from July 8th knew that was the pickpocket's favorite location. Others had a bag they stuffed their *won* into. After a few hours at the market, I learned that about eighty percent of North Koreans put their cash in their front pants pocket.

After spotting for a few days, I began to pick pockets myself. I brushed up against a mark and slipped my hand into his pocket. This way he had two distractions: the seller he was bargaining with and this rude young man who had bumped into him. I would grab whatever I found — sunglasses, a key ring — and saunter on.

Kook Cheol and the others were razor men. They carried the thin sharp blades between their index and middle fingers as they strolled through the market pretending to be looking for a bargain. When they saw a woman carrying a canvas bag or purse, they would sidle up to her and, while leaning over to look at a seller's wares, slice open the bottom of her bag. In their hand would go, and out it would come with a little cash or merchandise. Some guys even used long tweezers to reach into people's pockets without them feeling anything and extract their money. In many cases, your hand is too thick — the mark will feel it fumbling around in his pocket. So the thief stands to the side and just behind the victim and slips these long-nosed extractors (used in North Korea by dentists) into the bag.

In the market, we had not only the police on our side, but the sellers too. That's because if a trader shouted at a victim that he was being pickpocketed, his business suffered. The other *Kkotjebi* would single him out for rough treatment. Out of nowhere, he might find a shower of stones raining down on him. Or he would become the target of all the thieves in the market, who were punishing him for betraying one of their own. We felt that stealing was all we had, our only way to survive, and if the traders were going to take it away, we would fight back. But unconsciously, we made moral decisions. We avoided stealing from pregnant women, for instance, or young mothers with toddlers. It was just understood.

Kook Cheol and I would watch out for each other. I would take his guard hours when he wanted to go pickpocketing in the market; he thanked me by bringing me snacks when he sneaked back into the detention center. One day, I asked him to return the favor by taking my shift so I could go check on my mom. He agreed.

After two months in the center, I went out in search of my mother.

CHAPTER FORTY

I BELIEVED MY MOM was still with my stepfather, so I walked toward the train station, where his apartment was. On my way, I saw women standing along the side of the road; they were selling their bodies to get food. One of the women recognized me and called out. She was an old friend of my mother's, and she told me that my mom was no longer living with my stepfather. So I turned around and headed instead to the old Association apartment, thinking she might be there. I was still angry that she'd left me in the detention center, a place everyone knew to be full of depraved men, for so long. My blood was boiling.

When I opened the apartment door, a gust of musty air greeted me. I saw my mother and Hyo Sung's mom lying on sleeping mats, their heads almost touching. Their eyes were closed and they were as still as figures carved from stone.

My mother could barely raise her head to look at me. Her eyes were glassy and unfocused. I knew the signs of starvation; neither of them had enough strength to get up. I looked around the apartment for food, but there was nothing, not a bit of cornmeal or noodles. I had arrived just in time.

With what money I had, I went and bought some cornmeal cakes and brought them back to the apartment. My mother and Hyo Sung ate them greedily. When my mother finished, she told me they hadn't eaten anything in two days. Then she began to cry, her chest heaving with little sobs.

"What's wrong?" I asked.

"You just had your birthday, and I did nothing for you."

I had forgotten about my birthday. It always seemed to arrive during a crisis. I smiled. Knowing that she'd remembered made my rage vanish. "Don't worry," I told her. "I'm just happy to see you."

Without the Association, I couldn't earn enough to feed three people. I had saved some of the money I'd earned while working as the night guard, but I quickly realized that it wasn't enough. I'd have to go back to the detention center to find work. I left my mother all the money I had and walked back to the center, my heart heavy, thinking that I would have to rejoin Kook Cheol, pickpocketing at the market.

Finally, after a few more weeks at the center, I had saved enough money to keep the three of us alive for a little while. I also hoped I could earn a decent living with my new pickpocketing skills. I ran away from the detention center again and returned to the Association apartment. But there was another family living there now. I asked around and eventually was told that my mother had remarried and moved in with her "new husband."

I found their accordion house and met my new stepfather, a man named Sung Min, who was in his late forties, lean and jovial. "Oh, he's taller than I expected!" was his first comment when I walked through the door. He was a nice guy; I could see that my mother was happier with him than she'd been with my first stepfather.

I ate a meal of cold corn noodles and cucumber kimchi, perfect for a hot day, then fell onto my sleeping mat. Sung Min knew I was exhausted and didn't try to keep me awake or ask me when I was going to bring in money. I was grateful for that; my body was so worn out from the tension I'd felt at the center, the constant apprehension, that it simply gave out. I slept for three days, getting up only to eat and use the bathroom.

When I woke up, I found myself still haunted by the detention center. For months afterward, I would be walking through the neighborhoods of Hoeryong and spot one of the older boys whom I'd guarded there. They hated anyone associated with that place, with that humiliating time in their lives, especially guards. I knew the boys were angry because I'd been rude or smacked them if they didn't obey orders. The fact that I was younger than many of the people I guarded also infuriated them. They'd shout, "Remember me?" and I'd immediately start running as the sound of pounding feet rose behind me. Occasionally, my pursuers caught up with me, and I took a beating.

Sung Min didn't have enough money to support me. To save myself that summer, I had to get away from Hoeryong.

CHAPTER FORTY-ONE

I WENT TO THE mountains. Food had become so precious in North Korea that farmers hired men to guard their crops up there. These guards were guaranteed food and shelter until the crop was brought in. So I became a corn shepherd, a watcher over hot fields.

Who was my benefactor? you ask. Who took me from the streets and set me up in the clean, peak-washed air with plenty of (well, not plenty, but enough) fresh vegetables to eat? My small grandfather.

I was still angry with him for how he'd treated my mother and me, but those things are nothing when you're hungry. The reason we met again was simple: he needed someone to watch over his crops; I needed to eat. By now, I'm sure he knew I was a thief—how else did I survive, dirty, hardly any taller, but alive? My guess is that Small Grandfather didn't ask himself that question. Or perhaps he was still hoping my mother would go to China and send money back, and so wished to stay on good terms with me.

A famine can cause people to do odd things. Nothing is pure, and you must look at people's motivations again and again if you hope to discover only a piece of what is happening within them. The most cunning thought can be mixed with a sudden desire to save a stranger. The person who takes you in from the streets and saves your life one day can watch you take a piece of chicken at the next night's dinner and say to herself, "This boy is smothering my children." Rage appears alongside charity. Generosity and pure selfishness are not so far apart.

And so my small grandfather, as clear-cut a villain as I could find in my life, became more mysterious to me during the summers I worked for him.

By the time he was ready for me, Small Grandfather had already gone to the nearby mountains and built a tent on the small plot of land he owned. My aunt made up a package for me with enough food to last two days, until I could get up to the fields and live off the vegetables that grew alongside the corn. In the heaviness of the package I could feel my aunt's love. She was sorry about what had happened in the past, I knew. The package was filled with goodies I hadn't tasted in many months.

I went up there alone that first summer, though I was lonely and sad. I didn't know this part of North Korea, Beock Sung Lee, which was one hour southwest of Hoeryong. I was used to the noise and bustle of the city, and the mountains were silent and dark. Very few people lived up there year-round, and there's nothing to distract you from your memories. Even the need to find food had disappeared: there were rows and rows of vegetables behind me, and I could eat my fill. My mind, which had been so preoccupied by survival, now had time to roam.

It rained the first night. I closed up the tent as best I could and lay down on the thin plastic mat my small grandfather had provided. I wondered for the hundred thousandth time where my sister was, what she was doing at that very moment. Had she found a good Chinese man to marry, perhaps an old man in a rural village where all the young girls had gone to work in the factories? Was he kind and grateful for this lovely girl? I knew that she would be an excellent wife in such circumstances. She would simply transfer her sense of duty from me to this Chinese man. I had seen my sister in this way for so long I hardly knew how to imagine her otherwise.

Wondering soon became hoping, which led again to fantasizing. I imagined the impossible: becoming a millionaire. But could I ever achieve wealth in a land of dismal poverty?

The fastest way to become a millionaire in North Korea without being part of the government was to become a trader. Cross over into

China, buy things there, come back and sell them. But how many trips would it take to get rich off North Koreans? Innumerable, countless ones. It was absurd, the whole thing, but it didn't stop me from populating my dreams with crazy feats.

I didn't think of the *how,* of course, I thought only of the *what if.* What if I woke up one morning and smelled the food my mother was making and heard her chatting happily with Bong Sook? What if I opened my eyes and saw my sister folding up her sleeping mat and had that delicious sensation of knowing my stomach was soon to be filled with corn pancakes, as many as I wanted? What if I could see my freshly laundered school uniform folded on top of our chest and know that my friends would be waiting for me at school, where I would share my unlimited supply of store-bought snacks? Everything came back to food. Food had the power to bring my mother and sister back to me. It could reunite me with my friends and keep us safe. I lay in the tent, the raindrops pocking off the dried wheat plants that covered the plastic, and lost myself in these thoughts.

Soon, though, I realized my food was running out. If it kept raining, that meant the wood would be wet, and wet wood meant no fire to cook things on. I began to ration out my aunt's supply of goodies. My thoughts turned mournful and lonely. When I looked out the flap of the tent, there were no human figures to be seen. I missed my friends back at the market, not friends that you could trust to save your life, but friends to gossip with and laugh at the bumpkins from the countryside.

The fourth day, I woke to sunshine. I heard crickets in the field and the sun was blazing down on the corn stalks, turning their husks a shiny, almost plastic-looking green. I went to work. There was a lot to do: weeding the rows, patrolling the fields for intruders (every so often, I scared away kids doing the same things I did on my father's farm), going down the mountain and hauling up water from the small pump that served the village. This was the worst part. I rationed my water, not even washing my clothes, to avoid the long walk with the plastic five-liter container. When full, it was so heavy that by the time I got back to the tent, I felt my arms had stretched three inches. I'd hoped that a villager would be at the well filling his own jug and that I could talk to a human being for the first time in days. But there was nobody in sight and I returned to my tent, homesick.

I made one friend that summer, an ex-convict who was watching his brother's farm—just surviving, like me. He'd been in prison for three years for escaping to China. He regaled me with stories of his time there—how he had so much money he would wander the streets drunk, going into restaurants and ordering enormous mounds of lobster and beef and washing them down with pints of beer. He danced with Chinese girls and went to movie theaters and saw three films in a row, from all over the world. His descriptions of Bruce Lee flicks kept me enthralled for hours.

One day, the ex-convict told me, "Kwang Jin, if you ever go to China, the churches will give you money."

"What's a church?" I asked.

He looked dumbstruck.

"Um, it's a place where they worship God."

I didn't understand either of those ideas—worship or God—so I got straight to the part that most interested me.

"Why would these church people just give you money?"

I'd startled him again. I don't think he'd ever considered it. His mouth was slightly ajar.

"Why *would* they just give me money?" he said softly. "Oh! Because they're Christians."

"What are Christians?"

"The people in the churches."

"Yes, I know. But why do Christians give money to strangers?"

He was getting a little peeved. "It's just what Christians do. They give things away. They're not like normal people."

I sighed. "That makes no sense."

The ex-convict tried to explain, but I could see even he didn't understand what he was saying. In North Korea, there was no concept of doing things for other people out of kindness. Unconditional love was not something I was familiar with. You did things because of family obligation, or because of hunger or greed, or because there was no other choice. But what he was describing—people freely giving their hard-earned cash to complete strangers—was plain crazy.

We changed the subject. But the ex-convict's stories stayed in my mind. I thought of Christians as bizarre people, almost another species. I wanted to meet them, touch them, to confirm that such creatures existed.

I would soon get my chance.

CHAPTER FORTY-TWO

HAULING THE UNSHUCKED corn down to the city would have been very expensive for Small Grandfather, so my job also included slowly harvesting the crop, stripping off any leaves, and getting it ready for a pickup. I took a corn plant, snapped off the ears, shucked them, and tossed them onto a pile. At the end of the day, I would spread the ears out on the ground to dry. Every week or so during the harvest season, Small Grandfather showed up on his bicycle, we would bag up the dried corn, and he would pedal back to Hoeryong with it, to keep for the winter. Over the entire season I harvested more than four hundred kilos of corn, which could make you big money in North Korea. But it took a great deal of work and many long hours in the sun.

I had arrived in the mountains in late August but couldn't begin harvesting the main crop until late September, when the corn turned ripe. I spent the late summer looking forward to the days when the harvest was in and I could go to the village and trade for goods. In the city, an armful of corn was valuable; it might earn you two bowls of noodles. In the country, everyone grew corn, so you couldn't get very much for it. But an armful equaled ten pieces of candy, and that's what I wanted. I was still a kid at heart.

When September came, I anxiously checked the corn each morning, looking for stalks in the outer rows that got more sun and so ripened quicker. When I found a couple that were ready for picking, I snapped off the cobs and hustled down the mountain, heading straight for the store.

I marched into the little place, dumped the corn on the counter, and walked out with my boiled sweets. Instantly one was clacking around between my teeth and the others were deep in my pocket. I had to be careful: the road my small grandfather came in on ran right next to the store. I sucked the candy while keeping an eye out for his gray-haired head approaching down the road. I'd eaten nothing but vegetables for months, so the candy tasted like alien food. My body tingled from the sugar and I felt my spirits lift.

Small Grandfather was using me: he didn't pay me for my two months of work, apart from the corn I ate. So I began using him. I took a bit of the crop and stashed it away for myself. It gave me a warm glow inside to know I was stealing from him. My bitterness at what he'd done hadn't diminished. I even involved the ex-convict in my little plot. Since I couldn't hide all my corn near my tent, I went to him and said, "Please hide this for me until I can come for it." He knew the story of my family, and he had no loyalty toward a city slicker like my small grandfather. The ex-convict did as I asked.

I didn't hate Small Grandfather, exactly, but he treated me like a stranger. I was a piece in an economic system; I never felt he considered me his blood. So I treated him like a rube at the Hoeryong city market.

One of the hardest parts of being homeless was the constant risk of embarrassment. When I was working as a thief or a beggar, I often forgot what I looked like. It didn't matter how dirty your face was or how many holes your shirt had or if you had shoes or not, because everyone else around you was in the same boat. But when I saw someone I knew from my old life, I felt a rush of shame and despair. I saw myself as they saw me, as a kind of half man, half bird of prey. I had felt the same way about others who became homeless. They weren't their old selves anymore. They were poisonous insects, only human-sized.

So when I saw my old teachers in town, my face flushed. I'd run away so they couldn't see me. The same with my ex-classmates.

In the countryside I thought I was invisible to others, but even in the small towns there were schoolchildren, and some days they would march by when Small Grandfather and I were out walking. I would see long lines of children in their uniforms heading down the road. Sometimes they carried a large school flag and sang patriotic songs. When they saw me, they stared. You don't see as many *Kkotjebi* in the countryside, since they tend to flock to the cities. So I was a novelty.

One time, we were leaving the mountain, pulling a cart back to the city with a load of corn inside. In North Korea, pulling a cart means you are taking the place of oxen. It's something poor people do. It means your family is so desperate it cannot even spare you to go to school.

That day, more schoolchildren came by, and their looks were pitying. I was their age, but here I was, sweating like a horse. I felt the shame crawl over my face like maggots. My small grandfather saw my reaction, or sensed it—how much in North Korea depends on sensing rather than seeing!—and he told me something I'll never forget.

"Are you embarrassed?" he asked.

"Of course I am," I snapped.

"You shouldn't be."

We were silent for a moment, the axle of the cart squeaking and grinding as we pulled it over the uneven road.

"I once read this Japanese book," he said. "Very good book."

I snorted. I didn't want to hear about any book, Japanese or otherwise. I was steaming. *I have a job,* I wanted to yell at the children. *I'm a shepherd! I'm just like you!* But I said nothing.

"It was about three thieves who were stealing from people in the countryside," he continued. "They were caught and sentenced to prison, a prison located on a faraway island. They stayed there for many years. Finally it was their time to be released, and a merchant ship came and picked them up and the thieves made their way through the island channels back to the mainland. Although the thieves had eaten three meals a day, they had learned nothing during their imprisonment

190

—there were no classes or workshops to learn anything—and so they went back to their old ways. On the ship they robbed things from the seamen's quarters, and the sailors caught them. What do you think the sailors did?"

Why is he telling me this story? I thought. "I don't know."

"They threw them overboard! And although these men had been on an island for years, do you know they hadn't even learned to swim? So they drowned."

I looked at Small Grandfather, but he just kept walking along, his eyes facing straight ahead. This, apparently, was the end of the story.

For years, I dismissed his little tale. It was a simple one of wrong-doing and punishment, and my small grandfather was a great fan of people getting what they deserved. (How much mercy had he shown my mother? Or me, for that matter?) But I think I did him a disservice. He wasn't so clear-cut a character, in retrospect, and his mind was deep if not particularly kind. When I think of the story now, I believe he was telling me that my predicament, living as a shabbily dressed teenager with nowhere to call home, was not my fault. The government hadn't educated the three thieves, or given them a trade, but instead pitched them back into the world with only one option: to steal. In my most charitable interpretation of the story and his reasons for telling it to me, my small grandfather was saying: Don't blame yourself. Your torn clothing and your matted hair are not who you are. Take heart.

It was a very unusual thing for him to say. He'd been a supporter of the government, but he was telling me subversive stories about how officials didn't take care of their people. It made me think of Small Grandfather as a sad person. Perhaps he didn't feel right about what he'd done to my mother and me.

Maybe I misunderstood this old man. I sometimes believe that, deep inside, he felt remorse. Maybe.

CHAPTER FORTY-THREE

IN 2004 I turned fourteen, and when the harvest came in we stored away the crop for the new year. It's traditional in North Korea at this time, September 12 to be exact, to go to the cemetery and pour alcohol on the graves of your ancestors, thanking them for the good harvest. Then you take a portion of the new corn and make a meal.

It's like Thanksgiving in America in many ways. A celebration. The whole family gathers from all parts of North Korea; the roads are clogged with people on their way to join their kin. Only the rich go by motorcycle; everyone else forms parallel lines on each side of the roads, heading to their home place on foot. Once they get there, kids escape from their parents and play with their cousins for hours at a time. Everyone eats well. It was always one of my favorite holidays.

But this year, September 12 only served as a reminder that my family had been thrown to the winds. I went to my father's grave alone with a small bottle of homemade liquor that Small Grandfather gave me. It's traditional to say some words over the grave, such as "Father, I'm here. Thank you for your sacrifice over the years." But those words were merely ritual. I couldn't think of anything from my own life to say. Despite Small Grandfather's story, I was embarrassed by what had become of me, and felt there was nothing to be thankful for. I couldn't say what I felt inside: "I'm tired and I don't know what to do." That wouldn't have been right. So I just stood there quietly, my mind drifting through memories of my family, the sad times and the happy times.

The fall hadn't brought a bounty. All I had was what I'd managed to steal from Small Grandfather. My mother was living with another man, my sister was in China and in unknown circumstances. When you are alone on Thanksgiving, far from the ones you love, with nowhere to call home, the holiday is empty and painful.

When my work for Small Grandfather was done, I went to Sung Min's apartment. He was working as a security guard at a hospital, not making much money. He would steal a box of nails or some lumber from his job, and my mother would go and sell it in the market. But they were losing weight; their skin hung on their bones in dry, loose ridges.

I stole at night and slept during the day. One morning I returned to the apartment and found my mother gone. "She's been arrested again," Sung Min told me mournfully. She'd gone to see a broker about smuggling her into China, and he had informed on her. My mother was sitting in a jail in Manyang, on suspicion of plotting to escape North Korea.

My heart dropped. This was the third time my mother had been arrested. The authorities were sure to give her a long sentence.

I knew Manyang, of course. I went to see my mother, bringing some cornmeal powder and two aspirin that I'd bought. The guards wouldn't let me see her, so I left my little gifts and asked them to pass them to her. I left with a heavy heart.

Later, my mother wrote Sung Min that she had cried when she'd'd been given the aspirin and told I'd brought it. She was seriously ill at the time, and the medicine helped her recover. When I heard that, I wished I'd spent all my money and bought her a dozen. But perhaps it wasn't just the aspirin that gave her strength; it was knowing that I was thinking of her.

Time went by. I lived on the street. That year was the same thing repeated day after day, with no weekends or holidays. Get up at noon. Wait for dark. Steal. Eat. Sleep. There are entire months that are blank to me.

The summer of 2005 came and Small Grandfather hired me again to watch his corn. After we had harvested the last of the shucked ears, gathered wood for the coming winter, broken down the camp, and organized everything for next year's planting, my small grandfather surprised me. "Do you want to go to school?" he asked.

"Yes, of course," I said.

"Then you will come live with me."

That was all. Suddenly I was readmitted to the house I'd been exiled from three years before. Perhaps this was the lesson Small Grandfather had been teaching me: you're not a thief at heart, you're a schoolboy who's had bad luck.

I was so excited to be a student again, a high school junior. I was fifteen now, and this was my chance to return to a beloved place that had become a vague memory to me.

CHAPTER FORTY-FOUR

MY FIRST DAY at school, I showed up bright and early. It was the same place where I'd been a student when I was ten, a one-story building of painted white brick. The classrooms had big windows with small square panes, dark green desks with yellow chairs, the paint fading after years of use. I felt as if I'd walked back into a world that had gone on seamlessly without me. Here were the same kids I'd known back in fourth and fifth grade, the same boys I'd wrestled and had adventures with years before, the same girls I'd played with (though Hyang Mi, my boyhood crush, was going to a different school). Everything was the same, as if I'd walked out the school doors only a few weeks before. But of course this was an illusion. Things inside all of us had changed.

I was wearing a new uniform, dark blue trousers with a five-button jacket. I was carrying a fresh new notebook in my bag. And I quickly found a few of my old friends: Ahn Jin Hyuk, Kim Goom Hyuk, and Kim Myung Il.

I had known the three in elementary school, and they were now in the cool group. The girls I'd known as awkward, lumpy-faced eleven-year-olds had blossomed into poised and beautiful creatures. I was shocked. Some mysterious change had occurred inside them. Their hair was combed. Their figures were full. I had been away for three years, so it appeared this had happened overnight.

School was strange to me. Myung Il, who'd been a bit of a clown in elementary school, was now known as Ax, because he was supposedly a scary guy. I said, "But it's Myung Il. He's not scary at all!" Ahn also surprised me: he challenged me to an arm wrestle one day and I scoffed at him. "Are you kidding me? I've been working on farms and fighting on the streets." But finally I agreed, and I couldn't believe it when he won. I realized he'd been eating well for four years, while I'd been subsisting on one or two meals a day. It was shocking that this boy was stronger than me.

The first class I walked into was English, and I immediately sensed trouble. I could speak at that time perhaps three or four words: "Hi," "OK," "no," and maybe one other. My brain was frozen in place as a twelve-year-old. Of course all the other students had been attending school regularly, and as soon as I walked in I heard this odd buzzing, the clipped sounds of English in Korean mouths. My classmates were so far ahead of me. I stared at my old friends and realized that the world had passed me by.

The teacher spoke indecipherable words. My friends, a little bored, began to write things down in their notebooks. I just stared at mine, an expanse of white that would never be filled up. Academically, I was doomed the first day I came back. There was no way I would ever catch up; North Korean schools don't have any remedial classes. If you've dropped behind, you're lost.

But socially I was in heaven. All the things my friends and I had dreamed of doing when we were twelve years old we could do now. When I walked out to the schoolyard after classes, my friends turned to me, cigarettes in their hands. I started smoking, which in North Korea is a symbol of adulthood. Then we flirted with the girls.

I had a bit of a mystique now. All the other *Kkotjebi* my classmates knew were dead or under the control of the Saro-cheong, which made me seem like I was special. They never faulted me for becoming homeless; they were more mature now and realized it wasn't my choice.

Not everyone was so understanding, however. The head of my school's Saro-cheong division was one of my teachers, an aggressive guy who kept tabs on the students' lives. He was an intimidating person who relished the power he had over us. On my fourth day in school, he saw me and walked over.

"So, you left the market?" he said with a smile.

I was a bit shocked. He was reminding me that I'd been a homeless castoff for three years.

I didn't know what to say. I nodded.

I could see that some of the students—I noticed two pretty girls in particular—were watching us.

"Are you going to continue coming to school this time?" he demanded in a loud voice.

"Yes." I grimaced.

"Good. Make sure you do."

I felt my blood boil.

I continued my lackluster ways in school, but now I had the very good excuse that I was way behind. During the school day, I would hang out near the hearth, located in a back room behind the main classroom. Here a fire was kept going all day to heat the building (there was no boiler or central heating system). My pals shared their cigarettes and gossiped, not bothering to do their work, because in North Korea good grades without family connections meant nothing. The fireplace was hooked up to a chimney, and if we spotted any teacher walking past the door, we'd blow the smoke from our mouths into the fire. We had loose cigarettes that we passed around one at a time. But it was a cool thing, an adult thing to do, and we were addicted.

One day a teacher passed by the back room and the boy who'd just taken a drag stared at him in horror. He managed to flick the cigarette into the fire without the teacher seeing, but there was still the problem of the smoke in his lungs. The teacher walked in and studied him.

"Breathe it out," he said calmly. Our friend only stared, his face growing redder and redder. "Breathe it . . ." With an explosive *pah!* the smoke came belching out of his mouth, right in the teacher's face.

The teacher grabbed my friend by the neck and hauled him away. The rest of us just laughed. But the others would go back to class and earn A's and B's, while I was sure my report card would be a list of miserable C's and D's.

Did I think of my father and his love of learning? I did, but I pushed those thoughts away. *This is asking too much. I'm not superhuman,* I told myself. *Let me enjoy my little taste of life while I have it. It's bound to be brief, like most of life's pleasures.*

I was right about that.

CHAPTER FORTY-FIVE

AFTER SCHOOL, I would stay out with my friends, smoking in the streets or hanging out at one of their houses. I wouldn't arrive back at my small grandfather's until midnight. He'd be waiting for me, suspicion written all over his face.

"Where have you been?"

"There were extra classes," I said. "I had to stay afterward to catch up."

The first time I lied, he looked at me dubiously, but didn't challenge me. But after I kept showing up at midnight reeking of cigarette smoke, he looked at me in a new way. Any trace of pity or sympathy, which had been hard to detect in the first place, was gone. Clearly I was a bad investment, a thing whose economic function had vanished.

"I have no hope for you," he told me one night. "Tomorrow you must leave my house."

The little idyll had lasted only a few weeks. Strange, it looms large in my memory now; I remember more details about that short time than I do about entire other years of my life. I was happy again. I'd been reunited with my old friends. I'd failed in Small Grandfather's eyes, yes, but when you find happiness after so many years of misery, you want to savor every second. And I had.

Some days, I wonder what would have happened if I'd taken school seriously. I could have studied hard, made Small Grandfather happy, and he would have let me stay with him indefinitely.

As it happened, however, I was out on the streets the next day.

I returned to Sung Min's house. Sung Min was kind enough to let me stay without asking anything in return. Since my mother's so-called marriage was enough for me to call this house home, I waited there to hear news of her sentence, whether she would be sent to a labor camp.

I still had money from stealing part of Small Grandfather's corn crop, and I spent it on food for Sung Min. We stayed in the attic, which was our secret place, and played a card game—famous in North Korea—called 44A. The game requires a great deal of strategy, and you can lose yourself in different theories of how to play it. We became obsessed, dealing cards for hours and inviting neighbors over to gamble with us. There was a guy next door, Chul Nahm, who'd been to China many times and made piles of cash, which, like most people who came into money, he had spent immediately. He was a funny guy, a talker who could meet a girl and five minutes later she would be his girlfriend. "Kwang Jin, money is like a drug," he would tell me. "Once you have it, you can't go back to a normal life." But he was half starving now, just like the rest of us, eating maybe one meal a day.

Chul Nahm was planning another trip to China, where his mother lived. He described to me the meals she would make, including a beef stew, simmering in an enormous pot that she would stir continuously. As he described it, the meat gave off so much fat that the pot didn't send up any steam. I thought about that a lot: a pot of meat as large as I was. I'd never seen such a thing. I told Chul Nahm that I would go with him to China. That was the first time I ever really considered leaving North Korea.

I was living day to day, with no conception of my future. When we ran out of money, I went to the liquor store and pawned my leather jacket, the one I'd stolen from a boy at the detention center, and bought three bottles of moonshine and some tofu. If I could eat and laugh a little with Chul Nahm, it soothed my mind and kept bad thoughts about Bong Sook away. The thought of escaping to China wavered like a mirage.

Then Chul Nahm disappeared. One day, I went to his house and he was gone. Perhaps he'd seen a chance and made a dash for the border. No one knew.

By early February 2006, I was out of money and Sung Min was broke too. I had to leave or I would become a burden to him. I had nothing to pack, not even a toothbrush. I started walking to a small town a couple of hours away, where a distant relative of mine lived. I called her Byeck Sung Aunt (Byeck Sung was the place where she lived), though she was really a fourth cousin. I had met her only once or twice before, but by now I had exhausted all my family options in Hoeryong City.

It was a raw spring day, with blustery sheets of rain sweeping along the road. I was miserable. As I walked, I saw kids and their parents holding their special Kim Jong Il birthday packages. Every year during his birthday week, all children below the age of ten receive gift packages to celebrate; each one has cookies, candy, and popcorn. The kids who had already gotten theirs carried them with great pride and anticipation of eating the boiled sweets. The holiday was two days away.

I arrived at my "aunt's" and knocked on her door. *Won't she be surprised,* I thought grimly. She opened the door and her face registered shock, but she welcomed me warmly into her home. This aunt lived with her husband and her white-haired mother-in-law, who was tiny and stooped and at least seventy years old. She also had a young boy and girl, who were dipping into their gift packages as I entered. They shared some of the popcorn and candy with me, and their mother gave me a half bowl of rice soup. My belly was grumbling and I accepted their gifts gratefully. I knew how much children looked forward to the packages, and to give even one piece of candy away was a big sacrifice. After we'd all nibbled on some of the treats, Byeck Sung Aunt put the packages on a shelf for safekeeping.

The next morning, I woke up and found her waiting for me. I had a shaky feeling in my stomach; I knew what was coming.

"Kwang Jin."

"Yes?"

"You can't stay here."

I dropped my head. It had been only one night.

I gathered my things and walked out with the family. Her husband had left to go somewhere—perhaps to work, I don't remember. At a crossroads, Byeck Sung Aunt and her children said goodbye. I waved to them and began walking back to Hoeryong. It was cold and gray outside, the light filtered through heavy, rain-bearing clouds.

After five minutes, I realized I'd left my gloves behind. I turned around, hurried back to the house, and pushed the door open without knocking. I saw Byeck Sung Aunt's mother-in-law reaching up to the shelf where the children's holiday packages were. I could see she was trying to get to the candy and popcorn. She turned with a stricken look on her face.

I stared at her in shock.

She scurried toward me and grabbed my left hand.

"Please, Kwang Jin. Please, you can't tell my son."

I was speechless. I looked around for my gloves. I didn't know what to do—I felt pity for the old woman.

She was jerking at my hand, begging me to keep silent. I tried pulling it away, but her grip was fierce.

"I must tell you what happened before," she said. "Kwang Jin, please allow me to tell you the story."

There was an awful fear in her eyes. I stopped pulling my hand away and nodded. I would listen to what she had to say.

She bowed her head, her hand still holding on to mine. "A few months ago I was starving, and my grandson had candy he'd received for his birthday. When the family was out, the temptation grew too strong—I am old, but I must eat too!—and I took some of it. When my son came home, he noticed that a few of the treats were missing and he questioned me. I admitted I'd had some, and he went crazy."

She looked up at me. She was crying now. "This son I cared for so preciously, do you know what he did? He took pliers and tried to pull out my teeth. He gripped my head and put the pliers in my mouth as

I screamed. I was so terrified, Kwang Jin. Please, *please,* don't tell my son."

I turned to go. I didn't care about the gloves any longer. I didn't doubt her story for a second. To treat your parent in this way, in North Korea —it was unheard of.

The woman wouldn't let go of my hand. She was begging me for something else. As I tried to release myself, I realized what she was saying. "Poison. Please buy me poison so I may join my husband."

I left that place thinking, *The world is too awful.*

I went to the railroad tracks and followed them to Hoeryong. I remembered someone I knew who lived in, of all things, a culinary school. The place was full of ex-soldiers who went there after doing their stint in the service. I'd visited him before and he was always glad to see me; he let me use his meal card so I could eat in the cafeteria. The food was terrible, corn noodles so soaked in water they were falling apart, but it was better than nothing.

I had run out of family and friends and had to depend on mere acquaintances to keep my heart beating. I thought of the candle flickering at the bottom of the mine shaft. Was there enough oxygen—enough food, enough shelter—for me to live?

It took me hours to get to the culinary school. On previous visits, when the guards at the front gate asked me whom I was visiting, I would always say "the uncle of Lee," and they would let me in. But when I got there this time, the guards turned me away. I was confused until I recalled it was the week of Kim Jong Il's birthday. Security was always at its highest in North Korea in mid-February. Even the most confident thieves would stay home, knowing that the police and soldiers would be everywhere on the streets.

This is ridiculous, I thought. *Where am I going to sleep tonight?*

I turned south and began walking again, tramping along the train tracks toward Hoeryong. It was a cold, gloomy day, around noon. A most ordinary day. I had no idea I was soon to be faced with the most important decision of my life.

CHAPTER FORTY-SIX

As I walked, I remembered a friend, Dong Hyuk, whom I hadn't seen in some time. He lived near the local maternity hospital, in a building set in front of a beautiful mountain range. I'd met him while working the farm during my stay at the detention center. When I cut my arm while harvesting, he treated the wound and drained the pus. I still had the scar, and it reminded me of how kind he'd been.

If I failed this time, I would have to sleep by the train tracks.

Finally I got lucky. My friend was at home and very happy to see me. *When will he ask me to leave?* I wondered. Together, we boiled up noodles on his coil heater. He had a bottle of corn whiskey, so we drank a few shots to celebrate my visit. I went to sleep that night knowing this was just another temporary fix of my eternal problem: the lack of a home. I couldn't stay for the holiday. Though I was starving, I felt embarrassed to even ask.

The next morning, before he could ask me to leave, I said goodbye to Dong Hyuk and returned to the railroad tracks. There is something especially sad about wandering aimlessly around on the biggest holiday of the year. It's a sign your life is going nowhere.

Again I started walking along the tracks, this time toward Manyang. I was wearing a dark coat and trousers. If anyone bothered me, I could say I was part of the track maintenance crew, who wore uniforms of the same color.

The sun was on my face. It was a warm day for February, and the countryside looked pretty and fresh. The mountains, my North Korea, were very beautiful. When the wind changed direction, I could smell the pine trees.

Suddenly a thought came to me. If I kept walking, I'd reach the Tumen River — which was off-limits to civilians — and the Chinese border. What if I crossed over? It was an idle thought, like, What if I found a gold bar on the tracks?

But I kept walking, and a debate sprang up in my head. Staying versus leaving.

North Korea is still my home. It's the place where I learned to swim and play soccer, to crawl and run fast.

What do you have to compare it to? You've never been anywhere else.

I know what to expect. There are no disappointments here.

People pull out their mother's teeth with pliers. That's not disappointing?

I know my way around Hoeryong. China is a mystery to me.

You have nowhere to sleep tonight.

I've survived three years on my own!

You will die without seeing Bong Sook again.

If anyone had stopped me that day, I would probably still be in North Korea. My thoughts of escape had come to me almost on a whim. I had never thought it was possible to cross over alone. Honestly, I probably could have remained alive physically. North Korea had taught me how to survive. I was a good enough thief. But I also knew that I would never be prosperous or happy, and that one long illness would be the end of me.

Despite that knowledge, it was something else inside me that urged me on: the sense of having lost every human connection I had in the world. There was a practical reason too. I wanted to earn enough money to bribe some high-up officials to get my mother out of prison and begin the reunification of my family.

Bong Sook had disappeared into China. I only had my mother left. I wanted to rescue her.

CHAPTER FORTY-SEVEN

As I walked beside the rails, I began to catalogue everything I'd ever heard about people who had escaped North Korea. Most refugees tried the border at night, I knew, when darkness hid them from North Korean guards. I was aware that guards often shot escapees who ignored their warnings. They were notorious for that. And Chinese soldiers often patrolled the far side of the river and sent the refugees back if they caught them. I heard that some escapees committed suicide rather than return.

Not many people tried crossing the border in Hoeryong; security was too tight. Most people went across farther north. I briefly considered that, but it was too far to travel and came with too many risks. I didn't want to ford the Tumen at night, either. I was still afraid of the dark. Another thing that worried me was that, growing up, I'd been told many times that the river itself was electrified with 33,000 volts of current. I didn't know if that was possible — my understanding of electricity was woefully lacking — but I also wondered if the ice-covered water would be too dangerous to try.

The sun was high overhead. Maybe no one expects people to escape at one o'clock on a clear winter afternoon, especially during Kim Jong Il's birthday week.

The farther I walked, the closer I drew to the river. Soon I could see China, a gray smudge across the ice to my left. Now the argument in my head became all in favor of going. *Mother needs money to get out of prison. I've run out of places to go for more than one night. Why not risk my life for a chance at something else? I'll get money and return home and buy Mother's freedom.*

I didn't want to examine my motives too closely. Whom was I running away for, my mother or myself? If I thought too much about that, I might discover something cold inside me.

I just said to myself: *I have no other choice.*

As I walked, the highway came into view to my right. A hundred yards up that road was a security checkpoint manned by North Korean soldiers—"tiger skins"—with automatic rifles. They checked the IDs of every driver and of the few walkers who came by. I expected they would stop me and my little adventure would be over. I would have to turn back toward hunger and isolation.

I walked on, stepping on the wooden ties that secured the steel rails to the earth. No one stopped me. I couldn't see any soldiers milling around near the railroad tracks either. Where had they gone? Had they chased someone into the woods? With every step, my heart trembled a little more. If I'd known the Bible at that time, I would probably have thought of Moses parting the Red Sea. But I could only think of getting a bullet in the back.

Twenty yards more. My heart louder. Nothing. No one.

I was ten yards from the point where the track swooped right along a curve in the bank. The security checkpoint hovered in my peripheral vision. I saw figures now, but no one called to me. Instead of following the curve of the tracks, I stepped quickly to the left and scooted down the bank toward the river, twenty yards away. The ice covering the water was hidden by tall rushes and trees.

I ran to the little copse of trees and pushed my way through them. I dug my shoes into the silty soil at the river's edge, getting enough dirt on them to steady my way on the ice. I'd often played on river ice as a boy. I knew how to walk it.

Am I doing this? I thought. *Is it real?* I was breathing hard from excitement. The absence of soldiers seemed like an invitation to escape. It was as if the universe had arranged itself for these particular five minutes to leave the border open to me.

But I was paranoid. What if it was a trap? What if the soldiers had hidden themselves in the rushes so as to entice me into escaping, and were waiting to pounce? I almost fell over in my hurry.

I broke through the last line of reeds and rushed onto the ice. China was seventy yards away. I knew the ice was thin in some parts. I'd heard of people falling through in a dash for freedom and freezing to death. Their bodies were found downstream in the spring, bloated and rotten.

A noise sounded behind me, a long, drawn-out yell. The soldiers! I glanced back in terror. It wasn't the tiger skins at all but people driving on the highway. They'd seen me and called out, *"Whooooooaaaaaah!"* I thought, *Are they yelling to the guards?* But no, they'd just never seen anyone try to escape in the daytime. Their yells were sounds of pure surprise.

I ran toward the center of the river, the sand on the bottom of my shoes scratching at the ice. The opposite shore was bouncing in my vision. I was shaking with fear but making good progress. The ice, I'm sure, groaned beneath my weight, but my ears were filled with the sound of my heartbeat. *Just let me make it,* I thought. *Just let me get there and I will be able to live for the first time in so long.*

I slipped and ran across the ice, the tails of my coat flapping in the breeze. The roars of the people on the highway grew more and more distant. I reached the opposite shore and dashed for the tall reeds growing out of the mud. I had to catch my breath. It was as if I'd dared myself to do something I never thought I'd try — and I had done it. I was in China. I was shaking with nerves and excitement.

CHAPTER FORTY-EIGHT

I WASN'T SAFE YET. I knew that Chinese soldiers and border guards patrolled the banks of the Tumen. And about three hundred yards downriver, there was a bridge used by trucks carrying goods and by the very few North Koreans with permission to enter China. It was heavily guarded. I could just make out its spindly form against the blue sky. If I could see them, they could see me.

All of a sudden, a black bird landed on a thick reed above my head and began to caw. My heart twisted in my chest. A raven! In North Korea, the raven is a symbol of death, known for landing on corpses. My nerves were so jumpy that I thought the bird was calling to Chinese soldiers. *Here! Here is the North Korean defector!* It made no sense, but I couldn't even bend down to throw a rock at the bird. Its cries were so loud in that little thicket.

I crept farther into the foliage and reached the other side. When I pushed the last bunch of reeds aside, I saw the riverbank, then snow and pines, and through them the pale trace of a trail.

The raven wouldn't stop cawing. I ran for the trail. I made it to the track, seeing no one. All I could hear was the wind in the pines.

It was about 2:30 p.m. My stomach was growling. I needed to find food and a place to rest for the night. I couldn't walk along the highway I knew was about a mile away. The risk of being spotted was too great, and the drivers would know from my face and my clothes that I was a

North Korean refugee. I decided to skirt through the mountains.

I walked up the riverbank and cut toward the rising slope, my feet crunching through the snow. After ten minutes, I began to see houses ahead, some small and not well cared for, others stately and big. The homes of people with money.

Go to the rich people, I thought. *They will be better able to take care of you.*

My heart was still pounding in my eardrums, but I was confident of finding help. Most of the people along this river were descendants of North Koreans. They spoke the language; they knew how things were in my country. My mother had found a second mom here.

I knocked on a door. It opened almost immediately. A man, maybe forty-five, broad face, Korean features.

"I was wondering if you could give me some leftover food."

He took me in. The clothes. My dirty face.

"Get away from here!" he cried. His eyes were wide and staring. What was the matter with him?

"I'm hungry, please . . ."

He slammed the door in my face. I turned away in shock.

My spirit was in turmoil. I might have expected this in North Korea, but that was because of the famine. The people there were selfish because they had to be. But here there was plenty of food! I didn't understand.

The tremor of a thought went through my mind: what if people are cruel not because of circumstances, but because they just are? I didn't want to believe it.

But the next hour confirmed it. I went to house after house, all of them big and well kept. Some had new cars or small trucks in the driveways, unimaginable luxuries for a North Korean. Sometimes an occupant opened the door a crack. I would see one black eye, a tuft of dark hair, sallow skin. I couldn't even tell if it was the face of a man or a woman.

"Please, I'm from North Korea. Would you . . ."

I rarely got further than that. One woman's face seemed to go into a spasm. "Get the hell out!" she shouted.

The Tumen River near Hoeryong wasn't a popular place to escape into China; it was too heavily patrolled. So maybe these people had little experience with refugees like me.

Helping a North Korean wasn't without risk, I knew. If caught, a Chinese person might face a fine of a few thousand *yuan*. It wasn't a small amount of money, but it wasn't a firing squad. I understood why North Koreans didn't assist me, but I couldn't comprehend why the Chinese, who had so many more resources, also refused to help.

My heart turned against the world at that moment. I thought: *Human beings are hard and faithless. Have I come to China only to starve?*

Finally I came to an abandoned house that had no front door to keep me out. Inside, I found broken things — dishes, chairs — strewn about. I went right to the kitchen, and when I pulled open a drawer, I heard a rolling sound. I ducked down and peered inside. *Sweet potato,* I said to myself. A small one, with dirt encrusted on the skin, but that didn't bother me. I grabbed the vegetable, brushed off most of the dirt with my sleeve, took a bite, quickly chewed, and swallowed.

My stomach erupted. A feeling of spicy heat. It wasn't a sweet potato, I realized, but a ginger root. I wanted to throw up. My stomach twisted and flipped. I ran out of the house looking for water, but there wasn't a stream or brook nearby. I haven't been able to eat ginger since.

I walked along the stone and dirt path that curled around the base of a small mountain with a worn-away summit. Trees came into view, but not the pines I was used to. These were fruit trees, neat rows of them. A farm.

My mouth began to water. I wondered what kind of exotic fruits they grew here, maybe apples or pears. There was a man cutting back the branches of a bare tree. I gave him a wide berth — he might be the owner, and I'd had enough of rich people.

I headed for another farmhouse four hundred yards away. It looked half abandoned, the panes of dirty glass and broken farm implements along the side of the cinderblock wall. *This looks like a North Korean house,* I thought. *A poor man lives here.* My stomach ached and gurgled from the ginger.

I knocked on the door and a man opened it. He was badly dressed, his clothes dirty and torn at the knees and elbows.

I gave him my little speech. His eyes brightened.

"Of course I will help you. I have to! You're my compatriot."

He invited me in. The house was unbelievably dirty. I'd never seen such a house, even in North Korea. My second dream of China was dashed. Not everyone had money.

The man brought me into the kitchen and sat me down. He was talking in Korean, bubbling with enthusiasm. I saw that he had a good heart.

He put some dishes on the table: white rice and something reddish that stank to high heaven. I recognized the food, decomposed tofu, a traditional Chinese dish in this region. It wasn't what I'd hoped for, but I dug in with chopsticks and ate. Next was an eggplant dish. I finished it within a couple of minutes. I was ravenous and couldn't worry about manners.

My plate was empty. I could have eaten the same meal again, but I was too shy and too distressed by my reception in China to ask for more. I did manage to ask for a cigarette. The man smiled and offered me some loose cigarettes. I took them and he lit one for me with a plastic lighter, which he then handed to me. I bowed my head slightly and slipped the lighter and the other cigarettes into my pocket. Then he reached into his pocket and handed me some bills.

I looked at them. I knew little about Chinese money and had trouble telling how much I had. Was it eighteen *yuan* or a hundred eighty? Finally I figured it out. Eighteen *yuan.* I thanked the man.

I was so happy having the money that I even thought of going back to North Korea with it. I could use the cash to bribe the guards at my mother's prison. But it was worth less than three dollars. I wouldn't have done much good with that.

I stayed only half an hour. When I left, I decided to go to the Japanese-style pagoda I'd always spotted from my school. I needed to organize my thoughts.

I reached the foot of the pagoda hill forty minutes later and climbed up. When I got to the top, I turned to the east and saw my homeland. It was so close! I saw the soccer field where I'd played for hours as a child. I saw the river I'd plunged into in past summers. I saw my old school, with students entering and leaving. I could see the house where I'd lived with my mom and dad and Bong Sook. Tears welled up in my eyes.

I'd been gone only a few hours, but a feeling of loss stole into my heart. I already knew that China wasn't the paradise I'd imagined. But mostly I felt nostalgia for things and people, even the street corners where I'd begged. *Have I left you forever?* I wondered.

I wiped away the tears. I couldn't return home empty-handed; that would be a disgrace. I decided to go to Kai San, the city where my mother had pointed out the house where she'd stayed with the Chinese broker. He would be able to tell me, I was sure, where to find Bong Sook. And behind the broker's house was that of her second mother, Cho Hee. Surely she would have the rest of the money for Bong Sook. With that, I could return home and possibly free my mother.

I walked for mile after mile, determined to get as close as I could to Kai San. But after a few hours, I could feel my legs giving out. Night had fallen. There was no way I could navigate through the countryside and the snowy mountains in the dark. I needed to find a place to sleep. I started down the hill and knocked on two more doors. Again the same response. Barks of suspicion and anger.

The wind had picked up. I climbed a slope and found a gulley where leaves had been trapped by two walls of rock, forming a deep bed. Here was as good a place as any. I turned away and fell backward, sinking deep into the leaves, which nearly covered my face. I could smell the rich, pleasant odor of decaying matter.

In ten minutes I was asleep.

CHAPTER FORTY-NINE

I woke at two or three in the morning, my feet nearly frozen. The moon was above me, its edge stamped sharp against the black sky. My feet were freezing. If it wasn't for the cold, I thought grumpily, I wouldn't have woken up until morning. It felt as though I'd been asleep for only a few minutes. Unrefreshed, I got up, feeling more miserable than I could remember.

I needed to make my own campsite and start a fire.

But what if I lit up some branches and then fell asleep? If I didn't burn myself to death, I'd send a signal to the local police: here is a vagrant, come and get him. I walked up and down the steep hillside, looking for a place where I wouldn't accidentally start a forest fire. Finally I found a section of the gulley that was protected from the wind. In the middle was a circle where no snow remained. I hunted around and found some old branches and dry moss for a fire. I put everything in the middle of the circle. By now my hands were shaking from the cold. I had the lighter the farmer had given me, and I lit a corner of the dry moss. A flame leaped up and soon the fire was roaring and for the first time in hours I was warm.

When I'd absorbed enough heat, I smoked a bunch of cigarettes, half asleep in front of the fire, then went back to my leafy bed and slept again.

Two hours later, I awoke, struggled out of the leaves, and stamped my feet on a rock. The fire was out so I restarted it, looking at the strange shapes of the forest and the unfamiliar mountains around me. Soon the wood was crackling. My homesickness increased as I contemplated another day of wandering and begging. This only got worse when I heard something odd floating through the pine trees: voices, North Korean voices.

I stood up, confused and scared. Were there agents in the woods, looking for me? But no, the voices weren't speaking, they were singing. I blew out a breath. I recognized the sounds which floated toward me from the Tumen River: soldiers doing their morning exercises in the camp at Hoeryong. I'd heard them before when I was sleeping rough. This meant it was 5 a.m.

I listened to the voices, relishing each word. It was like being alone at Christmastime, listening to someone far off singing carols. If I was home, I would have found some family and celebrated the holiday with them. But here I was on a mountainside, freezing my limbs off. I was fairly high up, and through the valley I could see sparks of light from the North Korean side. People were waking up and turning on their house lights. I wondered who they were and if I knew them. My homesickness overtook my hunger, but soon the pain came back.

I smoked a couple of the farmer's loose cigarettes, drifted off to sleep, and then snapped awake again. Finally I got up and began to walk, following a river that flowed twenty yards away, burbling in its gulch. I knew that if I kept the river on my right, it would take me to Kai San. A highway ran parallel to the river, and cars zoomed by in the semidarkness. I was afraid they were police. Every time I saw headlights, I would jump down into a ravine and hide. But after doing this four or five times, I realized no one was looking for me. I began ignoring the cars.

I tried another farmhouse. To my surprise, the couple living there were nice. More than nice. They invited me in, asking no questions, and gave me rice with chicken and some cabbage. "You must be from Book Jo Sun," the man said, which meant North Korea. I nodded. I noticed a girl, perhaps in her late twenties, watching me from a doorway. I was startled and stopped chewing the rice.

The girl was beautiful. And then I realized why she was looking at me: I had slept in a pile of leaves, some of which still clung to my clothes and hair. My face was dark with soot, and I was wolfing down the food like a starving animal. I smelled terrible. Embarrassed, I dropped my eyes. The girl retreated into her room.

She had a brother, who was also kind. After I'd eaten my fill and drank as much water as I could, he took me outside.

"Where do you want to go?" he asked.

"Kai San."

He nodded, pointing to a road that wound up the mountainside.

"If you take that road, it'll cost an extra day. There's a shortcut through the mountains. Do you see there?"

I turned and followed his pointed finger to a cut between the rock-strewn slopes. It didn't look passable, but he assured me it was.

"It'll take me away from the river," I said.

"Yes, but do you want to walk for another day?" He looked at me with concern.

I decided to follow his advice. I thanked the family and set out. It was scary; I was walking through a completely alien landscape without a landmark to guide me. I tramped across cultivated fields and small rock mounds. The snow began to deepen, coming up to my knees. My breath came out in ragged gasps as I pulled a foot out of one ice-encrusted hole and plunged it a couple of feet ahead. My anxiety mounted. I could feel the ground underneath was made of clay. With the sun on the snow, the clay was slippery. The wetter it got, the more it tried to hold on to my shoes when I walked. There was a sucking sound when I pulled my foot away.

After an hour of hard walking, I stopped. I looked back the way I'd come and saw the farmhouse. *If you turn back now,* I thought, *you can pick up the river route.*

But I pressed on. It took me four hours to reach a small city. When I came down the mountainside and saw it in front of me, I marveled at how big everything looked. It was Kai San, all right, but I had no idea how to orient myself or where my mom's friend's house was.

I picked up my pace. I spotted a man out for a walk, wearing a fedora-type hat, and asked him if he knew the two old men that my mother had spoken of.

He looked at me strangely.

"Are you here for the funeral?"

"What funeral?"

He shook his head and turned. "Take this second right, then go up until you see the red house on the corner. Take that left. Theirs is the second house in on the right."

I thought that the older of the two men I was looking for, the eighty-year-old, must have died. I thanked him, and in ten minutes I was standing at the door. I felt eager and nervous. At last I'd made it. Now I'd find out where Bong Sook was. I saw her face against the dark red sweater.

I knocked and an old woman opened the door. Probably a relative, here for the funeral. In the background I could see an elderly man with straight white hair looking at me. I asked the old woman if the other man, the fifty-year-old, was at home.

Her eyes, clouded with cataracts, regarded me. "He died two days ago."

My knees felt weak.

"My mother and my sister, Bong Sook, came through here after leaving North Korea. Do you know where my sister is?" I said this loudly enough for the old man to hear me. But his face registered nothing.

The woman shook her head. "Soon Ryul, the man who died, took care of all that. He told nothing to us."

The woman closed the door. I stumbled away, feeling dizzy and sick.

I was two days too late. My last connection to Bong Sook was gone.

If I couldn't find Bong Sook, I had to get enough money to go back and redeem my mother. I walked around the corner of the house and found a small lane behind it, on which fronted another house. This must belong to Cho Hee, the old woman who was holding on to the remainder of our money. I rapped my knuckles on the wooden door.

My mother's description of her second mom was so loving that I half expected an angel to answer, someone with beautiful, kindly features and light shining from behind her. I was fifteen; I still took things literally.

The door opened and a woman was standing there. She wasn't evil or bad-looking, only an old Chinese woman in a red knitted jacket.

"Hello," I said. "I'm Kwang Jin, Sook Hee Kim's son."

A tremor or some thought passed over her face, but she didn't nod or say anything at first.

After a long moment of silence she said, "Who?"

I tried to calm myself. I wanted to make sure I heard her correctly.

"Are you Cho Hee, the mother of Bae Sung Il?" In China, a person is called "the father of this one" or "the mother of that one."

"Yes, that's me," she said.

I was incredulous. "You don't remember my mother? She traded with you, she stayed here many times. And she left money here."

At that, her face hardened. I knew I'd made some dreadful mistake. Perhaps I should have asked about Bong Sook. That would have pulled on her heartstrings. Instead, I began with money. I could feel her wariness go up like a shield.

Cho Hee looked down and shook her head.

"I never knew a Sook Hee."

I was speechless. What should I do? I couldn't go to the police. I couldn't rob the woman; that wasn't in me. I shook my head and walked away, feeling there was nothing but darkness in the world.

CHAPTER FIFTY

My mother had told me about one other house in Kai San where she knew the family. I went there next. It was a much grander place. When I knocked on the door, a handsome, well-dressed woman opened the door. She wore makeup and had raven-black hair and kind eyes. Behind her, I could see fancy mahogany furniture gleaming in the living room.

I asked her about my mother.

"Oh, yes," she said. "She was captured in Hoeryong. I'm very sorry for you."

This showed me that information flowed between North Korea and China. So Cho Hee had to have known that my mother was in prison. She'd probably prepared herself for the day someone appeared at her door, and that was why she was so cold.

I wanted money to go get my mother. But the rich woman offered me nothing. I turned away from her door.

What to do now? There was a North Korean woman in the next district who knew my mother and Bong Sook. This my mother had told me before leaving that first time with my sister. I knew she would help me, but I didn't have her address. I began to walk west through Kai San. Perhaps I would bump into her.

I walked for a good two hours, searching for any woman who looked more North Korean than the other pedestrians, while scouting out places to stay. Finally I found an abandoned house on the outskirts of Kai San. Dusk was darkening the streets. Inside, I took the clothes I was carrying and put them in a large dresser drawer, making a bed for myself. I laid the drawer on the floor and curled up inside it. *This is better than the mountains,* I thought. *At least I'm out of the elements.*

I stayed in that house for a week. In the mornings and early evenings I would go begging for food. In the afternoons I would sit and think of what to do. But my options were limited. Things hadn't turned out the way I'd expected.

My training with the Association helped a little bit. When I begged at a house, I would mark the front walk or wall with chalk to show that I'd already been there, something we'd always done. If my chalk was used up, I would memorize the door colors or the gates or where the TV antennas sat on the roofs. If I came just once, the residents would think I was passing through and might not think to report me to the police. If I went to the same place twice, the people would know I was staying in the area. Also, if you keep knocking on the same doors, people feel you're pestering them and they're more likely to get you in trouble. North Koreans who'd been to China had told me again and again: "Keep moving. Don't stay in the same area for long or you'll be caught."

I got enough to eat from knocking on doors. Barely. But my fear of being sent to prison never left me.

The sixth day, I knocked on a door and a woman opened it. I knew immediately that I'd been there before. In fact, this was the first house I'd come to.

"You're back," the woman said.

"I'm sorry," I said. "Please don't report me." I turned hurriedly to go.

"No!" she called. "If you're still around, you must really be in trouble. Wait here."

The woman was gone for three or four minutes. When she returned, she had packed a bag of food.

"You must go to a Christian church," she said.

The word "Christian" brought back the corn summers and the tent in my small grandfather's field. The only time I'd heard that word before was when the ex-convict who'd been watching his brother's farm had mentioned it to me, then failed to explain what it meant.

"How do I find this church?" I asked.

"Look for a cross."

I was confused. "A cross?"

The woman looked surprised. She bent down and traced a cross on the ground.

"Have you never seen that?"

"Oh, yes," I said. "On the walls of hospitals." It was the symbol for a medical building in North Korea.

"This is not a hospital. Look for it."

I thanked the woman and walked toward the market, looking for a cross. But there was nothing. None of the walls or gates had the familiar lines etched in them. I stopped an old man. "Do you know where I can find a cross?"

"Look up!"

"Look up?"

He pointed to the sky.

"Look up."

And there I saw one, lit against the dark gray clouds. I walked over and knocked on the door. When someone answered, behind him or her I could see young men in their early twenties bent over these strange-looking flat boxes, tapping on them. It was the first time I'd seen a computer.

I told the man at the door that I was from North Korea and was sleeping in the mountains, hoping this would make him feel sorry for me. I needed food and money. I guess I was pretty blunt. Because of the story the ex-convict had told me, I just expected them to help.

"What does this look like, a bank?" the man said, frowning.

I froze. I felt I'd said something wrong, but I didn't know what. Fear prevented me from saying anything else.

The man sighed and turned away. A couple of minutes later, he returned with a small bag. "Here," he said. "Come back tomorrow."

The bag had some rice and Chinese vegetables in it. I quickly ate the food outside on the sidewalk, then went to the abandoned house I'd spotted to sleep.

CHAPTER FIFTY-ONE

The next day, soon after the sun rose, I was back at the church's door. This time, the man gave me twenty *yuan,* the equivalent of about three dollars.

So it's true, I thought. *Christians are real.*

The church members even gave me new clothes. I took a shower there — more precious than food — and scrubbed every part of my body until I was scraping off skin. Others came to the church to become reborn; I was reborn in physical form. I'd been a walking garbage heap who now emerged as a clean-cut young man who might be a computer programmer or a bank clerk. The Christians hadn't touched my soul yet, but my body was spotless. Now I looked like a real Chinese teenager, down to my new white sneakers. I asked the church members where I could buy a bus ticket to Yanji, the biggest city in the area.

I still thought like a street person. I said to myself, *If one church gave me twenty* yuan, *I'll hit every church I can find and clean up.* Ten churches meant two hundred *yuan.* A fortune!

I took the bus to Yanji. When I came out of the station, the sight before me was overwhelming — tall skyscrapers, a torrent of honking cars, blinking lights in every imaginable color, people walking by in clothes so fashionable and well tailored that I felt dizzy. It was as if I'd landed on another planet, down to the traffic lights, which I'd never had to deal with before (there were so few cars in North Korea, you could walk right through a red light). To calm my nerves, I bought a pack of cigarettes from a street vendor; I handed over five *yuan*, hoping that would be enough. The vendor handed me my change and I shoved it in my pocket with great relief.

I walked all morning and finally found a church with a Korean sign out front. The sight of the words in the familiar script gave me a feeling of homecoming. Inside was a small lobby where a few parishioners were sitting around a card table. I approached them and blurted out my story. One man turned to me and said, "You need money? My son can't even find a job!"

I was so shocked I was sure I heard the man wrong. But the looks on the faces of the others left no uncertainty. These were my people, and yet they were filled with contempt for me. I retreated to a couch, my emotions — resentment, anger, confusion — released in quiet tears. Eventually a church member brought me four steamed buns and begrudgingly handed me twenty *yuan*. I ate a bun and left, eager to get away.

I walked around the city for several more hours. As the sun sank in the sky, I grew tired. I found myself at the foot of an enormous bridge that seemed to arch into the sky. A river flowed to my right and passersby streamed by on my left. I envied them, people with actual destinations, whereas I was lost and alone in this huge, clashing place.

It began to rain. I needed to find shelter for the night. I ended up in the poor area of the city, where I spotted an apartment building with broken windows. Walking inside, I found a room with nothing but an old mattress on the floor. I collapsed on it and closed my eyes, my feet throbbing. Soon I heard a thin, rattling sound that terrified me — I was afraid someone was coming — and it kept me up for all but a few hours. In the morning light, I saw a Diet Coke can and realized that mice had been pushing it around, making the noise. The three remaining buns from the church were frozen solid; I wished I had eaten them the night before. I went back to Kai San, tired and homesick.

I returned to the half-wrecked building I'd been staying in for a week and came up with a new strategy. I asked a Korean-Chinese street vendor about churches in Tumen City, and she told me there was a big one across from the bus station. My plan was to take the bus there, memorizing the locations of all the churches on the way, then walk back, hitting every place I'd spotted on my return trip.

When I got to Tumen City, I looked across the street from the station, but the building there had no cross on it. I found out later that the church was being renovated and Mass was being held elsewhere. I thought I had ended up in the wrong place and fear immediately seized me. I wandered the streets of Tumen City looking for crosses. When I found one, I walked into the church. I saw a verse on the wall, Matthew 11:28: "Come unto me all you who are weary and burdened, and I will give you rest." I felt it had been written especially for me. The words penetrated to my heart, and my hopes revived. A middle-aged woman walked by, nicely dressed, and I poured out my story to her. She listened kindly, then handed me fifty *yuan*, just like that. I was overjoyed. Outside, I bought some traditional Korean food before spotting an old man selling pineapple slices. Pineapple in North Korea was super-expensive, and I never dreamed I'd ever get to try it. I decided to buy a slice with my newfound riches. I popped it into my mouth, thinking it would taste like nothing I'd ever eaten before. But the pineapple slice was sour and watery; I nearly spit it out. Disenchanted, I walked to the train station, stole a bicycle, and rode back to Kai San.

I remembered there were eight or nine churches along the way, but my bad luck returned: they were all closed, apparently because it was a weekday. It wasn't until the next morning that I found an open church, where three or four Korean-Chinese men were sitting around a big pot of meat; they dipped into it with chopsticks as they chatted. They eyed me suspiciously as I came through the door. I made up a new story on the spot, telling the men I was headed to Hoon Choon to find my long-lost sister. Could they help me with some money to get there? The men looked at one another, their expressions alternating between boredom and disgust. Finally one handed me fifteen *yuan*, and I pedaled off toward Hoon Choon before doubling back to continue my cash-gathering mission on the way to Kai San. Passing the church again, I saw the men were now standing outside, talking to another man, straddling a motorcycle. They shouted for me to stop.

My heart froze. I instantly weighed my options: obey their order, make a run for it up the mountain, or take my chances on the bicycle. I knew the motorcycle would be too fast for me, so I hopped off the bike a few feet away from the men. They began to question me roughly and made me turn out my pockets. When the folded notes of different denominations spilled out, one of them yelled, "I knew this guy was lying!" Two of the men started beating me, bloodying my lip and nose. When they'd had enough, the man holding my money returned it and told me to get lost. "You're lucky we're Christians," he said.

My face was throbbing painfully. I pedaled up and down the nearby hills, wondering what to do next, and then made my way back to Kai San, where I found the abandoned house and tried to fall asleep. When I took off my shoes and socks, I was shocked at the sight of my feet. It had been weeks since I'd slept somewhere without my shoes on. My feet were swollen, clammy, and pale white, like a drowning victim's. I knew if I didn't find a warm, dry place to stay, they were going to get worse.

The next day, I went back to the church in Tumen City, the only one where I'd found real kindness and understanding. The members welcomed me and offered me a room in the church where I could sleep. They returned with a plate of white rice and thick, sweet Chinese sausage, which I quickly devoured. I hadn't expected such treatment; I thought they might give me another fifty *yuan* and send me on my way.

Though I'd found a place to stay, I was terrified of seeing the generous woman again. By now, word must have reached her that I was telling the same story all over the area and milking Christians for everything they were worth. I was under the impression that all Christians were rich, and felt no guilt about taking their money. When I saw the woman, however, she only smiled at me, her eyes all warmth with no trace of suspicion. I found out that she was, in fact, the pastor's wife.

One evening a few days after I'd arrived, I was half asleep in the church lobby when I heard some of the parishioners talking. They were gathered around passing the time before Mass began. "Pastor's teeth are terrible," I heard one say. "They give him so much pain he can't sleep at night. But with three children, who can afford a dentist?"

I felt as if something — a sharp sword — had cut through me. The pastor's family was poor! And he was suffering from health problems. Yet his wife had given me fifty *yuan* as if it were nothing. I became curious about who these people were and what made them so different from the men and women who turned me away.

I memorized the Apostolic Creed and read the Bible every chance I got. The pastor's wife and the parishioners were overjoyed at this, so much so that I would turn the pages whenever I saw a church member coming, without comprehending the stories told on them. My interest in Scripture was the only way I could pay back these kind people for their love and concern. But the biblical world bewildered me completely.

I couldn't stay at the Tumen City church indefinitely. A local pastor who led the congregation began to look around for someone to sponsor me. Eventually she found a Korean-Chinese grandmother, about seventy-five, a strong Christian, very young in spirit, who had been looking for a North Korean teenager to help her with the dishes and household cleaning.

"I'm not looking for a boy," the old woman told the pastor. "They're too dangerous. Please find me a girl."

But he persisted. Everyone in that area of China was hoping to find a female North Korean defector to help around the house, because they were vulnerable and easy to exploit. Their popularity made them quite scarce. The pastor hammered home this point, but the woman was adamant.

At last she relented. "I'll tell you what," the grandmother said. "If it is God's will, I will take the boy."

"And just how will you know if it's God's will?" the pastor asked.

"When I meet him I will ask him if his name is Joseph. If he says yes, then I will know."

The old woman and the pastor made a secret deal. If my name turned out to be Joseph, I would have a sponsor and a permanent place to stay, which very few North Korean boys ever found. The pastor came to me and, despite his word to the woman, told me what had happened.

"You must say that you are Joseph," he said. "It's the only way."

I was offended and hurt. My name was all I had left of my father, all I had left of my childhood. Everything else had been sold off or taken from me. To give away my name for some hot food and a roof over my head was too much.

"I won't do it," I said emphatically.

But the pastor, who was a very determined person, didn't relent. "You *must*," she said. She wouldn't let the subject rest, no matter how many tears I shed. I couldn't stay at the church any longer, and the old woman was my only remaining hope of staying safe in China.

Eventually I agreed to at least meet the old woman. She came to the church and found me in my room. She sat down and greeted me. I nodded to her.

"Are you Joseph?" the old woman said in her no-nonsense way.

I looked at her wrinkled, kind face, which was tense with expectation. "Yes," I said.

The old woman's eyes went wide and she clasped my hand in hers. I could feel them trembling. *Old woman,* I thought, *let me tell you what is going to happen. I am going to let you call me Joseph, and I am going to your home and I will steal all your money and all your valuables. I will take them and go back to North Korea and live under my real name. I will buy my mother's freedom and live happily with her and never see you or China again.*

That was my plan. I was filled with a lingering bitterness.

The grandmother lived in an apartment building in Yanji, which was in the Yanbian Autonomous Prefecture, about thirty miles from Tumen City. We took a bus to her neighborhood. I went along willingly but didn't trust the old woman. After we arrived at her home, I started calling her Grandma but felt no emotion in my heart.

North Korea—and my mother—seemed to recede farther and farther away each hour I spent in China. I stayed in my room in Grandma's apartment, out of sight of the police. I watched the people on the street and exercised and cleaned the place. I was in limbo, but the possibility of a new life seemed right around the corner.

Grandma wasn't the usual seventy-five-year-old Chinese woman. She lived with her son — a kindly man of few words whom I called Uncle — but was very independent. Grandma even had a boyfriend. His name was Mr. Lee, and he was at least six feet tall and handsome, with white hair; he was about eight years younger than Grandma. Mr. Lee spoke some English and Russian. It was this elderly gentleman who, on first meeting me, saw my ragged clothes and went out and bought me a red jacket and a couple of pairs of jeans and sneakers, clothes that any Chinese teenager with a little money would wear.

I was so moved by his gesture, I sat on my bed with the jeans in my hands, their creases sharp and fresh, and tried to hold back my tears. It was another stage in my becoming human again. All teenagers want to look cool; somehow Mr. Lee knew that. I quickly shed my old outfit and tried on my new clothes, turning this way and that as I studied myself in the mirror. After a few minutes, my happiness faded. I realized I couldn't wear my new jeans outside, trapped as I was in Grandma's spare room. This depressed me. I undressed and put my old clothes on again.

I was still far from being able to function in normal society. I wasn't free, I had no real home, and my confidence was gone. When Grandma's granddaughter visited, she was cute and very sweet. She brought bananas, which I'd told Grandma I'd never eaten. It was obviously a gift for me. "Hi, Joseph, how are you?" she said. Grandma smiled and left the room.

I shook my head. To talk to this dazzling creature — it was unthinkable. She'd never seen the degradation I'd seen; she'd never been a scavenging animal as I had been. I felt that I was another species almost. I couldn't make small talk or tease her.

"Hi," I said shyly, then turned and retreated to my room. It wasn't just the difference in our backgrounds, but also my secret, that I'd left North Korea in part to help my mother and still hadn't returned. The guilt was something that accumulated every day, growing heavier.

For the first week, I never left the apartment. Grandma insisted on this. She'd kept a North Korean refugee before and the experience had broken her heart. All she would say about him was that he was in his thirties, very religious, a heavy smoker, and a good and gentle man. (I, too, was a smoker, though I tried to hide this from her, knowing she disapproved.) The mystery refugee had been snatched off the streets by Chinese police and she'd never seen him again. Grandma was afraid the same thing would happen to me.

Grandma worked with a South Korean church, which paid some of her rent and reimbursed her for any North Koreans she took in. But still, had she been caught, she would have had to pay a five-thousand-*yuan* penalty. That was big money for her. She was taking a risk by even allowing me to visit her.

I was safe and had plenty of food to eat; in North Korean terms, I was a great success. But my state of mind was very unsettled. I kept seeing my mother in my daydreams. I wondered if she was expecting me to visit her with enough money to buy her freedom. Did she say to herself, "My son will come tomorrow"? That thought kept sleep away many nights.

I also thought of Bong Sook. Now that I was in China, I was closer to my sister. But I had no idea how to find her. I didn't know if she had a new name or what prefecture she was living in. I didn't have the power yet to search for her. To ask about a missing North Korean girl would be reckless in the extreme.

To find Bong Sook, I first had to free myself.

CHAPTER FIFTY-TWO

ONE EVENING, GRANDMA called to me that she was going out. I heard the click of the front door and waited a few minutes, listening in case she returned for a forgotten purse or something. When I was sure she was gone, I got up from my bed, walked down the hallway, and turned into her room. Days before, I'd watched her from the hallway as she stuffed something beneath her mattress. I knew what it was: money. Like so many older Chinese people, Grandma didn't trust the banks and kept a good amount of cash at home.

Her room was neat and plain, with a cross on the wall and an electric blanket on the bed, covered by a pink duvet with little flowers on it. I lifted the mattress and saw three or four hundred *yuan* (about fifty U.S. dollars). I didn't want to pick up the money and count it, thinking Grandma might have a system, piling the bills a certain way so she could tell if they had been moved. I was suspicious of everyone, and assumed Grandma was too.

So I stood there staring at the stack of wrinkled cash. Should I take it and go back to Hoeryong? Was there enough to redeem Mother? I had no idea. Three hundred *yuan* was a small fortune in North Korea, but I didn't know how much it took to bribe a guard. (Later, I realized it wasn't nearly enough money for what I wanted to do.)

My arm began to ache from holding up the mattress, but I barely felt it. My mind was a buzzing cloud of thoughts. Mother and North Korea, a country I still loved, were competing with this other world I'd found, a world represented by the rich variety of food I saw every day, food that I could eat anytime I pleased. That meant a lot to me.

If I took the money and disappeared, Grandma would be heartsick. I didn't want to hurt her. She'd been good to me. She had even thrown a small party for my birthday. Mr. Lee and Uncle had come, and we'd eaten kimchi and chicken and fried pork, and I'd had three glasses of wine. Though that amount of alcohol barely got me tipsy, I'd pretended to be half drunk, to Grandma's delight. At the end of the meal, she'd emerged from the kitchen with a vanilla cake topped with pineapple and orange slices, candles blazing. It was the first real cake I'd ever tasted in my life.

How could I betray her trust?

A voice inside my head said, *You can't go back. You won't make it, you'll be caught, and it will be another miserable chapter in your life.*

But I knew I was making excuses. I couldn't admit the truth: I wanted to stay. I had plenty of food here. I had a few people who took care of me. I had encountered new things — unconditional love, ethics, Christianity — that I wanted to experience.

I set the mattress back down on the money without touching it. *Let's wait and see what happens,* I thought.

Did every day I resisted stealing the money mean another day closer to death for my mother? I didn't want to think about it. I became an expert in not thinking about such things.

Slowly, I saw that Grandma really cared for me from the bottom of her heart. She treated me as her blood, as her own grandson. Eventually the name Joseph would lose its bitterness for me. I would accept the name as my own, in tribute to the new life I'd found and to Grandma's true heart. Joseph Kim. That was me.

One day Grandma came to me and said, "Put your new clothes on, Joseph. We're going to the market."

"Yes, Grandma," I replied calmly. But I was very, very excited. It would be my first time out of the apartment.

I took the new jeans down from the top of the clothes pile, put on a fresh white shirt and my red jacket. Sneakers, too, tied perfectly with the loops of equal size. Grandma told me we were going to the grocery.

I'd observed that North Korean refugees who'd been in China a while looked different. Their faces are different. Smoother. Lotioned. North Koreans tend to hunch their shoulders and walk stiffly, but after a month or so in China they walked faster while appearing more relaxed. Their shoulders unclenched; their posture improved. Their clothes, of course, looked smart and modern.

I was terrified that despite my red coat and the Nikes, my face and my body were going to give me away. I didn't have any lotion, but I put on some of Mr. Lee's gel to give my hair a nice sheen, hoping that would help me blend in. Still, I was almost shaking with nerves.

The police can come for me anywhere, I thought. *This wall I sleep next to is no protection against them. I might as well go outside and be a person.*

We walked out of the apartment, down the stairs, and out into the street. It was spring and there were crowds everywhere. The noise, after being cooped up in my room for so long, was like the blast of a ship's horn. I held Grandma's arm like I was guiding this old woman around, but that was only for show. Really, I was clinging to her.

We made it to the bus stop and joined the line of people there. Suddenly a woman turned to me and stared. I froze. My pulse went slam-slam-slam in my ears. Grandma turned to look at the woman, and the stranger spoke to her, keeping her eyes on me.

Grandma said a few words, then turned to me.

"She says my grandson is very pretty."

I was offended. "Pretty?" But I smiled at the woman. Grandma nodded and gave me a look. She was quite proud of me.

Next to the woman was an attractive girl about my age. The woman whispered to her.

Oh, God, please don't let her play matchmaker, I thought.

We got on the bus. Grandma paid the fare and she found us seats. When an elderly man got on, short and stooped, I stood up and gave him my seat and he thanked me profusely. By now Grandma was beaming.

The grocery market was another wonder. We walked the aisles and I stopped to touch some of the goods. The broccoli fascinated me. Soft miniature trees. White broccoli cost more than green. Why? Grandma didn't know.

"What do you want to eat?" she asked. But it was too overwhelming. I pointed to some things — tomatoes, shrimp — and she gathered them up, along with the items on her list. How did she know which products to choose from the thousands stacked on the shelves? Had she memorized where they were placed in the never-ending aisles? I thought I would never master the market.

We went home on the bus, and when the apartment door closed behind us, I felt relieved. But I knew I'd be venturing out again soon.

I ate constantly. When I finished breakfast, twenty minutes later I would be nibbling on a banana or popping a few grapes in my mouth. I wanted to know the food was still there, always available. It's like a brother you left in the park one day and almost lost forever. You keep going to his room to check on him.

Two days later, I asked, "When are we going out again?"

She took me to her church. It was an underground church, meaning it had no official certificate allowing it to operate, unlike the ones that paid bribes to government bureaucrats. There were only thirty congregants. The pastor was from South Korea, and he introduced me to his three daughters. They were each blindingly pretty. I, on the other hand, was as talkative as a rock.

"Say hi." Grandma nudged me.

I couldn't even make eye contact. I'd never been exposed to the Western way of flirting. I had no idea what they wanted from me and was sure that if I said anything, it would be the worst possible thing I could have done. So I stayed quiet.

The next week, we went to a super-church, the biggest one in the province. There were at least a thousand people jammed into a huge building. It was the evening service, and a youth chorus sang hymns from the stage.

I spotted a young man walking up the aisle wearing a bright white suit with white shoes. I'd never seen anyone dressed all in white before. The thought of doing that in North Korea—you would be covered in mud in half an hour. His skin looked so fresh and smooth against the white. I was mesmerized.

"You like his suit?" Grandma whispered to me.

I nodded.

"One day I'll get you one just like it," she said. "And one day you'll come here and talk to anyone you like."

That day will never come, I thought. To be like this young man? Impossible.

As time went by, Grandma grew more confident that I wouldn't be spotted on the street and taken back to North Korea. She began letting me go out alone, handing me two *yuan* to take the bus. Sometimes I saved the money to spend on cigarettes and walked wherever I was going. When I took the bus, I sat in the back and spoke to no one, but the feeling of being out on my own was precious to me. At first I didn't know how to tell the driver I wanted to get off. I went to the bus depot and waited for the bus to turn around, watching the other passengers. Finally I caught what they were saying: *Xiàchē,* which meant "I want to get off."

Each of these little discoveries was rewarding for me. You don't recover your humanity all at once. It's like climbing out of a deep pit, one shaky handhold at a time.

CHAPTER FIFTY-THREE

EVERY NIGHT GRANDMA and I read from a well-used Korean Bible with a scratched and worn black leather cover. We sat together in the living room, which had tall windows looking out over a busy street. We sang hymns together and talked about the meaning of proverbs. I was still lost. To begin with, the concept of B.C. and A.D. was alien and confusing. I didn't yet know Jesus' story, so I couldn't figure out what those terms meant. I felt my head spinning.

Grandma arranged for a young man from the church to come read the Bible with me. We went over many passages and I puzzled out what they meant. All these strange names: Joshua, Moses, Noah. To me, they were like characters in a foreign mythology. Just penetrating to what they were actually doing in the stories required a great deal of effort. What it all meant was beyond me.

But the young man told me something I never forgot. "If you pray to God for something selfish," he said, "he won't hear you. If you ask him for a Mercedes-Benz to drive fast and catch girls, it will never arrive. But if you want the car to drive old people to the doctor, if you want to do good, he will hear that prayer."

Everything about Christianity was backward. What I'd learned in life was that if you didn't constantly put yourself first, you would die.

I had food and shelter now, but as the days went by, I grew more and more depressed. I felt lonely and so filled with fear that I thought of sneaking back into North Korea again, though it meant risking starvation. I decided I would start collecting as much money as I could for the trip back. You can even yearn for a prison, so long as it contains the people and places you love.

One night, Grandma turned to the back of her Bible and picked out a hymn. We began to sing it together, her voice frail and reedy, mine faltering over the words. The hymn was "Father, I Stretch My Hands to Thee."

> *Father, I stretch my hands to Thee,*
> *No other help I know;*
> *If Thou withdraw Thyself from me,*
> *Ah! whither shall I go?*

I felt something pierce my heart. *This* I understood; this was my life. The thing that had been haunting me, the feeling that I was a hunted animal whose luck was running out, came over me again. That night, alone in my room, I began to cry. I closed my eyes tightly and attempted to talk to God for the first time. "I don't know who you are," I said. "I don't understand the Scripture. But I'm surrendering myself to you. If you fail me, I have nothing left to fall back on. Please help me. Please show me the way."

Was that a prayer? I didn't know. Exhausted, I curled up in the wool blanket that was my mattress and quickly fell asleep.

Over the next few weeks, I read more and more of the Bible, and the strangest thing happened. My worries, my alienation, began to melt away. I felt refreshed in my soul. *What's happening to me?* I wondered. I found it hard to believe that the Bible stories I'd been hearing in the churches I'd visited were real.

The world was changing for me. The sun that shone through the glass was the same sun. The trees outside my window were the same trees, the food was the same I'd been eating for weeks. But I had new eyes to see all of these things. The world had lost its terrors; I felt like a child who'd come home after a long, painful journey.

I was in no less danger of being caught and taken to a labor camp.

But I felt God walked beside me now. His love covered me like a thick, warm cloak. I knew He would never forsake me.

I didn't understand the Bible intellectually at that point. (I would struggle with concepts like the Trinity for months.) But in my soul, I was no longer a fugitive. God had shown me that He was everywhere in the world, and that He cherished me beyond reason.

My first experience of Him was one of a deep and transforming love.

CHAPTER FIFTY-FOUR

ALL OF GRANDMA'S dumplings and rice and beef with orange had an effect: I was getting chubby. Uncle took me to a Korean-style sauna one afternoon and noticed a thin roll of fat around my belly. I hopped on the scale. Four pounds heavier than the week before.

I began skipping rope in my room at four in the morning. Downstairs was a store, so they didn't care. I tied a clothesline from my doorknob to my dresser and jumped back and forth over it. I ran on the street—two, five, ten miles. I would jump over trash cans, and people actually stopped and stared at me in surprise. I was getting stronger.

One of the places I ran to was the Yanbian University of Science and Technology. It lay behind a stout black steel fence. The first time I went, I looked through the railing at the gleaming green grass with all these young students playing and studying and chatting on it. It was too perfect; it looked fake. I couldn't believe anyone could live this way, studying and flirting in this beautiful world. I started ending my daily runs at the fence, and for five or ten minutes I would stare at the students. Why were their lives and mine so different? Did they always have to be that way? I was afraid to speak to the students, afraid I would discover something in them that told me: *This is why you are kept outside.*

Then I would run home.

It's strange, but I measured progress in material things: a new shirt, sunglasses, cigarettes of my own. My great desire was a cell phone. To be without one in China was to be a nobody. I even knew which model

I wanted, a Nokia with a sliding cover. I would see someone pull one out and think, *When I have a phone like that, I will be happy*. It wasn't so much the physical object that entranced me as it was the idea that I could reach anyone I wanted, anytime I pleased. It didn't occur to me then that I had, in fact, no one to call.

I still felt closed off. I didn't know how much I'd been affected by my time in North Korea, but I was far from the swaggering boy I'd been in the markets.

Eventually I got to know one of the ministers at a church, and one night he put his arm around me and said, "Joseph, do you know how amazing it is that you survived? You must pray to God and thank Him and ask Him what He has planned for you after such a miracle."

I did wonder about that, and I asked God, "Why me?" No answer came, but I felt compelled to make the most of my new life.

My pastor told me about a missionary who was going to visit me at Grandma's. She wanted to give me some encouragement and an allowance as a refugee. When she arrived, I was startled by her appearance. The woman was of average height and very overweight. Her clothes and eyeglasses weren't fashionable; even after only a few weeks in China, I knew what was stylish and what wasn't. I thought, *Why are you dressed like this?*

We sat in the living room and she asked me, "What do you want?"

I'd never thought of that before. I had new shoes and a jacket. All my needs were taken care of, except for a cell phone. And that was too much to ask for.

The silence went on and on. Three minutes later, she said, "Joseph?"

It was summertime. I looked up. "A soccer ball?" I said.

The woman laughed out loud, then her eyes filled with tears. I didn't understand. I thought I'd offended her. She nodded and left shortly afterward.

Two weeks later, she picked me up in her van. We were going to the mall to buy me a soccer ball, along with some clothes. I was so excited that someone had taken me zooming along the highway on a glorious sunny day. It made me feel special. After we'd picked up the items at the mall, we headed back home. On the way, the missionary told me why she'd cried the last time she saw me. She said that whenever she visited North Korean refugees, they immediately asked her for one thing: money. Unlike me, these refugees often had no sponsors, and were living hand-to-mouth in the mountains. They asked for cash to help them survive, and not just a little cash either.

So when I asked the missionary for a soccer ball, she had been moved. It might also have been the fact that South Korean teenagers my own age were taking exams and preparing for college and good careers, while my only thought was for a simple toy. In fact, I never thought to ask for money or anything extravagant; it would have been rude and, honestly, I didn't need any at the moment. All my needs were being met.

Then the missionary turned to me and asked if I wanted to go to America. My response was automatic. I said no.

She was shocked and a little angry.

"Do you know that this is a one-in-a-thousand chance? I have many refugees who would die to go to America. Why do you say no?"

America was big and strange and far away to me. It was thousands of miles from my mother and sister. And I'd always been taught that it was the enemy, full of big-nosed, big-eyed, vicious people who'd killed my countrymen. I guess I was still brainwashed from all those years ago.

"I have a special feeling for you, Joseph. You're not like the other boys. Please consider this."

She told me she'd be back in a week for my decision.

CHAPTER FIFTY-FIVE

WHEN I GOT home to Grandma's, I showed her my new sneakers and the soccer ball. I didn't talk about going to America. It was such a new and unexpected idea, like defecting to the enemy, that I wouldn't have known what to say. And I was afraid of hurting her by announcing that I might leave China.

That night, confused and unhappy, I opened my Bible. I began reading in Matthew, one of my favorite gospels, and soon came to chapter 26, verse 39, which describes Jesus at Gethsemane. "Going a little farther, he fell with his face to the ground and prayed . . . 'Yet not as I will, but as you will.'" I closed my eyes. I knew exactly what was in Jesus' heart at that moment. He's physically spent, hopeless, filled with black despair. His body fails him; he can't take another step. And so he delivers himself into his father's hands.

In my own small way, I needed to do the same thing. "God," I whispered, "I don't know what to do. Do I stay with Grandma or go to America? I feel powerless to decide. I leave it in your hands."

No voice or vision came to me as I lay on my bed that night. But my confusion melted away, and I found in its place a conviction that my way in life was through America. It was clear in my heart that I had to go. I felt relief and joy wash through me. I put the Bible down on the desk next to my mattress and finally fell asleep.

• • •

I knew nothing about America except that it was full of people with large eyes who hated North Koreans. I tried to picture a typical American city, but I couldn't do it. All I could do was multiply what was outside my window: shopping malls many times bigger, streets many times busier. (Even then I somehow knew that America was big.) I decided to research the United States by watching a lot of movies. Grandma's TV had about two dozen channels, and I would flick through them for hours on end, looking for movies with white people in them.

Uncle found me watching a movie one day.

"What are you doing?" he said as he sat next to me on the couch.

"Learning about America," I said. I could talk to him in ways that I couldn't to Grandma, who feared I would leave her.

He looked at the screen in confusion. "America?" he said. "This movie is German!"

"But it has white people!" I protested. It was some kind of action film, and I'd been staring at the houses in it with fascination. I couldn't believe the places these people lived.

He laughed. "Lots of places have white people," he said. "Don't you know this?"

I shook my head. Uncle took the remote and searched for American films. The first one he came across starred Sylvester Stallone. An early scene in the movie really impressed me. Nothing much happened in it. Stallone wakes up one morning, takes a shower, dresses in a black leather coat and black leather gloves. He opens the refrigerator and takes out bread and a bottle of wine. He eats the bread and drinks some wine and gets up and leaves.

This was astonishing. America was so advanced, he didn't even have to wash his own dishes. I washed the dishes three times a day at Grandma's. Three times a day, at breakfast, lunch, and dinner, there were several main dishes, side dishes, soup bowls, glasses — I was at the sink for hours. If I went to America, I was sure I wouldn't have to wash another glass.

North Korea had trained me to think of concrete things. The obvious dishwashing gap between American and Chinese life impressed me to no end.

I watched more Stallone films. In them, the bad guy lost and the good guy won. Always. This was familiar to me from North Korean spy movies, and I liked that. Another thing that impressed me was that when the good guys shot their guns, the bullets went through walls. My old gun obsession flickered. Americans can shoot through *bricks?* Those must be very powerful guns. Everything in America seemed *more.* Of course, when I went to live in America, I found out the bricks were actually drywall, which explained everything.

One last thing impressed me about Stallone: I really liked his leather gloves.

I went to my underground church and spoke to the pastor. After the service, we went for a walk. He had his arm around my shoulder. I asked him if I should go to America.

"Yes, I think you should. There you can study."

That didn't move me. I'd never been interested in studying.

"And in America you can go to a store twenty-four hours a day, any time you want. There is always something happening, even at night."

I thought about that. It wasn't an abstract thing. *Life goes on twenty-four hours a day there.* At the moment he said it, I felt my desire for that kind of unlimited freedom grow inside me.

America was limitless, I decided. I wanted to see what that was like.

The missionary woman didn't return the next week, or the week after. I thought, *She's forgotten about you, Joseph. You missed your chance.*

I began to pray. "Jesus," I said, "I'm not sure if I want to go or if it's just curiosity. If it's your will, I will respect that. But please guide me down the correct path."

The thing that anchored me to China was Grandma. Going to America would take me away from her, and I knew that would hurt her terribly. I was the second refugee she'd taken care of, the ghost of the other North Korean she had lost. "If you weren't here, Joseph," she told me once, "I'm not sure how I would go on." That weighed on me awfully. I felt I was losing one person after another: my father, Bong Sook, my mother, and now, possibly, Grandma. Was there something about me that made it impossible to stay with the people I loved?

As the weeks went by, the desire to leave burned hotter and hotter inside me. But there was no word from the missionary.

Finally she called Grandma and arranged a time to see me. We went out to eat. Over lunch, she said: "Joseph, I'm sorry I've left you alone for so long. There are so many refugees who need my help. I haven't forgotten about you or my offer. But I have another possibility as well."

"Yes?"

"You know Shenyang? It's a city about a day's train journey from here. They have a Christian school, for Chinese students only. If you don't want to go to America, I will try to get you a Chinese ID so you can study there."

I thought of the school behind the fence, the students on the lawn, studying. This appealed to me.

"I feel I will go," I said.

She smiled. "Good, Joseph."

"But only if I can take Grandma with me."

The woman's eyes were watchful.

"Very well. But in order to get into the school, you'll have to practice your Chinese at a shelter I know of. You don't speak it well enough yet."

I said fine, so long as they took Grandma too. We were a unit.

I went back and told Grandma. It was a big step for her. She'd have to give up the lease on her house, leave Uncle, leave Mr. Lee and her loved ones, and move into a shelter with me one hour from home.

She hugged me and said she was ready to go.

CHAPTER FIFTY-SIX

THE SHELTER, IN Yanji, was partially funded by an American non-profit group called Liberty in North Korea (LiNK). While the shelter workers looked for a family we could live with, I studied and explored the city, and Grandma cooked and made new friends.

LiNK wasn't a Christian group, but the people who ran this particular shelter were strong believers. Every day, I and the other refugees there read the Bible from four in the morning until nine thirty at night, with short breaks for meals. I had never studied so much in my life. But now I had a motivation. I believed that the people who studied hardest would be chosen to go to America. That was the system in North Korean schools—the ones with the highest grades were selected for university and for special treatment. So at nine thirty, when we were finally allowed to rest, I kept my desk light on and read for another hour and a half. *Choose me,* I was saying.

I memorized book after book of the Old Testament. One night, I was writing an essay on Genesis when my nose began to bleed. The workers at the shelter became concerned and told me I was studying too hard. "You need to rest," one of them said. I only smiled. I wanted to be recognized as the best and hardest-working student, and the nosebleed proved I was.

Our existence was a difficult one, eating the same food every day and knowing nothing but study and sleep. We couldn't go outside, because of the fear we'd be caught by Chinese police. I felt like I was in Noah's

Ark, trapped all those months after the flood, when the creatures in the ark couldn't see sunlight or taste fresh air.

Sometimes American or Canadian activists came to meet me and the other refugees. They didn't speak Korean and we didn't speak English, so they stared at us and talked among themselves. They brought good cookies and lots and lots of Coca-Cola, but that's really all we shared.

When the visitors came, I felt as though I was behind glass. We were an endangered species; their eyes got big when they saw us: "Here are the North Korean refugees you've heard so much about." I knew these people were there to help us, but something inside me rebelled against their stares. Especially because some of them were Asian but spoke only English. This was shocking to me.

One day another group came through. One guy caught my eye. He was young, his hair was cut in a stylish way, and his clothes were American and very hip. Everything about him, in fact, was cool. He was visiting the shelter with another American activist, Carol Chang.

"How are you today?" he said in Korean.

"Fine," I said.

The young man smiled. He told us his name was Adrian and began to ask me and the other refugees about our lives in North Korea. I felt comfortable with him and soon described my struggles and how I'd ended up in China.

After I finished, Adrian looked at me with a warm and friendly smile. "So," he said, "do you want to go to America?"

I couldn't believe it was that easy. This guy didn't even know I was the top scholar at the shelter!

I thought about what Adrian had said. It had been two months since I'd come to this place. Nothing was happening. My existence seemed like a dead end.

"Yes," I said. My heart leaped when I said the word. Finally I'd admitted my true desire.

Adrian asked two other boys, Danny—who turned out to be the

nephew of Sung Min, my "stepfather" back in Hoeryong—and John, plus a young girl, if they wanted to go to America. Danny was tall and, at least to me, sophisticated for a North Korean refugee: he spoke very basic English, could name a number of South Korean pop stars, and seemed comfortable in his skin. He'd been living at the shelter with his mother, who wasn't going to make the journey. His mom was kind to me, constantly worrying about my diet and asking me if I had enough food or why I was sad.

John, on the other hand, was more like me, still finding his way outside North Korea. He was a bit of a clown, always looking to make us laugh.

The girl was an urgent case. Female refugees, especially teenagers, are at high risk for being sold into sex slavery. But the girl's neglectful mother, who lived ten hours away, refused at the last minute to let her go. Months later, I learned the girl had been sent to a North Korean prison camp.

Things happened fast. Adrian started preparing us for a long trip to an unnamed city, where we would begin our journey to America. He felt that even after months in China, we looked and behaved too much like North Koreans. So he took us to the market and told us to act like spoiled Korean-American teenagers who were bored out of their minds.

"Mr. Adrian, how do we do that?" I asked.

"Push each other around. Act a little rowdy."

The three of us looked at each other. We were so tentative because we barely knew one another. And besides, pushing someone in North Korea was a serious thing. You'd really have to fight afterward.

Passersby were staring at us, grouped awkwardly on the sidewalk.

Adrian sighed. "Joseph, put Danny in a headlock."

I grinned. This I understood. I snapped Danny into a quick headlock, and he started yelling for me to let him go. But I had him tight.

John shoved me back and I lost my grip. I saw disapproving looks in the eyes of people going by. They believed we were spoiled brats!

We did this for a while, horsing around and being, well, jerks.

"Good," Adrian said. "But you have to work on your voices. I want you all to say 'Yeah,' like you're annoyed."

It was such a foreign concept, the irritated sound that comes out of an American teenager's mouth. "Yeaaaaahhh?" We practiced until we were laughing hysterically.

Adrian took us to a fast-food restaurant for lunch. As we waited for our meals, he looked closely at our clothes. I was wearing my favorite things: a suit jacket and a pair of cotton pants. Adrian's face turned sour.

"You know how you look, Joseph?"

"Trendy," I said.

"No, you look like a North Korean refugee."

I was shocked. This was my coolest outfit!

"We'll have to get you guys some clothes," Adrian said.

Before we left the restaurant, he told us to stop trying to appear invisible in public. When you slump your shoulders, he said, it's clear you're trying to minimize your body, to disappear. We had to do the opposite: be loud, boisterous, and flashy. That's the way American kids were.

Adrian took us to a hotel in a taxi. When we arrived, there was a line of employees in sharp uniforms bending their heads to welcome us. I was so impressed. No one had ever done anything like that for me. Behind the workers rose a building — it was probably twenty stories high, but in my mind it stretched through the clouds — where we'd be staying. I was super-excited.

Our hotel room was so big, so amazingly luxurious. Adrian left us there to take care of some business, and John and I began jumping from one bed to the other. It was such a beautiful place; the beds and pillows and duvets were so soft, I couldn't believe I'd get to sleep on them.

Then we spotted the minibar, which had cans of soda and little bottles of whiskey and cognac. When Adrian got back, we asked him if we could try one each, and he said yes. (Later, it turned out he'd thought we were talking about the sodas, not the alcohol.) It was like a party. Adrian called down to the front desk to get extra blankets. *One phone call,* I thought, *and they bring you blankets. This is another world.*

Adrian turned on the TV, changing channels until he found an American football game. We sat on the edge of the beds and watched while Adrian tried to explain the rules. But we were too excited and our brains were going crazy. Eventually he gave up, and we played martial arts, doing scissor kicks and chopping each other to the carpet. The first time I was knocked down, I stayed there, thinking that the carpet was the softest thing I'd ever lie on.

Adrian insisted on sleeping on the floor that night. We couldn't persuade him otherwise. As I slept on the soft duvet, I felt like my life was going to change drastically. I was being carried along on a wave, not knowing what was coming next. But I didn't resist.

Adrian took us to a clothing store in a shopping mall. He wanted to make us look like trendy Korean-American teenagers. John turned into a surfer type, with clothes covered with the logos of American board makers. Danny became a hip-hop kid, with baggy pants and a shirt with a rapper's face on it. I was the skater type: baseball cap turned to the side, bright graphic T-shirt, narrow pants. I studied myself in the store's mirror. I didn't really convince myself, but Adrian had done this before, so I trusted him. Danny laughed and shoved me toward the glass. I turned and chased him out into the mall. We felt like we'd been reborn.

The train journey was the next day: twenty hours, with Chinese security officials checking everyone's tickets multiple times. That made us all nervous.

"If they ask you anything, just shake your head," Adrian said, "like you can't be bothered to deal with some minor official. Then point to me. Remember, you're spoiled, sleepy American kids. Don't act like you're back in North Korea."

Grandma was away visiting relatives. I had to make a decision. "You can start your journey now and see Grandma later," one of Adrian's coworkers said to me. I felt somehow that if I didn't leave China this time, I would never go. I would never see America and experience its freedoms.

I called her on the phone.

"Grandma, it's me."

She was so relieved to hear from me. I told her the activists had let me know I'd be able to see her the next day, before I left for America. She was very emotional on the phone but managed to hold her tears back. After I hung up, I made sure I had memorized her cell phone number.

The next time I saw Grandma would be for the last time. I knew we'd both cry. But for once in my life they would be hopeful as well as sad tears.

This is the price you pay for seeing America, I told myself. *I'm so close now, I can't turn back.*

CHAPTER FIFTY-SEVEN

THE NEXT DAY we went to the Yanji train station. It was nighttime, and the place was enormous. It had these tall glass walls that overlooked the city, and it was like standing at the foot of a bed of luminous plants, each bud a lit-up house or an apartment. It was magical. I was staring at it when Adrian came over to me and whispered, "Take a good look, Joseph. You may never see it again."

That hit me hard. *You may never see it again.* It was true. But more than Yanji, I might never see Grandma again, or Bong Sook, or my mother. It was as if each light down there on the bed of darkness was a person, a place, a memory of mine, and I had to take them all in now, because I would never be so close to them again. I began to cry. *I'm leaving the land that I share with Bong Sook.*

Was I doing the right thing? Why did I want to leave everything I'd known and loved? I couldn't answer.

Danny met us at the station. Soon it was time to get on the train. Adrian gave us our instructions again. "If anyone talks to you, don't say anything. Just come see me and say, 'Hey.' That way I will know something is going on. Above all, don't talk to anyone but me."

He went off to pick up the tickets. John and Danny and I looked at each other.

"Hey," I said to John.

He laughed. "Heee-eey."

"Not like that," I said in Korean. "Like Adrian. *Hey.*"

252

We kept practicing. Anyone walking by must have thought we were idiots, saying the same thing over and over again. But even this one word — so casual, so short, so *American* — made us uncomfortable. We couldn't get it to sound right.

There was only one thing to do. We decided we'd pretend to be deaf-mutes.

We found our seats in the train compartment. A middle-aged couple sitting across from us said hello in Chinese. We nodded our heads. When they started talking to each other, we realized they were Korean. This was bad. Danny, John, and I knew that if they heard us talking, we would be in trouble. We gestured to our mouths and ears. I think the couple understood.

It was a long journey, and I fell asleep on one of the pull-down bunk beds across from the couple. Danny was below me. After an hour or two, I was deep in my dreams when the train came to a sudden stop. My head slid forward and slammed against the wall.

I woke up instantly. "What's going on?" I cried out. I didn't recognize anything around me. I looked down and saw Danny's horrified face turned toward me and realized I'd spoken in Korean. I looked across at the couple. They were reading newspapers, which obscured their faces. I didn't know if they'd heard me or not. Danny, John, and I stared at the papers worriedly. We were in a panic. Should we run, go find Adrian? But we were frozen in place. We didn't dare move.

We stayed awake for another three hours, the train swaying and rattling over the rails. I couldn't go back to sleep. I felt I'd endangered all of us. But the Korean couple never left their seats.

The train pulled in at 8 a.m. The terminal in the unnamed city — it was really Shenyang — was even bigger than the station we'd departed from. We stopped at a burger chain for a quick meal, and I ordered a burger with lettuce. For some reason, I'd gotten it into my head that Americans ate only beef and bread and butter, so I thought, *Here's my chance to have a last piece of green vegetable.* The burger was horrible, so I munched on some French fries while studying the passersby with wide eyes. The people each seemed to have their own sense of fashion. Their suitcases were in all different colors. That just amazed me. I never imagined you could have an orange suitcase.

We rushed through the station and found taxis. Adrian wanted to travel in two. He, Danny, and I jumped in the first taxi, while Carol and John followed in the second. This made me nervous. I had no idea where we were headed, and our splitting up made things more ominous.

We arrived at a rundown hotel, a big disappointment compared to the one the day before. We stared at the dingy sheets on the thin bed and thought this was not a good sign.

I asked Adrian when I could see Grandma.

"What are you talking about?"

My heart sank. It turned out that Adrian didn't know about Grandma, didn't know I was desperate to see her for the last time. He'd been consumed with the details of getting us out of China safely. There was no chance now of seeing Grandma before we left.

It felt like the air had left my lungs and nothing replaced it. I hung my head. Again I didn't get to say goodbye to someone I loved. Someone who'd risked her life for me.

"I saw her," Danny told me.

I stared at him. "You did?"

"Yes. She was very sad she didn't get to say goodbye."

I felt daggers in my heart.

I sat down and wrote Grandma a poem that was inspired by a movie I'd loved as a kid, about the occupation of Korea. In the movie, some Koreans go to work for the occupiers and become more Japanese than the Japanese. But others sacrifice their lives fighting for independence. The poem said that even when you burn bamboo, the ashes line up in a straight line. That is, the bamboo retains its shape even when it has vanished into smoke. The same for white rice: you can smash it into a paste, but it is always white.

It was a poem about righteousness, about keeping your values no matter what. I believed Grandma had done that. She'd sacrificed so much for me. I wanted her to know that I would always remember that. I gave the poem and a letter I dashed off to one of Adrian's associates and asked her to send it to the shelter.

Adrian left the hotel to make a phone call, and I was alone with Danny and John. Our anxiety began to spike, like frightened puppies left in a box. We wanted to make sure we could get out of the room in case we had to escape. As we fiddled with the doorknob, one of us inadvertently locked it. We couldn't get it open again. The three of us kept getting more and more nervous, whispering, "Why won't it open?"

"What do we do?" Danny said.

Was the lock controlled from the front desk? Was someone on his or her way up to arrest us? At that point, I would have believed anything. Our thoughts ran away with us. Finally we got the lock to work, and two minutes later Adrian walked in, his face tight. He'd brought us cookies and chocolate pies, but we were so wound up that we couldn't eat them.

"It's time to go."

We gathered our things. *We're getting on the plane,* I thought, *and the food on board will be delicious.* We were all so excited that we left the snacks on the table.

We got into taxis. I thought we were headed to the airport and that I was moments away from being free. China was connected to North Korea, but America was an ocean away. It was possible to start over there. I wanted to. I'd left so much behind.

We didn't go to the airport, of course. Instead, after fifteen minutes, we pulled up in front of a building with a black fence around it and Chinese policemen guarding the entrance. Adrian hustled us out of the cab. We stood on the sidewalk, staring at the passersby. Where was the plane? What were we doing here?

Adrian made a call. Soon a young Asian woman in a smart suit emerged. She nodded to Adrian, and he motioned for us all to follow her. John and Danny and I fell into line and we walked through the gate.

It was the U.S. consulate. We walked quickly toward a door and inside. Adrian was separated from us. Men with black wands—I had no idea what metal detectors were — approached us and began waving them over our bodies. Adrian's hands were in the air as men swarmed over him. *Are we being arrested?* My heart was beating like a rabbit's and our faces were sheened with sweat.

I thought of running. I turned to look at the door and the gate beyond. If I could get there, I could find the train station. I could get back to Grandma.

I was ready to bolt. Adrian saw the look of terror on my face. His hands were still up in the air. He began vigorously shaking his head back and forth.

"You're safe!" he cried out in Korean. "You're safe!"

EPILOGUE

I LIVE ON A quiet street in Brooklyn now, in a two-story wood-frame house with yellow aluminum siding, where I rent a one-bedroom apartment. When I leave for work in the morning, I turn left and walk to the subway station, about fifteen minutes away. I pass Indian restaurants, bagel shops, a Tibetan crafts store. I slip by people of all colors, walking the streets in the slanting light of early summer, most of them young and busy-seeming, on their way to work or school or something more mysterious. Some of these people, I'm sure, are newcomers like me.

I'm twenty-four years old and work for a private education company, helping to develop their curriculum. I attend Borough of Manhattan Community College, where I'm in my second year of studying international business. In the spring I will apply to my dream colleges as a transfer student: Yale (where Adrian founded LiNK), Princeton and Amherst, plus a few other schools. I finally got my phone—an older-model iPhone, not the Nokia I lusted after back in China—and its contact list is surprisingly full of people who care about me and whom I care about.

I have friends and colleagues I go to dinner with. I take vacations and worry about my bills. I've been to Europe. In other words, I am a fairly typical American.

There are still things, nine years after leaving North Korea, that I find strange about America. Sometimes I miss the simplicity of my life there. In North Korea, if you have food and a place to sleep, you are beating the odds; you can feel satisfied with your life. In America, there are so many shades of gray between the black and white that is a North Korean life. To pass a homeless person on the street or to turn down an invitation to an event involves a moral calculus that, though most Americans might barely register it, is still palpable to me. Whose feelings will you hurt, what amount of selfishness is permissible in life? These are things I never thought of while I was in the Hoeryong city market.

I am a much happier person than I was when I first came to this country. But my journey to the West and my journey *within* the West was far stranger than I could have imagined.

I spent four months in the embassy in Shenyang. It was a difficult time. Danny, John, and I were put in a room with two North Korean couples who had also escaped. None of us understood the defection process, and we were all impatient to be in America. As in my first days in China, I couldn't walk outside and remained a kind of prisoner.

I spent a lot of my time wondering about Adrian and the others who had helped me. Why would they do such a thing, take such risks for people they'd never met? It seemed important to me to figure this out, a clue to the world I was going to. I decided that Adrian must be the richest man in America; surely he lived in the tallest skyscraper in New York. He must have lots of extra money and time, and so he liked to travel the world doing nice things for people, to amuse himself or whatever. I looked forward to seeing his house. I wondered if I would look out the windows and see clouds slipping by at eye level.

I also spent some of my spare time ogling the American ambassador's car, a new black Ford. I thought all cars in America would be this sleek and powerful and black, and that I would own one someday. And I thought about Bong Sook.

After four months, we were given new white dress shirts, black pants, black shoes, and new sunglasses. We flew to Tokyo — where Danny and I had an unsettling encounter with a bathroom hand-dryer that startled us with its roar—and then boarded a plane for Los Angeles. I was so excited I could barely contain myself.

After a long flight of sixteen hours, we came down through the clouds and I began to see houses and cars below. When we got near the airport, I spotted a line of cars, not black like the ones I'd fantasized about, but yellow. (They were taxis, of course.) *My dream car is not so common in America,* I thought sadly. I still wanted one.

At LAX we were in for a shock. We were to be separated right then and there. Danny was going to Salt Lake City, John to Seattle, and the two North Korean couples—whom we'd grown close to in the consulate—to Kentucky. I was frightened. I spoke maybe four words of English and was headed to a place called Richmond, Virginia, alone. One of our guides put a sign on me that said *Minor,* and after many tears, I got on another plane.

When I landed, Carolina Velez, my social worker, was waiting for me. She was Colombian, quite emotional, and very compassionate— we remain friends to this day, which doesn't always happen with caseworkers. She reached out to hug me and I stepped back in terror. I'd never really been hugged before—there is no culture of embracing in North Korea—and I didn't know what she wanted. We drove to my foster home, which was in a rural area surrounded by woods where deer occasionally flashed through the underbrush.

This was not the America I'd imagined from the movies. I wondered if I'd done something wrong to be sent here, but was too afraid to ask. My foster parents were an African-American couple who had two American children they were caring for as well. I got my own bedroom, and I stayed in it that night, looking out at squirrels scampering across the lawn. I couldn't communicate with my new parents. I felt scared and lonely and lost.

My foster father was kind (and so tall I had to crane my neck to look up at him). My foster mom, who ran the household, had to be strategic with her budget. She was very strict about food, for one thing. There was nothing in the fridge or freezer, and her foster children were forbidden to eat outside of regular mealtimes. The food was locked away except for some condiments. I found this odd, but I was too timid to ask for more. Later, I realized she had to feed a few hungry teenagers, so it was necessary to be careful with the groceries.

Three days after my arrival, Carolina told me I had to go to high school.

"But I never finished middle school!" I said through the translator. "Besides, I don't speak English." *And I never studied in North Korea,* I added silently. *Why would I begin now?*

The rules said I had to go, however, and my foster parents took me to a department store to buy school clothes. Nothing in the men's section fit me, so we went to the children's racks and they chose a few button-down shirts and khakis. The clothes were uncool, but I didn't complain.

School was a nightmare. It was a tough place. It was also ninety percent African American, which made me stick out even more. Some of the boys in gym class tried to get me to say swear words, while others pointed at me and laughed. One boy tried to teach me how to play basketball, but when it came time for the game, I just grabbed the ball and ran, infuriating everyone on the court.

I was desperate to fit in. Adrian came to visit me, but was allotted only ten minutes — perhaps out of an excess of caution — by Catholic Charities, which ran the foster program. Adrian bought me a package of Reese's Pieces, which were precious to me because they were a gift from him and because I wasn't getting enough to eat. I didn't devour them on the spot, however. Instead, I brought the candy to school. In the hallway that morning I went up to two or three kids, complete strangers, and handed them the chocolate treats. "You want be friends?" I said in my broken English. The kids freaked out.

I made one friend, a boy named Chen, who was from China. Chen was kind and less clueless than me, and he soon became my anchor, just the latest in a long line of people who'd shown up to help me when I most needed it. But I had no idea how to socialize with real Americans.

At home, I felt like an alien. My English was still spotty. But what confused me most was that I was hungry all the time. Maybe my foster parents thought I was getting enough food, since I never complained. But I couldn't understand why I'd traveled from China, where Grandma stuffed me full of exotic foods, only to end up starving in America. I began volunteering to wash the dishes every night, so that when everyone left the kitchen, I could sneak the ketchup bottle out of the cupboard and suck from its spout.

After a month in Richmond, Adrian called, concerned that he hadn't heard from me. I told him that I didn't know how to use the phone and was afraid to make my foster parents angry by experimenting with it. On his second visit, he and Hannah Song, a LiNK colleague, picked me up and brought me to their offices in D.C. I thought, *Now, finally, I am going to see how the richest man in America lives!* We arrived at a modest two-story house, filled with twenty-somethings sitting on couches and the kitchen table, tapping away at laptops. I thought this must be the home of one of his friends, but it turned out to be the LiNK office. I learned that some of the workers here held part-time jobs to support their work with North Korean refugees, even though they'd graduated from places like Yale and other top schools. They were struggling to make ends meet.

I was astonished. These people were sacrificing the American dream to help people like me. That moved me tremendously.

During the trip, I met Hannah's boyfriend, John, and together we went to a mall to buy me some clothes. Once there, we couldn't find any shorts with a twenty-seven-inch waist, which saddened John. He took out $100 from his wallet and handed it to me. "The next time I see you," he said, "I want you to have a thirty-two-inch waist." That was the most money I'd ever held in my hand. I was so grateful. That $100 would buy many slices of pizza in the school cafeteria. Even now, I'm a couple of inches away from meeting John's target, and every time he sees me, John buys me steaks to get me closer to that thirty-two-inch waist. Though he's very successful, John is always humble, and he has become like an older brother to me, one whose generosity and kindness I hope to emulate one day.

I returned to Virginia inspired by their example, but I was still flailing in most parts of my life. My report card came that May: all D's, except for an A in world history (where the students barely did anything) and an F in math. I didn't really care.

One evening, after a typically tense day at school, I found my foster mother had made chicken wings for dinner. I was famished and quickly ate my portion. I really wanted more, but there wasn't enough for the other members of the family. So I left the last wing on the serving plate, and it was soon snapped up. I closed my eyes, thinking of another long night in my room, with the hunger — a mere shadow of what I'd felt in North Korea, but still hunger — aching in my belly.

I opened my eyes and looked down. There on my plate was a chicken wing. Someone had quietly left me the last one. I looked up. My foster father was looking at me, his eyes filled with . . . compassion, I suppose. I smiled at him. We said nothing, but inside I was moved. This man had shared his last piece of food with me.

That night, I lay on my bed and thought of one night in Hoeryong, in the Manyang house. My father and sister had gone to the mountains to look for firewood and I'd been left alone. I was eight or nine years old. I decided I would be a big boy and cook a meal for my family, so they would have something warm to eat when they came home from hours of foraging. I put some rice in the pot with water and lit the fire underneath. I stirred the pot, feeling the resistance of the rice against the spoon, sticky and wet.

The door opened and my father came in, his arms full of branches. Bong Sook followed behind. They were chatting as they entered. My father's eyes fell to the pot and saw me stirring the rice. It was the first time I'd ever tried to cook for him, and his eyes lit up as if I'd surprised him with a wonderful and unexpected gift.

I spooned the rice into three bowls. My dad and sister dumped the wood in the corner and came to sit down. With my first bite, I realized I hadn't let the pot simmer long enough. The rice tasted awful. But my father couldn't stop smiling and he scooped it into his mouth with great pleasure.

I thought of that night now, in bed in my foster home. Since then, I'd become quite good at preparing rice and other dishes. *Father,* I thought, *I wish I could make you rice again. I am a much better cook now, and you would be so happy.* I began to cry into my pillow.

*I was never a good son to you, Father. But from this day on, I will be different. I won't lie—*something he always hated—*or fight with people. I will study and earn good grades and I will do something for our people. I will help them in your memory. This is how I will honor your sacrifice.*

I have always been skeptical of moments that change people's lives. Progress is painful and slow; in my experience, it doesn't come in a flash from the sky. But from that moment forward I was a different person, in school at least. I began to study voraciously, and worked on my math and English especially.

I felt I had to move on from my foster parents, however. One morning I came down to the kitchen and saw a cold hamburger and some fries sitting on a plate. I began to eat. I realized the house was empty; everyone had left without telling me where they were headed. That was all I would have to eat until the family came back that evening. This only happened once, and I'm not sure what caused it. My foster mom, perhaps thinking my English wasn't good enough, never tried to explain. But I somehow sensed it was time to leave.

All that night I worried about how I would tell Carolina. Finally, the next morning, I called her and told her what was happening. She started to cry. "I can't believe this," she said. "To come to America and be hungry!" Within a week she'd found a new foster family for me. I know my first foster dad and mom did their best, but food was such a powerful thing for me that I had to leave their home. They were sad when I left. I know this.

My new foster mom, Sharron, was a single parent and a loving person. That first day she embraced me, then led me into her kitchen. She opened the fridge and said, "Joseph, this is your home and you can eat whenever and how much you want." Carolina had told her about my previous home.

That September, I went to a new school, the second best in the state, and made the dean's list. For the next six semesters, I never dropped off the list. And I won the award for academic excellence three years running. My father would not have believed it.

Not everything was so sweet in my life. I still struggled to fit in at school. I went from being the "weird Asian kid" to the "crazy Asian kid." I learned to swear, something that delighted my American classmates, and acted like a clown, especially around girls. I dyed my hair yellow at one point, wore it in bangs down to my chin, pierced my ears, and wore super-thin stovepipe pants and bright, outrageous shirts. Adrian nearly stopped speaking to me when the earrings appeared.

The worst time was lunch. I had no one to sit with for those eternal, agonizing forty-five minutes, so I would gobble up the school lunch alone at my table, then pick up my books as if I was late for an important meeting or a study session. There was no meeting or session, of course. I just made a circuit of the lunch hall and returned to my empty table, hoping no one had noticed. They had noticed.

There were some bright spots. I played pickup games of basketball and sometimes sank five jumpers in a row. I took up soccer, mastering a bicycle kick that had my schoolmates looking at me like I was some kung fu David Beckham. I made some friends, though I never told them I was North Korean. I feared that Kim Jong Il would send his agents to kidnap me, as he'd done to defectors in Japan.

All in all, I survived.

After high school I moved to New York, in July 2011. I shared a small apartment with a roommate and began working, going to college classes, and enjoying the city. My life was finally beginning to resemble the one I'd hoped for. But a few months after I arrived, I slid into a depression. It was my first time being on my own in America; I often found myself alone in my room, thinking about the past and my family. On weekdays, I was busy with a full load of classes and a part-time job, but on weekends the empty hours seemed endless. I would get a takeout meal from a Korean or Thai restaurant, lay the food out on my table, look at it, and say to myself: "How can you eat this when your mother may be starving? What kind of person enjoys his pad thai when he doesn't even know if his own mom is alive or dead?"

The food turned bitter in my mouth, and I would open a bottle of whiskey. Often I finished it before the night was over. I lay in bed afterward, stupefied, my self-hatred at last subdued. But the next day it returned. I killed time by watching movies and grew ever more morose, until at times I felt anchored to the bed. I'd never learned how to express my deepest feelings. I was one of the lucky, I was far more blessed than my mother or father or sister. How could I possibly complain?

I suppose I was suffering from a form of survivor's guilt, complicated by the role I'd played in my own escape. Questions kept running through my mind: What if I'd gone back to North Korea? What if I'd been able to help my mother after all? My guilt and depression got so bad that there were days I couldn't leave my apartment.

Finally I started giving myself small chores, like taking the trash down to the street. Some days that was the only thing I accomplished. Then I assigned myself more ambitious tasks, like writing emails to five different people and taking long walks in the park. Eventually I worked up the nerve to travel to conferences on North Korea and related topics, where I was a featured speaker. At first it was simply the ego boost that lifted my spirits: "You are so brave," people told me. "Your survival is nothing less than a miracle." I enjoyed that. I liked being the center of attention, being recognized, after so many years as an invisible *Kkotjebi*.

But I felt I was being selfish, and I berated myself. *You want to emulate Martin Luther King Jr., but you are just a showman, out for your own ends.* Part of that was true. But I felt I was also helping people, those thousands of homeless boys and girls who were vulnerable to the North Korean state and the Chinese authorities. *I am not Dr. King,* I said to myself after a while. *I'm not perfect, but I'm doing my best to tell the world these people exist, and are in pain.*

Sometimes it's difficult for me to tell my story in public. My suffering ended the day I came to the United States, but I know that there are millions of North Koreans living in pain at this very moment. There are boys just like me whose fathers are in the last stages of starvation, girls who are being sold off in China, and mothers on their way to prison camps they will never leave. The children among them are not castaways; they are deeply loved, as I was.

While I sleep on my comfortable bed, covered with a warm blanket, homeless boys and girls in North Korea are starving to death or sleeping under bridges in withering cold. They will spend tonight desperately hoping tomorrow will be better. But that can't happen unless we all help make a place where these innocent people can live without terror or want.

I strongly believe that all North Koreans have the right to experience the life I have now. One day, I hope my countrymen will be able to taste freedom. This is what compels me to travel, to speak out and tell what I saw in places like Hoeryong. I can't do this alone. Only together can we bring justice and freedom to North Koreans.

This is their right as human beings. And I hope to see the day when they enjoy the same justice and freedom that I do.

After giving a talk at the TED Global Conference in Scotland in June 2013, I traveled to London and Paris, capping off my first trip outside the United States. On my way home, I found myself in the Edinburgh airport. My flight to New York would leave the next morning, and instead of getting a hotel, I decided to sleep in the terminal. I'm not sure what compelled me to do this: a strange mood came over me after all that time talking about being homeless. A curious nostalgia, perhaps. I thought back to those nights I'd spent inside the big, warm steam engine abandoned next to the railroad tracks in Hoeryong. The Scottish terminal was far more luxurious — there was piped-in music and a food court — but there was something in those lonely nights I missed.

From the gray pleather seat I slept in, I could see the night sky through the enormous plate glass windows. The terminal began to empty out, and soon there was no one around except a team of cleaners and one or two travelers, stuck like me for the night. I felt a kind of pleasurable melancholy seep through my veins. My memories of North Korea were precious to me, and the stars and moon brought them closer than they'd been in many months.

I looked at the night sky and talked to Bong Sook. "I've just told our story to seven hundred people," I said. "Everyone told me what a great speech I gave and what a hero I am. This isn't true, of course. If anyone is the hero of this story, it's you."

I told Bong Sook about my plans to find her. I'd spoken with different people, and they'd told me there were Korean-Chinese brokers who specialized in locating North Koreans in the border provinces of China. We'd agreed this was the best way to approach the difficult mission of finding my sister.

Right now, I thought, *we only share the stars. But I can look up at night and see that you are under the same sky. That will have to be enough until I find you.*

I focused on one particular star. *Why don't I know their names? I must learn them.* "I wonder what you are doing tonight, Bong Sook," I said softly. "Are you warm and safe like me? It's been so long since I waited for your return, dreaming like a baby brother of the delicious food you would surely bring. But now I just want to thank you for being my sister, for loving me and remembering me always. I will not forget you, as you never forgot me." I said a few more words, about my apartment in Brooklyn and my everyday life. Then I drifted off.

I slept peacefully that night. In the morning, I boarded the flight to JFK, and the plane ascended slowly into the sky as the muffled roar of the engines shook my seat. The stars were gone now, replaced by a pale blue sky and long ribbons of clouds. *Take everything from me,* I thought, *and I will still have those constellations. The hidden stars that draw me to those I love.*

ACKNOWLEDGMENTS

I AM SO THANKFUL for the opportunity to share my story. It's a privilege but also a burden, because this isn't just my story, but the story of millions of other people in North Korea today. Rudyard Kipling once said, "If history were taught in the form of stories, it would never be forgotten." My hope in telling my story, our story, is that the lives of the North Korean people would not be forgotten. I owe a huge debt of gratitude to so many important people in my life who have helped me to make it this far and have been a part of shaping who I am today.

First and foremost, I would like to thank my mom and dad for bringing me into this world. Dad, you made so many sacrifices for our family, things I probably couldn't have done. Mom, sometimes I felt so resentful. I wondered how differently things could have turned out if we had made different decisions. But I love you and am waiting to be together with you and Bong Sook again.

Adrian Hong, thank you for helping to bring me to the United States so that I could experience the true definition of freedom. You have remained a great mentor and friend through your continued support and care over the years. Angela Hong, thank you for always being so thoughtful. To the Hong family: Living in your house during the summer of 2008 was one of the happiest times in my life. I owe a very special thanks to my foster mom Sharron Rose: You are the epitome of kindness and generosity. To Carolina Velez: You were my lifeline when I first came to America, helping me through my resettlement as my case manager. Hannah *noona* (Hannah Song): Thank you so much for being my sister, for always believing in me more than I believe in myself, and for loving me the same way that I imagine Bong Sook would have if she was with me now.

I would like especially to thank some of my generous supporters who have made it possible for me study and live in New York City: Terry and Gregor Hong, Bernard and Christine Moon, Dave Park, PJ Kim, Peter Kang and Seiwook Lee, Eliot and Jen Kang, Jensen and Juhee Ko, Cathy Danchik, Edie Weiner, and Julia Rhee.

Eddie *hyung* and Mr. D (Eddie Song and Damon Adams): although I may not express it often, you have both been incredible mentors to me and have helped me grow immensely both personally and professionally. Eddie, I am thankful that you always expected perfection from me. Your tough love and your belief in my potential always encouraged me and pushed me to work harder. Mr. D, thank you for showing me what it means to remain optimistic even during the most difficult times. I don't think I've met anyone who is as tenacious as you.

Meghan Song and the Saulsbury family: Thank you for always welcoming me into your home and treating me like a part of your family. Mr. (David) Song: You remind me of my father when I listen to your wisdom and advice. It makes me wonder what it would be like to speak to him if he were alive now. Mrs. (Julie) Song: I am so blessed to have you in my life — you are always feeding me, worrying about my health, and you truly treat me like your own son.

To my LiNK *noonas* Jimin Oh, Jane Chung, Lori Kim, and Carrol Chang: You were there to welcome me when I first arrived in America and I will never forget how much you loved and cared for me. Thank you for always supporting me and cheering me on. Eunice *noona* (Eunice Lim): I can't wait to tell Bong Sook one day how much you and Sam *hyung* took such good care of me, as if I were your own brother. You are always praying for me and reminding me of God's love. Thank you for not letting me forget.

To my two best friends, Asein Ta and Ming Zheng: Thank you for standing by my side at times when I'm sure others would have left me.

John *hyung* (John Park): I am inspired by your generosity and humility. The day we first met, you assured me that I could always count on you. Thank you for always being there for me as my brother, just as you promised. PJ Kim: From traveling with me to interviews to helping me with speeches, I am thankful for your constant support and wisdom. Justin Wheeler: You have been a great friend and brother to me, and I am humbled by your sacrifice and your work to inspire a generation of young people to care for my people. Sokeel Park: I never say it enough, but I really appreciate how hard you work and how much you love the North Korean people. Thank you for helping me whenever I need something, for making me laugh, and for always being there for me as my *hyung*.

To my special *noonas* in South Korea, Jamie Hong and Hailey Lee: I will never forget spending the summer of 2009 with you in California, or the first time I had the *dong geu rang ddeng* you made for me. Thank you for always caring about me and checking up on me. Jennifer Welsch and Matt Wood: I'll never forget going to Yosemite and traveling to Westside Ministries, UIUC, and other events and conferences together. Jenn, you always were a great sister to me, and Matt, you were always so encouraging.

Elliot Lee: You have provided me with helpful guidance on things I wouldn't have otherwise known. Thanks for traveling with me, helping me to go suit shopping, and teaching me many things. William Kim: Thank you for always picking up my calls when I needed you. You have provided me with advice, constructive feedback, and encouragement throughout the years. David Park: I am thankful for your unwavering support and for taking me to my first live European soccer game in Yankee Stadium — it was unforgettable! Ji Un Kim: Thanks for making sure I always had food to eat. Paul Suk Jae: The first time I ever visited New York, you picked me up from Chinatown and took me all around the city and spent several days with me. Thanks for your hospitality and for helping me prepare for an exam. Andy Kim: I'll always appreciate how you would call me out of the blue to see if there was anything I needed. Daniel Pincus and La Wang: I am grateful for your friendship and for the many friends and influential people you have gone out of your way to introduce me to.

I want to thank all past, present, and future LiNK (Liberty in North Korea) interns, nomads, and staff who have dedicated their lives to the lives of the North Korean people. Thank you for believing in us. You inspire me with your determination and commitment to bring justice, peace, and liberty to North Korea. Please keep up your hard work—you are the hope for so many North Korean people who have lost their hope.

To Marianna Tu and Bryan Garcia at America Needs You: Thank you so much for your calls and emails, constantly checking up on me and helping me to stay strong. You always encourage me to fulfill my dreams, and because of that I truly believe one day I will.

To my friends who have been there for me throughout the years, thank you for continually praying for me and staying in touch: Andrew Lovely, Kenneth Hau, Hannah Ryu, June Park, and Stephanie Cho. I also want to acknowledge these friends who have brought me tremendous support at different times in my life and have always accepted me as I am: Robert Young, Sung Kook Oh, Danny Lee, Yeon Jeong Kim, Cameron Lee, Julie Han, John Kim, Scott Yang, Lyn Kim, Edward Cheng, Julie Lam, Morgan Porter, Hwang Bin Im, Jason Oh, Harim Lee, and Gabe Cruciani.

A huge thanks to everyone who made this book possible, including Terry Hong for the introduction, Scott Waxman for your ongoing encouragement and support, Bruce Nichols for your tireless help with all the editing, and Joan Cho for your help in proofreading and correcting Korean names and geographical locations.

To my coauthor, Stephan Talty: I'm not sure I could ever express quite how grateful I am to you. Because of you, my story and the stories of millions of other North Koreans will not be forgotten. Thank you for your friendship and your patience with me throughout this process, and for your commitment to helping me tell my story as thoroughly and accurately as possible. I hope, through your beautiful writing, that others may come to have a more compassionate perspective of the North Korean people.

For those I have forgotten or did not mention here, please forgive me and know that I am so thankful for every person who has helped me along the way. Without you, my story would not be possible.

And finally, to my sister, Bong Sook: *Noona*, it has been more than ten years since we separated and since I last saw you. I wish you were here with me now—you would be so surprised by how much I have grown up. I do so many things now that I couldn't do before. I cook my own meals, I wash my own clothes, and I even iron my dress shirts myself. I can't wait to do some of these things for you, just like you always did for me. *Noona*, you probably don't know this, but I went to China to look for you. Sometimes I wonder, if I had escaped just a few days earlier, could I have found you? Would our lives have turned out differently and would we be together? Sung Ryul died two days before I made it to his house, and I felt that the whole world turned black. Why did it seem like I was always just a few days late? After I left North Korea, my journey was so difficult, but I met many good people along the way who helped me. What was your journey like, and were there good people to help you too? Since coming to America, I wanted to find a way I could honor Father, so I studied hard and did my best to try to figure out how we could prevent stories like ours from happening to other families in North Korea. I still have so much to learn, but I am determined to make my hope of a better future for our people into a reality. *Noona*, I wonder if we'll ever be together again. Will we have a chance to make up for all the time we have lost? Sometimes I lose hope and want to give up, but I never have. I never will. I know we will find each other again, and I will work hard to make that day come as soon as possible. Please wait for me. I love you.